STOCHASTIC MODELS OF CONTROL AND ECONOMIC DYNAMICS

This is a volume in
ECONOMIC THEORY, ECONOMETRICS, AND MATHEMATICAL ECONOMICS
A Series of Monographs and Textbooks
Consulting Editor: KARL SHELL
A complete list of titles in this series appears at the end of this volume.

STOCHASTIC MODELS OF CONTROL AND ECONOMIC DYNAMICS

V. I. ARKIN

I. V. EVSTIGNEEV
Central Economic Mathematics Institute
Academy of Sciences of the USSR
Moscow, Vavilova, USSR

Translated and Edited by

E. A. MEDOVA-DEMPSTER
Department of Applied Mathematics
Technical University of Nova Scotia
Halifax, Nova Scotia, Canada

M. A. H. DEMPSTER
Department of Mathematics Statistics and Computing Science
and
School of Business Administration
Dalhouse University
Halifax, Nova Scotia, Canada
and
Balliol College
Oxford, England

1987

ACADEMIC PRESS

Harcourt Brace Jovanovich, Publishers
London Orlando San Diego New York
Austin Boston Sydney Tokyo Toronto

ACADEMIC PRESS LIMITED
24/28 Oval Road,
London NW1 7DX

United States Edition published by
ACADEMIC PRESS INC.
Orlando, Florida 32887

British Library Cataloguing in Publication Data

Arkin, V. I.
Stochastic models of control and economic dynamics.—(Economic theory, econometrics and mathematical economics)
1. Econometrics 2. Stochastic systems
I. Title II. Evstigneev, I. V. III. Medova-Dempster, E. A. IV. Dempster, M. A. H. V. Series
330′.01′5192 HB139

Library of Congress Cataloguing in Publication Data

Arkin, V. I. (Vadim Iosifovich), 1937–
Stochastic models of control and economic dynamics.
(Economic theory, econometrics, and mathematical economics)
Translation of: Veroiatnostnye modeli upravleniia i ékonomicheskoi dinamiki.
Includes index.
1. Economics—Mathematical models. 2. Central planning—Mathematical models. 3. Statics and dynamics (Social sciences) 4. Control theory. I. Evstigneev, I.V. II. Medova-Dempster, E. A. III. Dempster, M. A. H. (Michael Alan Howarth), Date. IV. Title. V. Series

HB141.A7613 1984 330′0724 84–14517
ISBN 0-12-062080-4

Printed by St Edmundsbury Press Ltd,
Bury St Edmunds, Suffolk

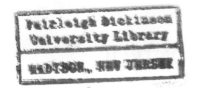

CONTENTS

PREFACE

This book is devoted to recent results at the interface of probability theory, optimal control theory, and mathematical economics. The results in question concern problems of stochastic control in discrete time (the stochastic maximum principle) and the probabilistic analogues of classical models of economic dynamics.

In the deterministic theory of controlled dynamical processes in discrete time, a central role is played by versions of Pontryagin's maximum principle. This principle serves as an effective tool for the investigation of a variety of optimization problems, among them a wide class of models of economic dynamics and the intertemporal distribution of resources. Translated into the language of economic models, the maximum principle yields a sequence of statements about the existence of optimal dual variables (prices) supporting an optimal programme in problems of economic planning over a finite horizon.

From the point of view of optimal control theory, the essential feature of most models of economic dynamics is that they define optimization problems with a convex structure. In particular, this is the case for the models described in this book. (The history of their creation is connected with the names of Leontiev, Kantorovich, von Neumann, Gale, and others.)

On the other hand, the theory of economic dynamics has its own class of specific questions connected primarily with problems of planning over an infinite horizon. (Such problems have an important economic meaning in that they permit the elimination of so-called economic end effects; for details, see §1 of Chapter 1.)

For planning problems over an infinite horizon, we are interested in two main types of proposition: turnpike theorems and the existence of optimal programmes. A turnpike theorem is an asymptotic result capturing the intuitive idea of the stationarity of optimal trajectories of economic development for planning problems over sufficiently long horizons. Such results may be compared with theorems from the qualitative theory of differential equations, where the asymptotic properties of trajectories are investigated by methods based on solutions with intuitively obvious formulae.

It is important to stress that we consider the economic models treated here to be extreme idealizations. Only by such idealization is it possible to construct a sufficiently complete mathematical theory. On the other hand, the main ideas and methods developed in this theory pervade the whole spectrum of economic models from the most abstract to those which support practical calculations.

The basic mathematical tool used in deterministic control problems is finite dimensional convex analysis. In many questions in mathematical economics, an important role is also played by various fixed point theorems and the theory of convex measurable multifunctions (multivalued mappings). In the stochastic case, the mathematical theory required becomes infinite dimensional, and a richer arsenal of methods must be brought to bear on the questions at issue.

We emphasize that the extension to the stochastic theory is not simply a formal generalization of the corresponding deterministic scheme. In the first place, the system of basic definitions must be changed. This change is necessitated primarily because in stochastic problems a new constraint appears: in constructing the control at each time period only the information available to the system up to the current period can be used (it is said that the control must be a *nonanticipative* function of the available information).

From the practical point of view, it is most natural to choose the current control as a function of the current state of controlled system. Such controls are termed *Markovian*. This concept is a central object in traditional schemes for the control of Markov processes based on the method of dynamic programming.

By means of dynamic programming, the analysis of an optimization problem is reduced to the investigation of a nonlinear functional equation (Bellman's equation) which, under the appropriate assumptions, is a necessary (and usually sufficient) condition for an optimum. The optimality theory for controlled Markov processes thus essentially reduces to the theory of the Bellman functional equation.

We also note that in dynamic programming we must always contend with a family of optimization problems depending parametrically on the initial state of the system, and in fact we investigate the family as a whole. In this sense, it may be said that the approach of dynamic programming has a global character.

Another approach (the one to be systematically presented in this book) consists in the investigation, as an optimization problem, of an individual problem of optimal control with a fixed initial state. In this approach we must consider, as well as Markov controls, the processes generated by these controls (i.e., the random trajectories of the system). The equations describing the dynamics of the system are considered as constraints on the pair consisting of a control sequence and the corresponding trajectory. Thus the problem arises of finding a constrained optimum in the space of corresponding pairs.

However the class of admissible pairs is defined, the resulting optimization problem does not, as a rule, admit the application of the calculus of variations to its solution. A related question concerns the natural extension of the class of admissible controls to non-Markovian controls—the nonanticipative controls—depending on all the past history up to the current period. In Chapter 3 it is shown that such an extension of the problem does not change the optimal value of the objective functional, and it follows that the necessary optimality conditions obtained for the wider class of controls also serve for the class of controls of Markov type. Furthermore, for the class of nonanticipative controls it is possible to obtain the main results for stochastic analogues of Gale's model.

The derivation of the stochastic maximum principle given here is based on general methods from the theory of optimization problems in function spaces. However, the main step in the argument is the translation of the necessary optimality condition given in abstract terms into the language of the original problem. To this end, delicate results of measure theory, connected with the representation of linear functionals on spaces of measurable functions, and measurable selection theorems are needed. For the results concerning models of economic dynamics presented in this book, the methods of convex analysis are also specifically required.

Having made these preliminary comments, we now briefly describe the contents of the book by chapter.

Chapter 1 is introductory in character; it is devoted to results for a general model of economic dynamics in the deterministic case. In this book we are interested primarily in stochastic models, but we begin with the Gale deterministic model by way of illustration in order to introduce the reader to the class of ideas constituting the mathematical theory of economic dynamics.

In §7 of Chapter 1, connections between Gale's model and the theory of optimal control are discussed. The introductory part of the book is written at the level of mathematical undergraduates and is meant to serve as a background for the subsequent text.

Chapter 2 is devoted to the stochastic maximum principle. It is proven first for a general class of problems in function spaces. From this abstract result the analogous proposition is derived for the optimal control problem over a finite horizon in which the class of admissible controls allows dependency on all the past to date. In this same chapter a version of the maximum principle is stated for a probabilistic generalization of Gale's model (an existence theorem for supporting prices). The account of economic models given here is independent of the control theory results since such models constitute "simpler" objects and consequently make it possible to obtain more precise results (as regards both the methods of construction of their stochastic analogues and the conditions under which the maximum principle is established).

Chapter 3 considers the Markovian case. The main result is the general theorem on the sufficiency of Markov controls, which we use to obtain the Markovian version of the maximum principle as a corollary of the maximum principle of Chapter 2. It should also be mentioned that in this chapter a new method not relying on the use of dynamic programming is given for the construction of optimal Markov programmes for convex problems.

Chapter 4 begins with the definition of a stationary dynamic economic model, used in Chapters 4 and 5, which is designed for the probabilistic version of optimal economic planning theory over an infinite horizon. In Chapter 4 the turnpike theorems are stated in weak form, and the existence of an optimal programme over an infinite horizon is proven.

In Chapter 5 the turnpike theorems are presented in strong form and a construction necessary for their proofs (approximation of programmes) is described.

In the appendices, the formulations of some general results are added for convenience. Proofs are given only for propositions which from our point of view have some methodological interest.

We emphasize here that the arrangement of the contents of the book allows the reader who is interested solely in economic models to avoid the theory of optimal control. To this end one need only read Chapter 1 excluding §7, then §4 of Chapter 2, and Chapters 4 and 5. The reader who is interested primarily in optimal control can start from §7 of Chapter 1 and then read Chapters 2 and 3.

The system of references in the book is the following. Theorems, corollaries, lemmas, and formulae are separately numbered in each chapter. When a theorem or a formula in another chapter is referenced, the number of the chapter is mentioned; for example, Theorem 2.1 is the first theorem of Chapter 2. The chapters in the book are divided into sections, and the sections are divided into subsections. The reference system should be obvious from the following examples: §2.4 is Subsection 4 of Section 2 of the current chapter and §2.5.1 is Subsection 1 of Section 5 of Chapter 2. A roman numeral refers to an appendix; for example, §III.2 is Section 2 of Appendix III. A similar system is used in the appendices with regard to theorem references, so that Theorem II.1 is the first theorem of Appendix II.

PREFACE TO THE ENGLISH EDITION

We wish to thank the translators warmly for their kind efforts in helping to address the English edition of this book to a wider audience. We are extremely grateful for their diligence and meticulousness in translating our work.

In this edition we have taken the opportunity to make a number of minor revisions.

We hope that the publication of our book in English will help to stimulate research in the application of probabilistic methods to control theory and economics.

Moscow
March 1987

V.I.A.
I.V.E.

TRANSLATORS' PREFACE

The English edition of this book has been prepared from the Russian edition (published by Nauka, Moscow, 1979) in collaboration with the authors. No attempt has been made to translate the Russian text literally. Indeed, as well as taking the opportunity to make minor corrections, several proofs have been altered, the notation has been substantially modified for clarity and consistency, and an attempt has been made to amplify the exposition to make it more accessible to Western readers with the current standard mathematical background in the fields of stochastic optimization, theoretical economics, and control theory. The book should now be amenable to careful study by senior undergraduate and graduate students in mathematics, economics, and systems theory who have mastered basic advanced courses in measure theory, probability and stochastic processes, and linear and nonlinear functional analysis. Economists should also possess some basic knowledge of the problems and applications of economic growth theory, although the former are elegantly reviewed in the very general context of the Gale model in Chapter 1. For researchers, we have appended—in conjunction with the authors and with the help of a number of colleagues—chapter-by-chapter references which treat topics related to points raised in the text. These mostly concern research appearing in both the Western and Soviet literature in the seven years since the original edition was published and are intended as a guide to this rapidly expanding field.

Several words are in order regarding terminology, conventions, and notation.

In general, we have tended to use what we consider to be the most common current terminology—for example, "mathematical programme" or "optimization problem" for "extremum problem," "supporting" for "stimulating" prices, etc. We have retained the original numbering and cross-reference scheme of sections, subsections, and results within chapters, but for ease of reference we have added an explicit statement of assumed technical conditions in the statements of theorem, but *not in those of lemmas* (where this was judged too unwieldy to be useful). All such conditions—both maintained throughout and assumed only in certain parts of the text—are displayed and indented and set in italics for easier referral.

We have attempted to remove the often confusing designation of a function by its value in the original text by the insertion of the words "given by" and a similar—less successful—attempt has been made with regard to measures. Our hope is that the result will be easily understandable without being excessively pedantic. We have also maintained—with less than total enthusiasm—the author's notation for (finite dimensional) vector product (as simply juxtaposition) and for the action of a functional (where it is important to note that, however such action is denoted in the text, the dual element appears first, i.e., leftmost).

Two major notational innovations appear in the English edition of this work. The first continues the crusade of one of us concerning the introduction of a compatible notation for random variables, vectors, sequences, functions, sets, etc., into branches of the mathematical sciences with an already-well-developed deterministic notation. This is effected simply by writing random entities with their usual symbols in boldface. This notation allows one to distinguish between, say, a random variable $\mathbf{b}$ and its realization $\mathbf{b} = b$. When an abstract probability space $(\Omega, \mathscr{F}, P)$ is involved, we may speak more precisely of $\mathbf{b}$ versus the realization $b(\omega)$; this introduces the usual schizophrenia between the probabilist's and analyst's interpretation of random entities. In the latter's view, b becomes a measurable function of Ω to $\mathbb{R}$, and this view has been taken where necessary in the text—for example, when speaking of elements of Lebesque function spaces and for arguments of certain abstract functionals on such spaces. Nevertheless, the boldface notation accords with the intuitive probabilistic viewpoint and results in considerable notational simplification, clarification, and consistency in the bulk of this text—as in others involving stochastic models in established fields. For example, it should be noted that equations or inequalities between random entities are mostly required to hold "almost surely (a.s.)" in this work, whereas the analogous pointwise statement of this requirement is used much less frequently and is denoted by "a.s. $[P]$" (or occasionally, when in the analytic mode, in terms of "almost everywhere" as "a.e. [P]"). Furthermore, due to the widespread use of Kolmogorov canonical constructions of probability spaces in the text, the notation $\mathbf{b} := b(\omega)$ is often useful and the indicator function of a set Γ as an elementary random variable is denoted by $\mathbf{1}_\Gamma$ in order to allow the compact use of the expectation operator in lieu of the integral.

The second notational innovation concerns a method for marking the logical structure of elaborate proofs. It has become common practice to denote the end of proofs by a symbol such as the "□" used in this text. It is perhaps fitting, in a book so largely devoted to developments concerning his elegant economic model, that David Gale's observation that the same symbol could equally well be used to denote the *beginning* of proofs is implemented herein. Moreover, we have used this idea recursively—in which one of us, in deference to the birthplace of the general notion, terms "Erice notation"—to make subdivisions of proofs, proofs of lemmas within theorem proofs, etc., appear as logical material within stylized brackets as "□ . . . □". The sole exception to this rule is that a single □ is used to terminate the statement of a result either not proven or proven later in the text under a specific statement or heading such as "Proof of Theorem 5". (With regard to the ultimate goal of the notation in terms of computing machine storage, selected proof-level retrievability, and natural-language user-friendliness of mathematical proofs essentially expressed in a suitable formal logic, a bracket "□ □" with void content could have been used for this purpose.) The aim of the notation generally is, of course, to expose proof structure by making the details of any proof at various logical levels parenthetical material to be carefully studied only at the reader's discretion. It might therefore be hoped to be of some pedagogical use.

Finally, we would like to thank the National Science and Engineering Research Council of Canada, Balliol College, Oxford, and the International Institute for Applied Systems Analysis, Laxenburg, Austria, for partial support of this project. We wish to express our gratitude to Leslie Stockhausen for meticulous preparation—on a MICOM 2001 word processor—of the document from which this book was printed. A number of colleagues have kindly provided encouragement, suggestions, references, etc. In particular, we wish to thank M. Ali Khan, J.-P. Aubin, D. P. Bertsekas, T. F. Bewley, A. Cellina, M. H. A. Davis, Y. A. Ermoliev, S. D. Flam, T. Kurz, H. J. Kushner, R. Marimon, L. W. McKanzie, R. Radner, R. T. Rockafellar, G. Salinetti, W. R. S. Sutherland and R. J.-B. Wets.

Halifax, Nova Scotia E.A.M-D.
March 1987 M.A.H.D.

1 DETERMINISTIC MODELS

1. THE GALE MODEL

1. Technology, Utility Functions and Programmes

The *Gale model* is specified at each time $t = 1, 2, \ldots$ by a convex set Q_t (the technology set), whose elements are pairs of nonnegative n-dimensional vectors (x, y) and a concave real-valued function[1] F_t defined on Q_t (the utility or social welfare function).

The pairs (x, y) specify *technological processes* (x as *input*, y as *output*), and the set Q_t is interpreted as the *technology set* of possible technological processes in the *time period* $(t-1, t]$. To say that $(x, y) \in Q_t$ means that the expenditure of the input vector x at time $t-1$ yields the production of the (not necessarily unique) output vector y at time t.

The components of the vectors x and y may be specified as amounts of some *products* (*goods*) existing in the economy.[2] The function $F_t(x, y)$ is supposed to measure the aggregate satisfaction (*utility*) of the technological process (x, y).

[1] A function F is said to be *concave* if $F(\alpha z + (1-\alpha)z') \geqq \alpha F(z) + (1-\alpha)F(z')$ for all z, z' and $\alpha \in [0,1]$. Further, if for $z \neq z'$ and $\alpha \in (0,1)$ the strong inequality holds, the function is called *strictly concave*.

[2] It may be preferable to use the term "goods" because "product" in the Gale model is interpreted in a very wide sense, so as to refer, for example, to different kinds of services. However, the authors prefer to use the traditional (Soviet) term.

The assumptions regarding the convexity of the set Q_t and the concavity of the function F_t are typical in the theory of economic growth models. The convexity of the technology set Q_t means that it is possible to *mix* technological processes in arbitrary proportions. The concavity of the utility function F_t reflects the nature of the preferences of society for *variety* in general—"half an apple and half an orange are better than either a whole apple or a whole orange."[3] A sequence of vectors

$$\{z_1, z_2, \ldots\}, \qquad z_t := (x_{t-1}, y_t) \tag{1}$$

—finite or infinite—is called a *programme* if

$$z_t \in Q_t, \tag{2}$$

$$y_t \geqq x_t\,^4 \tag{3}$$

$(t \geqq 1)$.

The first condition, (2), means that all elements z_t of the sequence are feasible from the technological point of view; the second condition, (3), is the *resource restriction*—the input (or *expenditures*) at each step must not exceed the output from the previous step. The vector y_0 is called the vector of *initial resources* (or the *initial vector*, i.v.) for the programme (1) if $y_0 \geqq x_0$; i.e., input at time zero does not exceed initial resources.

2. Optimal Programmes over a Finite Horizon

An *optimal programme* over a *finite horizon* (planning period) $1, 2, \ldots, N$ is defined for some fixed nonnegative initial vector y_0 as follows. Find a programme ζ^0 among all programmes $\{z_1, \ldots, z_n\}$ with initial vector y_0 such that the sum $F_1(z_1) + \cdots + F_N(z_N)$ is a maximum. Sufficient conditions for the existence of optimal programmes are that

> *at least one programme exists, the sets Q_t are compact and the functions F_t are upper semicontinuous.*[5]

In the sequel these conditions will be assumed to hold.

[3] Gale [2]. See also the example in §6 (a model which *explicitly* involves consumption).

[4] For two vectors $x = (x_1, \ldots, x_n)$ and $y = (y_1, \ldots, y_n)$, we define $y \geqq x$ $(y > x)$, if $y_i \geqq x_i$ $(y_i > x_i)$ for each i.

[5] A function F is called *upper (lower) semicontinuous* at a point z_0 if

$$\limsup_{z \to z_0} F(z) \leqq F(z_0) \quad (\liminf_{z \to z_0} F(z) \geqq F(z_0)).$$

3. Optimal Programmes over an Infinite Horizon

For an *infinite horizon* 1, 2, ... it might be possible to find a maximum of the sum $\sum_{t=1}^{\infty} F_t(z_t)$; however, this sum is not convergent for most interesting models, and hence *Ramsey's definition of optimality* is used.

We shall say that the real sequence $\{\delta_k\}$ overtakes the sequence $\{\delta'_k\}$ if $\delta_k \geqq \delta'_k$ for all k from some K onwards. By definition, an *optimal programme* ζ^0 among all infinite (horizon) programmes with given initial vector y_0 is the programme whose sequence of partial sums $F_1(z_1^0) + \cdots + F_N(z_N^0)$ *overtakes* the corresponding sequence for any other programme. If the series $F_\infty := \sum_{t=1}^{\infty} F_t(z_t)$ is convergent for each programme, an optimal programme maximizes F_∞.

Conversely, if exactly one programme exists which maximizes F_∞, it is optimal by the above definition.

The existence of optimal infinite horizon programmes (in "stationary" models) is one of the main results of the theory to be presented.

The problem of the existence of an optimal programme over an infinite horizon is important from the economic point of view. Some problems in dynamic economic theory are impossible to solve within the limits of a finite time period. For example, the question of determining an optimal ratio between *consumption* and *capital accumulation* in an economy is one such problem.

Specifically, we should like to determine what amounts of resource should be optimally allocated to the production of current consumption goods and what amounts should be allocated to the production of capital equipment to be used for producing consumption goods in the future. The solution of this problem over a finite horizon shows that in the last period all available resources should be consumed—but this is undesirable, as usually there are concerns beyond the planning period. One method to avoid this "end effect" is to introduce additional constraints which guarantee sufficient resource supply in the final period, but how much should this supply be? The higher the supply required in the future, the higher must be sacrifices in the present. To answer this question is to extend the initial planning period, but the problem arises anew on a longer interval, and so on. If this is so, however, the planning decisions must actually be based on consideration of an infinite horizon. For this purpose, the present opportunity and value systems must be extrapolated, and then an optimal infinite horizon plan must be found. What the resulting programme specifies over a thousand-year period has little meaning for us; it is only important to know what it specifies in the "near" future. The extrapolation task and the optimization over an infinite horizon may be solved again when the near future is left behind and the situation has changed, and so on.

4. Prices

In this section we shall be concerned only with those programmes whose initial vector is some fixed vector $y_0 \geqq 0$.

A *price system* (or *price*) is any sequence of nonnegative n-dimensional vectors $\{p_t\}$ $(t \geqq 0)$. If $x := (x_1, \ldots, x_n)$ is some vector of goods, the scalar product $p_t x := \sum_{i=1}^{n} p_{ti} x_i$ is defined as the *value* of the vector at time t. The ith component p_{ti} of the vector p_t is the current *price* of the ith good.

A central concept of this book is the concept of supporting prices. We say that a price system $\{p_t^0\}$ *supports* the programme (1) if the following conditions hold:

A. *The process* (x_{t-1}, y_t) *maximizes the function*

$$G_t(x, y) = F_t(x, y) + p_t^0 y - p_{t-1}^0 x \tag{4}$$

for all $(x, y) \in Q_t$ *at each* $t \geqq 1$.

B.

$$p_t^0(y_t - x_t) = 0 \tag{5}$$

for all $t \geqq 0$.

The function $G_t(x, y)$ is called the *total utility* of the technological process (x, y), and it has an obvious economic interpretation. The value $p_t^0 y$ in expression (4) is the *value of output* at time t, while $p_{t-1}^0 x$ is the *cost of input* at time $t - 1$, and so $p_t^0 y - p_{t-1}^0 x$ is the (*net*) *profit* from operating the technological process (x, y) expressed in terms of the prices $\{p_t^0\}$. Thus the total utility $G_t(x, y)$ may be interpreted as the (direct) utility (or social welfare) plus the profit from the process (x, y).

Equation (5) may be interpreted as stating that the value of the resources $y_t - x_t$ left *unused* by the programme (1) equals zero in each time period. Therefore a price system supports a programme if, and only if, in each time period, first, the technological process of that programme yields a maximum of total utility and, second, the value of unused resources equals zero. We emphasize that in formula (5) the vector y_0 is fixed at $t = 0$.

5. The Concept of Supporting Prices[6]

A number of theorems stating the existence of prices supporting optimal programmes will be provided in the sequel for deterministic and, later, stochastic models. (This is in fact the substance of the main results for finite horizon models.) Such theorems are important from the mathematical point of view, and they also have important economic consequences. They show that a system of supporting prices permits the *intertemporal disaggregation* of the solution of the optimal planning task. If such a price system is known and it is also known that total utility G_t achieves its maximum at a single point for each t (for example, if F_t is a strictly concave function), then the optimal programme can be found by maximizing the total utility for each $t \geqq 1$. In this case, the (globally) optimal plan need only appear to be optimal with regard to our myopic interests in each time period $(t-1, t]$. Thus the price system $\{p_t^0\}$ penalizes any deviation from the (globally) optimal programme and in this sense "supports" it. In the case when the optimum of total utility is *not* unique, the implication of maximization of total utility at each step may be interpreted as agreement between *myopic* objectives (maximization of G_t) and *global* interests described in terms of $\sum_{t=1}^{N} F_t$ $(N \geqq 1)$.

It should be noted that if the prices $\{p_0, p_1, \ldots, p_N\}$ support a programme $\{z_1, \ldots, z_N\}$ with initial value y_0, and $p_N = 0$, this programme is optimal among all programmes with i.v. y_0. This simple result will be demonstrated in §2.

6. Stationary Models

In this subsection planning over an infinite horizon is discussed for models in which technological possibilities and utility functions are constant in time; viz.,

$$Q_t \equiv Q, \qquad F_t \equiv F. \tag{6}$$

Such models are called *stationary*.

[6] It is important to note that in the definition of concepts similar to supporting prices in the mathematical economics literature, a variety of other terms (such as *stimulating prices*, *objectively determined prices*, and *shadow prices*) are often used.

The assumption of stationarity is, of course, restrictive. However, more realistic models of a *constant growth* economy,

$$Q_t := \lambda^t Q, \qquad F_t(z) := F(z\lambda^{-t}), \tag{7}$$

where λ is any positive number (the *growth rate*; see §6), may be transformed into stationary models. Moreover, some kind of stationarity assumption is difficult to eliminate in any realistic model; any probabilistic prediction of the behaviour of a system over long time periods is usually (if not always) based on some assumptions of stationarity.[7]

In stationary models, important rôles are played by *stationary programmes*, i.e., programmes for which z_t is independent of t (i.e., $z_t \equiv z$), and *stationary prices* $p_t \equiv p$. The programme $\{\bar{z}\}$, which maximizes $F(z)$ among all stationary programmes, is called the *turnpike*. Some conditions must be added to this definition to guarantee the uniqueness of the turnpike.

7. An Overview of the Theory of Stationary Models

A proof of the existence of stationary press supporting the turnpike is a central result of the theory of stationary models. (It is easy in the deterministic case but more difficult in the stochastic case.) This result is used to construct infinite (horizon) optimal programmes, and it may also be applied in the investigation of the asymptotic properties of optimal programmes. It may be shown that finite (horizon) optimal programmes approach the turnpike as the planning interval increases and that infinite optimal programmes approach the turnpike as $t \to \infty$. These results also hold for so-called good infinite programmes, which have the feature of being close to optimal programmes. These statements are called *turnpike theorems*. Turnpike theorems for finite programmes are of two types—weak and strong. *Weak turnpike theorems* assert that, for a sufficiently large planning interval, optimal programmes spend most of their time *close* to the turnpike. However, the locations of the "excluded" periods when an optimal programme deviates considerably from the turnpike are not mentioned in weak turnpike theorems. These

[7] We emphasize that this is not, of course, a *serious* prediction over a thousand years, but is used only for those periods nearest to hand. However, to give a basis for tomorrow's decisions, it is necessary to investigate the behaviour of the system into the future on a sufficiently long time interval. This argument leads directly to mathematical programmes over an infinite horizon (as noted above).

periods are characterized exactly in *strong turnpike theorems*, which establish that the excluded periods may only be placed close to the two ends of the planning interval. (In the middle of this interval an optimal programme must be close to the turnpike.)

Results of the previous type motivated the use of the term turnpike. The following analogy is given by way of further explanation. Suppose we would like to drive from a town A to a town B and that the main road (the turnpike) passes close to A and B. The (time) optimal journey is first to drive to the main road from town A, then to drive along the main road and finally to turn away from the main road to reach town B only near the end of the trip. Strong turnpike theorems show that optimal programmes of economic growth are analogous to our example. These results are important because they establish the proximity of the optimal programmes to a special programme with a simple structure. The turnpike is actually a maximal stationary programme. Relative to the difficulty involved in finding the optimal programme of given finite length, the turnpike can easily be determined. Turnpike theorems display the basic structure of optimal programmes in terms of the turnpike.

Furthermore, strong turnpike theorems lead to the following conjecture. It is possible that a programme exists which exactly coincides with the turnpike over most of the planning period and gives approximately the same result as the optimal programme. In reality this is often the case, but, in general, statements of the existence of such approximating programmes and turnpike theorems (in the sense described above) are independent. The existence of simple approximating programmes of this form was first shown by Winter (for a different model); the analogous result will be proved in §5 for the Gale model. The facts and concepts described above will be the main reference points for our presentation of stationary models. In addition, some results which possess both economic interpretation and independent mathematical interest will be developed.

First we make a few comments on methods for defining technology sets.

8. A Parametric Form for Technology Description

In realistic models technology sets are often presented in the following form. For each $t \geqq 0$ a set U_t is given (the *control space*), and for $u \in U_{t-1}$ $(t \geqq 1)$ two functions $a_{t-1}(u)$ and $b_t(u)$ (the *input* and *output* determined by the control u) are specified. A set of technological processes on the interval $(t-1, t]$ is then described as

$$Q_t := \{(a_{t-1}(u), b_t(u)) : u \in U_{t-1}\}.$$

This description of Q_t is called the *parametric form* of the technology set.

An important rôle is played by models in which U_t is a convex set in m-dimensional Euclidean space $\mathbb{R}^m$ and the input and output functions have linear representations;

$$a_t(u) := A_t u, \qquad b_t(u) := B_t u$$

(the *von Neumann technology*). The matrices A and B have the following interpretation. Suppose A_t and B_t are given by sets of column vectors as

$$A_t := (a_t^1, \ldots, a_t^m), \qquad B_t := (b_t^1, \ldots, b_t^m).$$

The pairs (a_{t-1}^j, b_t^j) $(j = 1, \ldots, m)$ characterize the basic technological processes; if the jth process is implemented with unit intensity, its input and output (vectors) equal a_{t-1}^j and b_t^j, respectively. If the first process is implemented with intensity u_1, the second with u_2 and so on, the aggregate input and output are given by

$$A_{t-1}u := \sum_{j=1}^{m} a_{t-1}^j u_j, \qquad B_t u := \sum_{j=1}^{m} b_t^j u_j,$$

respectively (where u_j is the jth coordinate of u). Thus U_t may be interpreted as the set of possible *intensities* of the technological processes, and our control at each period is the choice of intensity levels for these processes.

In §§2–6 of this chapter we shall give precise statements and proofs of the results described in this section.

2. OPTIMAL FINITE HORIZON PROGRAMMES

1. The Existence of Supporting Prices

We shall prove that prices which support finite optimal programmes exist. Let the nonnegative vector y_0 (the initial supply) and the natural number N (the length of the planning horizon) be fixed.

Theorem 1. (Existence of supporting prices over a finite horizon.) *Suppose the programme* $\tilde{\zeta} := \{(\tilde{x}_{t-1}, \tilde{y}_t)\}$ *with i.v.* $\tilde{y}_0 = y_0$ *is such that* $\tilde{y}_t > \tilde{x}_t$ *for all* $t \geqq 0$. *Then prices supporting a family of optimal programmes with length N and i.v.* y_0 *exist.*[8]

The condition of Theorem 1 requires the existence of a programme $\tilde{\zeta}$ with strictly positive vectors of unused resources.

□ The optimal planning task may be set out as follows. Maximize

$$F(\zeta) := F_1(z_1) + \cdots + F_N(z_N) \tag{8}$$

over all

$$\zeta := \{z_t\} = \{(x_{t-1}, y_t)\} \tag{9}$$

subject to the constraints

$$\zeta \in Q := Q_1 \times Q_2 \times \cdots \times Q_N \tag{10}$$

and

$$g(\zeta) \geqq 0, \tag{11}$$

where

$$g(\zeta) := \{y_0 - x_0, y_1 - x_1, \ldots, y_{N-1} - x_{N-1}\}. \tag{12}$$

By assumption, $g(\tilde{\zeta}) > 0$ for some $\tilde{\zeta} \in Q$. This means that the *Slater constraint qualification* (see §III.2) holds for the mathematical programming problem defined by (8)–(11). Therefore the *Kuhn–Tucker Theorem* (see §III.2) may be applied to obtain a vector $p^0 = \{p_0^0, p_1^0, \ldots, p_{N-1}^0\} \geqq 0$ such that for all $\zeta \in Q$

$$F(\zeta) + p^0 g(\zeta) \leqq F(\zeta^0), \tag{13}$$

where $\zeta^0 := \{z_t^0\}$ denotes an arbitrary optimal programme of length N.

This inequality may be rewritten

$$\sum_{t=1}^{N} F_t(z_t) + \sum_{t=0}^{N-1} p_t^0(y_t - x_t) \leqq \sum_{t=1}^{N} F_t(z_t^0) \tag{14}$$

for any sequence (9) from the set Q. We define that $p_N^0 = 0$. Then the following result holds:

[8] We say that prices support a family of programmes if they support each programme of the family.

Lemma 1. (Characterization of supporting prices.) *Condition* (14) *holds for prices* $p_0, \ldots, p_N$ *with* $p_N = 0$ *if and only if they support the programme* $\{z_t^0\}$.

□ ⇒□ By substituting $\{z_t^0\} = \{(x_{t-1}^0, y_t^0)\}$ in the left-hand side of (14), it is easily seen that Property B holds in the definition of supporting prices, namely, $p_t(y_t^0 - x_t^0) = 0$.[9] From this it follows that

$$\sum_{t=0}^{N} F_t(z_t) + \sum_{t=0}^{N-1} p_t(y_t - x_t) \leqq \sum_{t=1}^{N} F_t(z_t^0) + \sum_{t=0}^{N-1} p_t(y_t^0 - x_t^0). \quad (15)$$

For $\zeta = \{z_t\} \in Q$ let $G(\zeta) := \sum_{t=1}^{N} G_t(z_t)$ [cf. (4)], and notice that the inequality $G_t(z) \leqq G_t(z_t^0)$ holds for all $z \in Q_t$, $t = 1, \ldots, N$ (i.e., Property A) if and only if $G(\zeta) \leqq G(\zeta^0)$ holds for all ζ. This is so because the terms in the sum $G(\zeta)$ are independent of each other, and $G(\zeta)$ achieves a maximum if and only if each term achieves a maximum.

From this we can conclude that Property A is equivalent to inequality (15), since the left- and right-hand sides of the inequality $G(\zeta) \leqq G(\zeta^0)$ are equal to the left- and right-hand sides, respectively, of inequality (15). This is easy to see by regrouping terms in the sum

$$G(\zeta) = \sum_{t=0}^{N} [F_t(z_t) + p_t y_t - p_{t-1} x_{t-1}]$$

and using $p_N = 0$ and $y_0^0 = y_0$. □

⇐□ Conversely, inequality (15) follows from A, and equation (14) follows from (15) and B. □□

Applying the necessity part of Lemma 1 to the Kuhn–Tucker prices p^0 establishes Theorem 1. □

The next statement also follows from Lemma 1.

(Sufficiency of supporting prices for optimality.) *If the prices* $\{p_0^0, \ldots, p_N^0\}$ *support a programme* $\{z_1, \ldots, z_N\}$ *and* $p_N^0 = 0$, *then this programme* $\{z_1, \ldots, z_N\}$ *is optimal.*

□ The proof is a consequence of formula (14). One must substitute an arbitrary programme $\{z_t'\}$ in (14) and notice that $\sum_{t=1}^{N} p_t^0(y_t' - x_t') \geqq 0$, since $y_t' - x_t' \geqq 0$ by the definition of a programme. Hence $\sum_{t=1}^{N} F(z_t') \leqq \sum_{t=1}^{N} F(z_t)$. □

[9] We assume $y_0^0 = y_0$ at $t = 0$.

Note. Sums of the form

$$G_k^l(\zeta) := \sum_{t=k}^{l} G_t(z_t) = \sum_{t=k}^{l} [F_t(z_t) + p_t y_t - p_{t-1} x_{t-1}] \tag{16}$$

similar to the sum in the proof of Lemma 1 will often appear in the sequel, and we shall need the following formulae:

$$G_k^l(\zeta) = \sum_{t=k}^{l} F_t(z_t) + \sum_{t=k}^{l-1} p_t(y_t - x_t) - p_{k-1}x_{k-1} + p_l y_l, \tag{17}$$

$$G_k^l(\zeta) = \sum_{t=k}^{l} F_t(z_t) + \sum_{t=k-1}^{l-1} p_t(y_t - x_t) - p_{k-1}y_{k-1} + p_l y_l, \tag{18}$$

which are easy to work out by regrouping terms in (16).

2. Supporting Prices as Lagrange Multipliers

To construct supporting prices we have investigated the mathematical programming problem whose solution is the optimal programme; we have also treated the resource restrictions (3) as the constraints (11) of the problem. The optimal Lagrange multipliers corresponding to these restrictions are the desired prices.

The fact that $p_N^0 = 0$ in the supporting price system p^0 is not accidental. It reflects the end effect: If in the planning task no account is taken of what happens after the end of the planning period, any unused resource supply has zero value in the last period N.

A few more remarks are in order on the interpretation of inequality (15).

The optimal programme, by definition, maximizes the functional F subject to the resource restrictions (3) over Q.

By virtue of (15) it also maximizes $F(\zeta) + p^0 g(\zeta)$ over Q without further constraints. What is the additional term $p^0 g(\zeta)$? We must consider an individual term in the expression $p^0 g(\zeta)$;

$$p_t^0(y_t - x_t) = \sum_{i=1}^{n} p_{ti}^0(y_{ti} - x_{ti}).$$

For a programme each such term is always nonnegative. But if the sequence ζ is not a programme, then the number $y_{ti} - x_{ti}$ representing the unused amount of the ith resource may be *negative*. In this case, the value $p_{ti}^0(y_{ti}^0 - x_{ti})$ may be interpreted as the *expenditure* required to buy the quantity needed of a resource in short supply. This value must be subtracted from the utility function. If $y_{ti} - x_{ti} > 0$, the corresponding value is *profit*. Thus the supporting price system $\{p_t^0\}$ "replaces" the system of resource restrictions (3) by permitting the *purchase* of resources in short supply and the *sale* of unused resources.

3. An Inequality

We prove here an inequality involving supporting prices, which will be needed below.

Lemma 2. *Suppose the prices $\{p_t^0\}$ support the programme $\{z_t^0\}$, and suppose $\{z_t\}$ is any other programme. Then*

$$\sum_{t=k}^{l} [F_t(z_t^0) - F_t(z_t)] \geqq p_{k-1}^0(x_{k-1}^0 - x_{k-1}) - p_l^0(y_l^0 - y_l).$$

□ It is sufficient to consider formula (17) for the programme $\{z_t^0\}$ (in this case, as we have seen, $p_t^0(y_t^0 - x_t^0) = 0$) and for the programme $\{z_t\}$. Subtracting the formula obtained for $\{z_t\}$ from that obtained for $\{z_t^0\}$ and using $p_t^0(y_t - x_t) \geqq 0$ yields

$$\sum_{t=k}^{l} [F_t(z_t^0) - F_t(z_t)] - p_{k-1}^0 x_{k-1}^0 + p_l^0 y_l^0 + p_{k-1}^0 x_{k-1} - p_l^0 y_l \geqq 0.$$

[Nonnegativity follows from the optimality of $\{z_t^0\}$ and the definition of supporting price; cf. (4) and (5).] The required inequality is immediate. □

3. WEAK TURNPIKE THEOREMS

1. The Programming Problem for the Stationary Model

We consider the stationary model (6). As was defined above, programmes of the form $\{z, z, z, \ldots\}$ are termed *stationary*, and the *turnpike* is defined as a stationary programme for which $F(z)$ is a maximum. When does the vector $z = (x, y)$ define a stationary programme? Obviously, it is necessary and sufficient that the following conditions hold:

$$z \in Q, \tag{19}$$

$$y - x \geqq 0. \tag{20}$$

The first condition requires the technological feasibility of z; the second imposes resource restrictions. Hence the technological process z defining the turnpike is the solution of the problem

$$\text{maximize} \quad F(z) \tag{21}$$

subject to the constraints (19) and (20).

The turnpike programme is *unique* if the following condition (which will be assumed in §3.3 and the remainder of this chapter) holds:

(∗) *The function given by $F(z)$ is strictly concave.*

2. Stationary Prices Supporting the Turnpike

Our first aim is to construct prices supporting the turnpike. By definition, prices $\{\bar{p}, \bar{p}, \ldots\}$ support the programme $\{\bar{z}, \bar{z}, \ldots\}$ if and only if

$$F(z) + \bar{p}y - \bar{p}x \leqq F(\bar{z}) + \bar{p}\bar{y} - \bar{p}\bar{x} \tag{22}$$

for any $z = (x, y) \in Q$ and

$$\bar{p}(\bar{y} - \bar{x}) = 0.^{10} \tag{23}$$

As long as $\bar{y} - \bar{x} \geqq 0$ and $\bar{p} \geqq 0$, the two formulae (22) and (23) are equivalent to one:

$$F(z) + \bar{p}(y - x) \leqq F(\bar{z}) \tag{24}$$

for any $z = (x, y) \in Q$. Thus prices $\{\bar{p}\}$ support the turnpike if and only if the vector $\bar{p}$ removes the constraint (20) in the mathematical programming problem (19)–(21) (see Appendix III).

[10] In order to satisfy expression (5)—corresponding to (23)—at $t = 0$, we assume that the programme $\{\bar{z}\}$ is given together with the initial vector $\bar{y}$.

From the Kuhn–Tucker theorem (§III.2) it is sufficient for the existence of Lagrange multipliers that the *Slater constraint qualification* holds:

(**) *Vectors* $\tilde{x}$ *and* $\tilde{y}$ *may be found such that*

$$(\tilde{x}, \tilde{y}) \in Q$$

and

$$\tilde{y} > \tilde{x}.$$

This condition, called the *productivity condition* for the model, will be assumed in this chapter. The productivity condition asserts the existence of a technological process for which input is less than output for all components. The productivity assumption does not seem too restrictive (because the vectors $\tilde{x}$ and $\tilde{y}$ may differ very little from each other and the zero vector).

Further, we assume the following condition to be imposed:

(***) $(0, 0) \in Q$

(the possibility of *zero* inputs and *zero* outputs). This assumption is purely technical. It may be trivially replaced by the following condition:

The technology set contains the vector (d, d) *such that for any* $(x, y) \in Q$, $x \geqq d$, $y \geqq d$

[i.e., the technology set contains the *minimal* process (d, d)].

3. Statement of the Weak Turnpike Theorem for Finite Programmes

Suppose y_0 is a nonnegative vector. We consider the optimal programme $\{z_1^N, \ldots, z_N^N\}$ with initial vector y_0 and designate $t_N(\epsilon)$ as the number of time periods t from the interval $1 \leqq t \leqq N$ for which $|z_t^N - \bar{z}| \geqq \epsilon$.[11] We say that the vector y_0 is *sufficient* if a strictly positive vector can be produced from it in a finite number of steps; i.e., a programme $\{(x_0, y_1), \ldots, (x_{j-1}, y_j)\}$ with i.v. y_0 for which $y_j > 0$ exists.

Theorem 2. (Weak turnpike theorem.) *Let a sufficient vector* y_0 *be given. Then for any* $\epsilon > 0$ *the sequence* $\{t_N(\epsilon)\}$ *corresponding to the family of optimal programmes is bounded.*

[11] The *norm* $|z|$ of the vector $z := (z_1, \ldots, z_m)$ is defined as $|z_1| + \cdots + |z_m|$.

This result means that the number of time periods when the optimal programme differs from the turnpike by at least ϵ is bounded by a constant $L(\epsilon)$ independent of N. In other words, the optimal programme stays in an ϵ-neighbourhood of the turnpike for all time, except possibly for $L(\epsilon)$ periods.[12] Hence, it follows in particular that $t_N(\epsilon)/N \to 0$; i.e., the proportion of the time when the optimal programme deviates substantially from the turnpike converges to zero.

□ We deduce Theorem 2 from the following more general fact.

Theorem 3. (Weak turnpike theorem for a good family.) *The statement of Theorem 2 is true for any family of programmes* $\{z_1^N, \ldots, z_N^N\}$ $(N = 1, 2, \ldots)$ *for which there exists a constant I such that*

$$\sum_{t=1}^{N} [F(\bar{z}) - F(z_t^N)] \leqq I. \quad \square \tag{25}$$

A family of programmes $\{z_t^N\}$, $N = 1, 2, \ldots$, satisfying the condition (25) is called *good*. (These programmes can be "worse" than the turnpike only by a maximum utility value of I.) It will be shown that optimal programmes with a sufficient i.v. generate a good family.

4. Proof of Theorem 3: The Pseudometric ρ

Let

$$G(z) := F(z) + \bar{p}y - \bar{p}x \qquad (z = (x, y))$$

be the total utility corresponding to the stationary prices $\{\bar{p}\}$ which support the turnpike. Let

$$\rho(z, z') := |G(z) - G(z')|.$$

In the formulation of turnpike theorems, the pseudometric[13] ρ appears to be a more convenient measure of the deviation of z from $\bar{z}$ than the norm in terms of ease of proofs.

[12] This type of result is sometimes called a turnpike theorem in *Radner* form. Radner [1] proved an analogous result for another model.

[13] By a *pseudometric* is meant a function possessing all the properties of a metric except $\rho(z, z') = 0 \Rightarrow z = z'$.

□ The proof of Theorem 3 consists of two steps. First, the turnpike theorem is established for the pseudometric ρ:

Lemma 3. *A constant K can be found such that for all N*

$$\sum_{t=1}^{N} \rho(z_t^N, \bar{z}) \leqq K. \quad \square \tag{26}$$

From this it follows immediately that the number of periods $t \in [1, N]$ for which $\rho(z_t^N, \bar{z}) \geqq \epsilon$ is bounded by a constant independent of N.

Second, we prove the following lemma, which permits a shift to the original norm $|\cdot|$ from the pseudometric ρ.

Lemma 4. *A function given by $\delta(\epsilon)$ exists, nondecreasing in $\epsilon \geqq 0$, such that $\delta(\epsilon) > 0$ for $\epsilon > 0$ and*

$$\rho(\bar{z}, z) \geqq \delta(|\bar{z} - z|). \quad \square \tag{27}$$

From (26) and (27) the required statement of Theorem 3 follows, since obviously

$$K \geqq \sum_{t=1}^{N} \rho(z_t^N, \bar{z}) \geqq t_N(\epsilon)\delta(\epsilon),$$

whence $t_N(\epsilon) \leqq K/\delta(\epsilon)$.

5. Proof of Lemma 3

□ Let $\{z_t\}$ be an arbitrary programme. From formula (17) (with $k = 1, l = N$)

$$\begin{aligned} \rho_N := \sum_{t=1}^{N} \rho(z_t, \bar{z}) &= \sum_{t=1}^{N} [G(\bar{z}) - G(z_t)] \\ &= \sum_{t=1}^{N} [F(\bar{z}) - F(z_t)] + \sum_{t=1}^{N} \bar{p}(\bar{y} - \bar{x}) \\ &\quad - \sum_{t=1}^{N-1} \bar{p}(y_t - x_t) + \bar{p}x_0 - \bar{p}y_N. \end{aligned}$$

In the last expression $\bar{p}(\bar{y} - \bar{x}) = 0$, since the prices $\{\bar{p}\}$ support the turnpike. Further, by the definition of a programme, $y_t \geqq x_t$, and hence $\bar{p}(y_t - x_t) \geqq 0$. Finally,

$$\bar{p}x_0 - \bar{p}y_N \leqq M,$$

where M is some constant (this is so because x_0 and y_N are both elements of a compact), so we can conclude that for any programme $\{z_t\}$

$$\rho_N \leqq \sum_{t=1}^{N} [F(\bar{z}) - F(z_t)] + M. \tag{28}$$

From this and the definition of a good family the lemma follows immediately. □

6. Proof of Lemma 4

□ Let

$$\delta(\epsilon) := \inf_{|z-\bar{z}| \geqq \epsilon} \rho(z, \bar{z}).$$

It then suffices to check that $\delta(\epsilon) > 0$ for $\epsilon > 0$. In the contrary case, a sequence $z_k \in Q$ can be found for which $|z_k - \bar{z}| \geqq \epsilon$, but $\rho(z_k, \bar{z}) \to 0$. Because the set Q is compact, we may assume by passing to a subsequence that z_k is convergent to some point $z_0 \in Q$ with $|z_0 - \bar{z}| \geqq \epsilon$.

For any $z \in Q$ we have

$$\rho(z, \bar{z}) = |G(\bar{z}) - G(z)| = G(\bar{z}) - G(z) \geqq 0, \tag{29}$$

since $\bar{z}$ maximizes the total utility. On the other hand,

$$0 = \lim_{k \to \infty} \rho(z_k, \bar{z}) = G(\bar{z}) - \lim_{k \to \infty} G(z_k) \geqq G(\bar{z}) - G(z_0), \tag{30}$$

since $F(z)$ is an upper semicontinuous function; it follows that the same property is possessed by $G(z)$ [as the sum of $F(z)$ and a linear function]. Comparing (29) and (30) we obtain

$$G(\bar{z}) - G(z_0) = 0;$$

i.e., z_0 is the maximum of $G(z)$. But the function G is strictly concave (it is the sum of a strictly concave function and the linear function $\bar{p}y - \bar{p}x$ This function can therefore achieve its maximum value only at a single point, and thus $z_0 = \bar{z}$. This contradicts the inequality $|z_0 - \bar{z}| \geqq \epsilon$ and proves Lemma 4 (and Theorem 3). □□

7. The Existence of Good Infinite Programmes

To prove Theorem 2 from Theorem 3 it is sufficient to check that the optimal programmes $\{z_t^N\}$ $(N = 1, 2, \ldots)$ make up a good family. For this in turn it is enough to construct an infinite programme $\{\hat{z}_t\}$ with i.v. y_0 for which

$$\sum_{t=1}^{N} [F(\bar{z}) - F(\hat{z}_t)] \leqq \text{const} \qquad (N = 1, 2, \ldots). \tag{31}$$

Indeed, from the optimality of the $\{z_t^N\}$, the sums in the left-hand side of (25) do not exceed the corresponding sums in (31) and consequently are bounded.

Infinite programmes possessing property (31) are called *good*. Such programmes by definition cannot be "infinitely worse" than the turnpike. Further, it will be shown that good programmes are similar to optimal programmes in terms of the properties they possess. The next lemma asserts that a good programme exists, and this completes the proof of Theorem 2.

Lemma 5. (Existence of a good infinite programme.) *A good programme with i.v. y_0 exists for any sufficient vector y_0.*

□ Without loss of generality we may assume that $y_0 > 0$. Indeed, for a sufficient y_0 a good programme can be constructed as follows. First, obtain a positive vector from y_0; i.e., initiate the programme $\{(x_0, y_1), \ldots, (x_{k-1}, y_k)\}$ with i.v. y_0 and $y_k > 0$, and then continue it by the scheme described below.

Therefore let $y_0 > 0$ and suppose further that $\tilde{y} < y_0$. [This inequality can always be achieved by multiplying the $\tilde{z}$ of the Slater condition (**) by a sufficiently small $\lambda > 0$ by virtue of (***) and the convexity of Q.] We take some number $\theta \in (0, 1)$ and construct the sequence $\hat{z}_t$ by the formula

$$z_t = \theta^t \tilde{z} + (1 - \theta^t)\bar{z}.$$

We shall show that for a suitable choice of θ (a) this sequence is a programme and (b) this programme is good.

(a) In view of the convexity of Q, we have $\hat{z}_t \in Q$, because $\theta \in (0, 1)$.

It is necessary to verify the inequalities

$$\hat{y}_t \geqq \hat{x}_t \qquad (t \geqq 1), \tag{32}$$

$$y_0 \geqq \hat{x}_0. \tag{33}$$

The second inequality follows from the chain of relations $y_0 > \tilde{y} > \tilde{x} = \hat{x}_0$. To obtain the first inequality we use the following identity:

$$\hat{y}_t - \hat{x}_t = \theta^t[\tilde{y} - (\theta\tilde{x} + (1 - \theta)\bar{x})] + (1 - \theta^t)(\bar{y} - \bar{x}), \tag{34}$$

which may be checked by direct substitution (we advise the reader to do so). Because $\bar{y} \geqq \bar{x}$, it follows from (34) that $\hat{y}_t - \hat{x}_t \geqq 0$ for all $t \geqq 1$ provided

$$\tilde{y} > \theta\tilde{x} + (1 - \theta)\bar{x}.$$

But this may be achieved by taking θ sufficiently close to 1 [since by (**), $\tilde{y} > \tilde{x}$].

(b) By the concavity of F,

$$F(\hat{z}_t) \geqq \theta^t F(\tilde{z}) + (1 - \theta^t)F(\bar{z}).$$

Consequently,

$$F(\bar{z}) - F(\hat{z}_t) \leqq \theta^t[F(\bar{z}) - F(\tilde{z})],$$

from which it follows that the sums in (31) are bounded. ◻◻

8. The Turnpike Theorem for Good Programmes

The final result of this section asserts that all good programmes are asymptotic to the turnpike.

Theorem 4. (Convergence of good infinite programmes to the turnpike.) *If $\{z_t\}$ is a good programme, then $z_t \to \bar{z}$ as $t \to \infty$.*

◻ As a consequence of the definition of a good programme and inequality (28),

$$\rho(z_t, \bar{z}) \to 0. \tag{35}$$

Suppose that, for some infinite set of periods t, $|z_t - \bar{z}| \geqq \epsilon > 0$. Then by (27) the inequality $\rho(z_t, \bar{z}) \geqq \delta(\epsilon) > 0$ is valid for some t, which contradicts (35). Hence $|z_t - \bar{z}| < \epsilon$ after some t; i.e., $z_t \to \bar{z}$. ◻

4. OPTIMAL INFINITE HORIZON PROGRAMMES

1. The Brock *H* Functional

The purpose of §4 is to prove the following theorem:

Theorem 5. (Existence and uniqueness of an optimal infinite programme.) *A unique optimal infinite programme with i.v. y_0 exists for any sufficient vector y_0.*

□ We sketch the main stages of the proof. First, a functional H (introduced initially by W. Brock) will be constructed. This functional may be interpreted as characterizing the deviation of an infinite programme from the turnpike. It will be proved that a *unique* programme with i.v. y_0 which minimizes H exists, and then it will be seen that such a programme is optimal.

For the programme $\zeta := \{z_t\} = \{(x_{t-1}, y_t)\}$ with i.v. y_0, let

$$H_t(\zeta) := G(z_t) - \bar{p}(y_{t-1} - x_{t-1}) \qquad (t \geqq 1).^{14} \tag{36}$$

Thus H_t represents the total utility minus the value of unused resources. We transform expression (36) to

$$\begin{aligned} H_t(\zeta) &= F(z_t) + \bar{p}y_t - \bar{p}x_{t-1} - \bar{p}y_{t-1} + \bar{p}x_{t-1} \\ &= F(z_t) + \bar{p}(y_t - y_{t-1}) \end{aligned} \tag{37}$$

and note that H_t may also be interpreted as the sum of utility and the value of the increment of output in terms of the prices $\bar{p}$.

For the turnpike $\bar{\zeta} := \{\bar{z}\}$ with i.v. $\bar{y}$, it follows from (23) that

$$H_t(\bar{\zeta}) = G(\bar{z}).$$

Therefore

$$H_t(\bar{\zeta}) - H_t(\zeta) = G(\bar{z}) - G(z_t) + p(y_{t-1} - x_{t-1}) \geqq 0, \tag{38}$$

and the sum of this sequence

$$H(\zeta) := \sum_{t=1}^{\infty} [H_t(\bar{\zeta}) - H_t(\zeta)] \tag{39}$$

exists. This is the functional from which we obtain the optimal pro-

[14] Expression (36) depends on y_0 at $t = 1$ and should therefore be rigorously designated $H_t(\zeta, y_0)$. However, for simplicity of notation we omit the argument y_0.

gramme by finding its minimum over the set Π of *all programmes with i.v.* y_0.

2. Properties of the H Functional

Lemma 6. $H(\zeta) < \infty$ *if, and only if, the programme* ζ *is good.*

□ By virtue of (37),

$$\sum_{t=1}^{N} H_t(\zeta) = \sum_{t=1}^{N} F(z_t) + \bar{p}y_N - \bar{p}y_0 \tag{40}$$

and hence

$$\sum_{t=1}^{N} [H_t(\bar{\zeta}) - H_t(\zeta)] = \sum_{t=1}^{N} [F(\bar{z}) - F(z_t)] + \alpha_N,$$

where the term α_N is bounded. From this the desired result obviously follows. □

Lemma 7. *A programme* ζ^0 *minimizing* H *on the set* Π *of all programmes with i.v.* y_0 *exists.*

□ We shall interpret programmes ζ as elements of the product space $Q^\infty = Q \times Q \times \cdots$, equipped with the Tychonov product topology.[15] Since Q is compact, Q^∞ is also compact. The set Π is closed in Q^∞ [inequality (3) obviously holds in the limit] and therefore is compact.

Further, one can see from (37) that $H_t(\zeta)$ is upper semicontinuous, since F is upper semicontinuous. Consequently, the functional H is lower semicontinuous as the sum of a sequence of nonnegative lower semicontinuous functions $H_t(\bar{\zeta}) - H_t(\zeta)$. Hence, H achieves a minimum on the compact Π. □

Lemma 8. *The programme* ζ^0 *is unique and good.*

□ Since from Lemma 5 good programmes exist, by virtue of Lemma 6 $H(\hat{\zeta}) < \infty$ for some programme $\hat{\zeta}$ with i.v. y_0. But $H(\zeta^0) \leqq H(\hat{\zeta}) < \infty$; i.e., ζ^0 is good.

[15] By definition, a sequence of elements $\zeta^k = \{z_1^k, z_2^k, \ldots\}$ of the space Q^∞ is considered a convergent sequence in the *Tychonov topology* if and only if z_t^k is convergent at each $t = 1, 2, \ldots$.

A strictly convex functional achieves its minimum at a single point on a convex set. By virtue of the concavity of F, the set $\hat{\Pi}$ of *good programmes with i.v.* y_0 is convex (see the definition of a good programme). Therefore it is sufficient to check that H is strictly convex on $\hat{\Pi}$.

To this end let $\zeta = \{z_t\}$ and $\zeta' = \{z'_t\}$ be elements of $\hat{\Pi}$ and $\zeta \neq \zeta'$; i.e., $z_N \neq z'_N$ at some N. Let $\zeta'' = \frac{1}{2}(\zeta + \zeta')$. Then $H_t(\zeta'') \geqq \frac{1}{2}[H_t(\zeta) + H_t(\zeta')]$ for all t, and this inequality is strict at $t = N$. Hence, from (39), since $H(\zeta)$ and $H(\zeta')$ are finite, $H(\zeta'') < \frac{1}{2}[H(\zeta') + H(\zeta)]$. □

3. ζ^0 is an Optimal Programme

□ To prove this we need the following fact.

Lemma 9. *For any programme* $\zeta = \{z_t\}$ *with i.v.* y_0

$$H(\zeta) - H(\zeta^0) = \sum_{t=1}^{\infty} [F(z_t^0) - F(z_t)]. \tag{41}$$

□ Using the definition of H and equation (40), we obtain for the left-hand side of (41)

$$\sum_{t=1}^{N} [H_t(\bar{\zeta}) - H_t(\zeta)] - \sum_{t=1}^{N} [H_t(\bar{\zeta}) - H_t(\zeta^0)] = \sum_{t=1}^{N} [F(z_t^0) - F(z_t)] + \beta_N, \tag{42}$$

where $\beta_N := \bar{p}(y_N^0 - y_N)$. We consider two cases.

If $H(\zeta) = \infty$, then the left-hand side of (42) tends to ∞ with N, which implies that the right-hand side tends to ∞ with N, because of the boundedness of β_N.

If $H(\zeta) < \infty$, then ζ is good, and by Theorem 4

$$\beta_N = \bar{p}(y_N^0 - y_N) = \bar{p}(y_N^0 - \bar{y}) - \bar{p}(y_N - \bar{y}) \to 0,$$

and therefore the limit of the right-hand side of (42) exists and is equal to the limit of the left-hand side, i.e., is equal to $H(\zeta) - H(\zeta^0)$.

It follows from formula (41) that the programme ζ^0 is optimal and the optimal programme is unique. Indeed, by Lemma 8, for any $\zeta \neq \zeta^0$

$$0 < H(\zeta) - H(\zeta^0) = \sum_{t=1}^{\infty} [F(z_t^0) - F(z_t)],$$

so that the sums $\sum_{t=1}^{N} [F(z_t^0) - F(z_t)]$ must be positive after some N. □□□

5. STRONG TURNPIKE THEOREMS AND WINTER PROGRAMMES

1. Formulations and Discussion

Let y_0 be a sufficient vector and $\{z_1^N, \ldots, z_N^N\}$ an optimal programme with i.v. y_0, $N = 1, 2, \ldots$. Suppose that the function F is continuous on Q and that the following condition holds:

(Int) *$\bar{z}$ is an interior point of the set Q.*

Then the following results are true.

Theorem 6. (Existence of a family of Winter programmes.) *For any $\epsilon > 0$ a constant $D := D(\epsilon)$ (independent of N) exists, and for any $N > 2D$ a programme $\zeta = \{z_1, \ldots, z_N\}$ with i.v. y_0 can be found such that*

(*a*) $z_t = \bar{z}$ *for* $t \in [D, N - D]$,
(*b*) $\sum_{t=1}^{N} F(z_t^N) - \sum_{t=1}^{N} F(z_t) < \epsilon$. □

Theorem 7. (Strong turnpike theorem.) *For any $\epsilon > 0$ a constant $L := L(\epsilon)$ (independent of N) may be found such that, for any $N > 2L$,*

$$|z_t^N - \bar{z}| < \epsilon \tag{43}$$

for $t \in [L, N - L]$. □

In Theorem 6, Condition (a) means that the programme ζ coincides with the turnpike everywhere except perhaps during the initial and final parts of the planning interval. (The length of these parts is restricted by a constant, independent of the length of planning interval.) Condition (b) states that the utility of the optimal programme exceeds by less than ϵ the utility of the programme ζ. If for any sufficiently large N a programme with the properties described in Theorem 6 is given, we term the resulting family a family of Winter programmes (see the discussion in §1.7).

Theorem 7 states that the optimal programme lies in an ϵ-tube with center on the turnpike for all time periods not less than L periods distant from the end points of planning interval. This result exactly coincides with the idea of the turnpike discussed in §1.7. Theorems of this type are sometimes called turnpike theorems in *Nikaido* form.[16]

2. Proof of Theorem 6: Construction of Winter Programmes

□ We notice first that the (Int) condition may be rephrased as follows.

There exists a $\gamma > 0$ *such that*

$$|z - \bar{z}| < \gamma \quad \Rightarrow \quad z \in Q. \tag{44}$$

Let $0 < \alpha < \gamma$. By virtue of the weak turnpike theorem there exists a constant $M := M(\alpha)$ such that, for any N, there are fewer than M time periods t when $|z_t^N - \bar{z}| \geqq \alpha$. Thus, for fixed $N > 2M$, among the first M periods $1, 2, \ldots, M$ (and among the last M periods $N - M + 1, \ldots, N$) we must find at least one time period $k := k(N)$ [resp. $l := l(N)$], for which $|z_k^N - \bar{z}| < \alpha$ (resp. $|z_l^N - \bar{z}| < \alpha$).

Consider now a sequence

$$\zeta := \{z_1^N, \ldots, z_{k-1}^N, (x_{k-1}^N, \bar{y}), (\bar{x}, \bar{y}), \ldots, (\bar{x}, \bar{y}), (\bar{x}, y_l^N), z_{l+1}^N, \ldots, z_N^N\}.$$

[The beginning and end of this sequence coincide with an optimal programme, the middle with the turnpike and the three parts are linked by means of $(x_{k-1}^N, \bar{y})$ and $(\bar{x}, y_l^N)$.] We observe that ζ is a programme. Indeed, Condition (3) obviously holds. It is also obvious that the technological restrictions (2) at $t \neq k, l$ hold, and the relations

$$z_k := (x_k^N, \bar{y}) \in Q, \qquad z_l := (\bar{x}, y_l^N) \in Q$$

follow from (44). It is also clear that y_0 is an initial vector for ζ, since y_0 is an initial vector for $\{z_t^N\}$.

We fix some $0 < \alpha < \gamma$ and construct such a programme $\zeta = \{z_1, \ldots, z_N\}$ for each $N > 2M$. We shall show that when a suitable α is chosen the family of programmes so constructed has the required properties.

[16] Nikaido improved Radner's theorem and obtained a result similar to Theorem 7 for another model.

The following equations hold

$$r := \sum_{t=1}^{N} [F(z_t) - F(z_t^N)] = \sum_{t=k}^{l} [F(z_t) - F(z_t^N)]$$

$$= \sum_{t=k}^{l} [F(\bar{z}) - F(z_t^N)] + [F(x_{k-1}^N, \bar{y}) - F(\bar{z})] + [F(\bar{x}, y_l^N) - F(\bar{z})]. \quad (45)$$

Note that r is nonpositive by virtue of the optimality of $\{z_t^N\}$ and that it follows from the last equation, by applying Lemma 2 to the turnpike $\{\bar{z}\}$ with supporting prices $\{\bar{p}\}$, that

$$0 \geqq r \geqq [F(x_{k-1}^N, \bar{y}) - F(\bar{z})] + [F(\bar{x}, y_l^N) - F(\bar{z})] - \bar{p}(\bar{y}_l - y_l^N)$$
$$+ \bar{p}(\bar{x} - x_{k-1}^N) \geqq \kappa(\alpha),$$

where $\kappa(\alpha)$ is independent of N and tends to zero as $\alpha \to 0$. We must choose α such that $|\kappa(\alpha)| < \epsilon$ and set $D := M(\alpha) + 1$. Then Property (b) of Theorem 6 follows from the above inequalities, and Property (a) is evident from the construction of ζ. □

3. The Turnpike Theorem for the Pseudometric ρ

Next we prove Theorem 7.

□ The following lemma is important in the proof:

Lemma 10. *For any $\tau > 0$ we may find an $L = L(\tau)$ such that*

$$\sum_{t=L}^{N-L} \rho(z_t^N, \bar{z}) < \tau. \quad □ \qquad (46)$$

From Lemmas 4 and 10, Theorem 7 can be derived. Indeed, for $\epsilon > 0$ set $\tau := \delta(\epsilon)$, where $\delta(\epsilon)$ is given by the function described in Lemma 4. Then, if $|z_t^N - \bar{z}| \geqq \epsilon$ at some $t \in [L, N - L]$, it follows that $\rho(z_t^N, \bar{z}) \geqq \delta(\epsilon) = \tau$, which contradicts (46). So, as in §3.4, we have proved the turnpike theorem for the pseudometric ρ and then concluded from this the desired result for the norm $|\cdot|$. It remains only to establish Lemma 10.

4. Estimation of $\sum\rho$

To prove Lemma 10 we need the following evaluation of sums such as appear in (46).

Lemma 11. *For any $1 \leqq k \leqq l \leqq N$ and any programme $\{z_1, \ldots, z_N\}$ with i.v. y_0, the inequality*

$$\sum_{t=k}^{l} \rho(z_t^N, \bar{z}) \leqq \sum_{t=1}^{k-1} [F(z_t^N) - F(z_t)] + \sum_{t=l+1}^{N} [F(z_t^N) - F(z_t)]$$
$$+ \sum_{t=k}^{l} [F(\bar{z}) - F(z_t)] - \bar{p}(\bar{x} - x_{k-1}^N) + \bar{p}(\bar{y}_l - y_l^N) \quad (47)$$

holds.

□ By virtue of (17) and the definition of the pseudometric ρ, we have that

$$\sum_{t=k}^{l} \rho(z_t^N, \bar{z}) = \sum_{t=k}^{l} F(\bar{z}) - \sum_{t=k}^{l} F(z_t^N) - \sum_{t=k}^{l-1} \bar{p}(y_t^N - x_t^N)$$
$$+ \bar{p}(\bar{y} - y_l^N) - \bar{p}(\bar{x} - x_{k-1}^N)$$
$$\leqq \sum_{t=k}^{l} [F(\bar{z}) - F(z_t^N)] - \bar{p}(\bar{x} - x_{k-1}^N) + \bar{p}(\bar{y} - y_l^N). \quad (48)$$

Moreover, by the optimality of $\{z_t^N\}$

$$\sum_{t=1}^{N} F(z_t^N) \geqq \sum_{t=1}^{N} F(z_t),$$

which can be rewritten

$$\sum_{t=k}^{l} F(z_t^N) \geqq \sum_{t=k}^{l} F(z_t) + \sum_{t=1}^{k-1} [F(z_t) - F(z_t^N)]$$
$$+ \sum_{t=l+1}^{N} [F(z_t) - F(z_t^N)]. \quad (49)$$

Using (49) to estimate the right-hand side of (48), we obtain immediately inequality (47). □

5. Proof of Lemma 10

□ Using inequality (47) for $k = k_N$, $l = l_N$ and $\zeta = \{z_t\}$ (described in §5.2), we obtain

$$\sum_{t=M}^{N-M} \rho(z_t^N, \bar{z}) \leqq \sum_{t=k}^{l} \rho(z_t^N, \bar{z})$$
$$\leqq [F(\bar{z}) - F(z_k)] + [F(\bar{z}) - F(z_l)] + 2\alpha|\bar{p}|$$
$$\leqq \psi(\alpha),$$

where $\psi(\alpha) \to 0$ as $\alpha \to 0$, since $|z_k - \bar{z}| < \alpha$, $|z_l - \bar{z}| < \alpha$ and the function F is continuous on Q. We need only choose α such that $\psi(\alpha) < \tau$ and set $L := M(\alpha)$ to prove Lemma 10 and Theorem 7. □□

6. REDUCTION OF CONSTANT GROWTH MODELS TO STATIONARY MODELS AND SOME EXAMPLES

1. A Reduction Scheme

We consider the model M given by formula (7), together with the model M', which is defined as

$$\begin{aligned} Q' &:= \{(x', y') : ([x'/\lambda], y') \in Q\}. \\ F'(x', y') &:= F([x'/\lambda], y'). \end{aligned} \tag{50}$$

We show that the model M may be reduced to the model M' in the sense that results concerning M can be automatically concluded from results concerning M'. The model M' is stationary, so the theory developed above is applicable to it.

The reduction of one model to the other is based on the following simple observation. The formulae

$$x_t' := x_t/\lambda^t, \qquad y_t' := y_t/\lambda^t, \qquad p_t' := \lambda^t p_t \tag{51}$$

define, as is easily checked, an isomorphism between programmes $\{(x_{t-1}, y_t)\}$ and prices $\{p_t\}$ in the model M and programmes $\{(x_{t-1}', y_t')\}$ and prices $\{p_t'\}$ in the model M', an isomorphism such that

$$F_t(x_{t-1}, y_t) = F'(x_{t-1}', y_t'), \qquad x_0 = x_0'.$$

From this it follows that optimal programmes with i.v. y_0 in the model M correspond to optimal programmes with i.v. y_0 in the model M'.

Furthermore, we have the equations

$$F_t(x_{t-1}, y_t) + p_t y_t - p_{t-1}x_{t-1} = F'(x_{t-1}', y_t') + p_t' y_t' - p_{t-1}' x_{t-1}',$$
$$p_t(y_t - x_t) = p_t'(y_t' - x_t'),$$

which show, together with the isomorphism defined by (51), that the relation of support between prices and programmes is preserved. The above statements permit one to conclude immediately the existence of optimal programmes and supporting prices in M from analogous results for the model M'.

Moreover, if $\{\bar{z}\} = \{(\bar{x}, \bar{y})\}$ is the turnpike of model M', then the following *weak turnpike theorem* obtains for model M by the statement of the weak turnpike theorem for model M':

Let $\{z_t^N\}$ be the optimal programme of length N with i.v. y_0. Then for any $\epsilon > 0$ the number of periods $t \in [1, N]$ for which

$$|(x_{t-1}^N/\lambda^{t-1}, y_t^N/\lambda^t) - \bar{z}| \geqq \epsilon \tag{52}$$

is limited by a constant independent of N. It is understood that the optimal balanced growth programme

$$\{\bar{z}_t\} = \{\lambda^{t-1}\bar{x}, \lambda^t\bar{y})\}$$

plays the rôle of the turnpike in the model M. This programme is the best among programmes of the form $\{\lambda^{t-1}x, \lambda^t y)\}$ (*balanced growth* programmes), best in the sense that it maximizes (independent of t) the value $F_t(\lambda^{t-1}x, \lambda^t y)$ amongst all such programmes.

Finally, defining a *good* programme as one for which sums of the form

$$\sum_{t=1}^{N} [F_t(\bar{z}_t) - F_t(z_t)] = \sum_{t=1}^{N} [F'(\bar{z}) - F'(z_t')]$$

are bounded from above, we obtain the turnpike theorem for good programmes:

$$\lim_{t\to\infty} |(x_{t-1}/\lambda^{t-1}, y_t/\lambda^t) - \bar{z}| = 0,$$

since the statement of Theorem 4 is true for the model M'.

2. A Model with Utility Function Defined on the Consumption Set

We consider here an important special case of the Gale model described in §1.1. For each $t \geqq 1$, let a set Θ_t, consisting of pairs of nonnegative n-dimensional vectors, and a function given by $\phi_t(c)$, defined on n-dimensional nonnegative vectors c, be given.

Define

$$Q_t := \{(x, y) \geqq 0 : \exists\, c \geqq 0, (x, y + c) \in \Theta_t\}, \tag{53}$$

$$F_t(x, y) := \sup\{\phi_t(c) : c \geqq 0, (x, y + c) \in \Theta_t\}. \tag{54}$$

It will now be convenient to modify the previous interpretation of the elements of Q_t as input–output pairs. It was stated in §1.1 that for a pair

$z = (x, y) \in Q_t$ the vector x represents input, the vector y represents output of the technological process z and the function F_t gives the assessment of utility of that process.

It is natural to suppose that consumption must play a main rôle in the provision of utility. At first glance, the Gale model does not permit one to account for consumption directly. However, consumption can be included in the technological process (x, y) if we postulate that y is, rather than a total output, an *intermediate* output, i.e., total output less the vector of goods directed to final consumption. For example, the case when *only* the consumption process yields utility may be considered; just this situation is described by (53) and (54). Θ_t is the "true" technology set: $(a, b) \in \Theta_t$ means that b may be produced from a. According to (53), $(x, y) \in Q_t$ if some vector $y + c$ may be produced from x, where c is a vector of goods which are consumed. This vector yields the utility measured by $\phi_t(c)$ in the process of consumption. The function $F_t(x, y)$ given by (54) is defined as the maximum utility which may be obtained if the vector x is fixed at the beginning of a cycle of production and consumption and the vector y is fixed at the end of the cycle.

Suppose that Θ_t is convex and compact. Then, if ϕ_t is concave[17] and upper semicontinuous, the function F_t possesses the same property. We leave the proof of this simple fact to the reader. In general, it is not complicated to formulate conditions on Θ_t and ϕ_t which guarantee the validity of all assumptions made earlier regarding Q_t and F_t.

3. The One-Sector Model

We suppose here that in the model of the previous subsection $n = 1$; i.e., the vectors x, y are one dimensional. Moreover, suppose that the technology set Θ_t is described in the following way: Θ_t is the set of pairs $(x, y) \geqq 0$ such that

$$y \leqq f(x), \tag{55}$$

$$x \leqq k, \tag{56}$$

where f is a given function and k is a number. It is usually supposed that f is a concave, monotonically increasing function. The uniform

[17] The concavity of ϕ_t exactly corresponds to the idea of "the preference for variety" mentioned in §1.

boundedness condition (56) is often omitted; under appropriate conditions all programmes with a given initial vector satisfy this restriction.

Models of this type often serve as a proving ground for testing new ideas regarding the Gale model. Many new facts have first been obtained for this relatively simple special case and have then been generalized to the multidimensional case. Currently several interesting results[18] awaiting generalization exist.

7. OPTIMAL CONTROL PROBLEMS AND MODELS OF ECONOMIC DYNAMICS

1. Formulation of the Optimal Control Problem

The theory of the Gale model was presented in the previous sections. This model has the property of convexity, which plays an important rôle in the proofs of theorems and is essential for the validity of the stated results. At the same time, the full range of dynamic economic models does not fall within the framework of this assumption. One nonconvex economic model will be introduced in the present section. The general optimal control problem serves as a natural common denominator for this model and Gale's model. We begin this section with a formulation of the optimal control problem.

Let the *state* of some *system* at time t ($t = 0, 1, 2, \ldots$) be described by the vector $y_t = (y_{t1}, \ldots, y_{tn})$ of Euclidean space $\mathbb{R}^n$. A set of *control* parameters U_t is given for each time period. If at time t the control parameter $u_t \in U_t$ is chosen, then at time $t + 1$ the system moves to the state

$$y_{t+1} := f^{t+1}(y_t, u_t). \tag{57}$$

The vector functions $f^{t+1}: \mathbb{R}^n \times U_t \to \mathbb{R}^n$, $t = 0, 1, 2, \ldots,$ and the initial condition y_0 are given. Further, the *constraints*

$$g^t(y_t, u_t) \leqq 0 \tag{58}$$

are imposed on the choice of a control when the system is in state y_t,

[18] See, for example, Brock [2].

$t = 0, 1, 2, \ldots$. The vector functions $g^t : \mathbb{R}^n \times U_t \to \mathbb{R}^k$, $t = 0, 1, 2, \ldots$, are supposed given, as is a time *horizon* N over which control of the system is to be effected. It is required to find a *control* $u^0 := (u_0^0, \ldots, u_{N-1}^0)$ and its corresponding *trajectory* $y^0 := (y_1^0, \ldots, y_N^0)$, which maximizes the (*objective*) functional given by

$$\Phi(y, u) := \sum_{t=0}^{N-1} \phi^t(y_t, u_t), \tag{59}$$

where $\phi^t : \mathbb{R}^n \times U_t \to \mathbb{R}$ are given functions.

An extensive literature[19] is devoted to different versions of the optimal control problem formulated above. In the present context the discrete form of the *Pontryagin maximum principle*, which is a necessary condition for an extremum in the problem defined by (57)–(59), is the main result.

2. The Discrete Maximum Principle

Suppose that the following conditions hold for the optimal control problem formulated in §7.1.

1°. Smoothness condition. *The functions given by* $\phi^t(y, u)$, $f^{t+1}(y, u)$, $g^t(y, u)$ *are continuously differentiable with respect to* y *for each* $u \in U_t$, $t = 0, 1, \ldots, N - 1$.
2°. Convexity condition. *For any* $y \in \mathbb{R}^n$, $u_1, u_2 \in U_t$, *and any* $0 \leqq \alpha \leqq 1$ *there exists a* $u \in U_t$ *such that*

$$f_{t+1}(y, u) = \alpha f_{t+1}(y, u_1) + (1 - \alpha) f_{t+1}(y, u_2),$$
$$g_t(y, u) \leqq \alpha g_t(y, u_1) + (1 - \alpha) g_t(y, u_2),$$
$$\phi_t(y, u) \geqq \alpha \phi_t(y, u_1) + (1 - \alpha) \phi_t(y, u_2), \qquad t = 0, \ldots, N - 1.$$

3°. Regularity condition. *There exist a pair of sequences* $\tilde{y} = (\tilde{y}_1, \ldots, \tilde{y}_N)$, $\tilde{u} = (\tilde{u}_0, \ldots, \tilde{u}_{N-1})$ *satisfying the system of difference equations*

$$\tilde{y}_{t+1} = f_y^{t+1}(y_t^0, u_t^0)\tilde{y}_t + f^{t+1}(y_t^0, \tilde{u}_t) - f^{t+1}(y_t^0, u_t^0), \qquad t = 0, \ldots, N - 1, \tag{60}$$

[19] See, for example, Boltyanski [1].

$\tilde{y}_0 = 0$ *and the restrictions*

$$g_y^t(y_t^0, u_t^0)\tilde{y}_t + g^t(y_t^0, \tilde{u}_t) < -\delta 1, \qquad t = 0, \ldots, N-1, \quad (61)$$

where $\delta 1$ *denotes a positive vector with all coordinates equal to* $\delta > 0$.[20]

Define the *Hamiltonian* function by

$$H^{t+1}(\psi, \lambda, y, u) := \phi^t(y, u) - \psi f^{t+1}(y, u) - \lambda g^t(y, u) \qquad (\psi \in \mathbb{R}^n, \lambda \in \mathbb{R}^k).$$

Theorem 8. (Maximum principle.) *Let* (y^0, u^0) *be a maximum for the problem defined by* (57)–(59) *and suppose that conditions* 1°–3° *hold. Then there exist vectors* ψ_{t+1}^0 *and* $\lambda_t^0 \geqq 0$, $t = 0, \ldots, N-1$, *such that*

$$H^{t+1}(\psi_{t+1}^0, \lambda_t^0, y_t^0, u_t^0) = \max_{u \in U_t} H^{t+1}(\psi_{t+1}^0, \lambda_t^0, y_t^0, u), \qquad (62)$$

$$\psi_N^0 = 0, \qquad \psi_t^0 = H_y^{t+1}(y_t^0, u_t^0, \psi_{t+1}^0, \lambda_t^0), \qquad (63)$$

$$\lambda_t^0 g^t(y_t^0, u_t^0) = 0. \quad \square \qquad (64)$$

Expression (62) states that the optimal control maximizes the Hamiltonian. The set of equations (63) is called the *conjugate* (*dual* or *adjoint*) system; equation (64) is termed the *complementary slackness* condition.

Next we sketch the structure of the proof of the maximum principle. (In fact we shall conclude the truth of Theorem 8 from a more general result.) A detailed proof of the analogous theorem for the stochastic case will be given in Chapter 2.

We consider a control $u = (u_0, \ldots, u_{N-1})$ as an element of a set $U = U_0 \times \cdots \times U_{N-1}$, and a trajectory $y = (y_1, \ldots, y_N)$ as an element of a space $Y := \mathbb{R}^{nN}$.

The sequences

$$F(y, u) := \{y_{t+1} - f^{t+1}(y_t, u_t)\}_{t=0}^{N-1},$$
$$G(y, u) := \{g^t(y_t, u_t)\}_{t=0}^{N-1}$$

are interpreted as elements of the spaces $Z := \mathbb{R}^{nN}$ and $H := \mathbb{R}^{kN}$,

[20] Here the subscript y indicates the partial derivative (actually the gradient) with respect to y in the formulae (60), (61) and below, and (as above) the superscript 0 is used to denote optimal quantities.

respectively. Then the problem of (57) and (59) may be rewritten

$$\text{maximize} \quad \Phi(y, u) \tag{65}$$

$$\text{subject to} \quad F(y, u) = 0, \tag{66}$$

$$G(y, u) \leqq 0. \tag{67}$$

From Conditions 1° and 2° it follows that

(1) *the functions* Φ, F *and* G *are continuously differentiable with respect to* y*; and*
(2) *for any* y, *the set*

$$\{(r, z, h): r \leqq \Phi(y, u),\ z = F(y, u),\ h \geqq G(y, u),\ u \in U\}$$

is convex.

The derivatives of the functions F and G are given by the following formulae. If $\bar{y} = \{\bar{y}_t\}_{t=1}^{N}$, then

$$\begin{aligned} F_y(y, u)\bar{y} &= \{\bar{y}_t - f_y^t(y_{t-1}, u_{t-1})\bar{y}_{t-1}\}_{t=1}^{N}, \\ G_y(y, u)\bar{y} &= \{g_y^t(y_t, u_t)\bar{y}_t\}_{t=0}^{N-1} \end{aligned} \tag{68}$$

($\bar{y}_0 = 0$). From these formulae, setting $\bar{y} = \tilde{y}$ and with the help of simple calculations, we can see that Condition 3° can be reformulated as follows:

(3) *There exist* $\tilde{y}$ *and* $\tilde{u}$ *such that*

$$F_y(y^0, u^0)\tilde{y} + F(y^0, \tilde{u}) = 0,$$

$$G_y(y^0, u^0)\tilde{y} + G(y^0, \tilde{u}) < -\delta 1,$$

where $\delta > 0$.

We note also that from formula (68) it can be concluded that the following condition holds:

(4) $F_y(y^0, u^0)$ *is a surjection of* Y *onto* Z.

Next we use the following general result (a necessary condition for a maximum in a smoothly convex mathematical programming problem): Consider the function given by

$$L(\psi, \lambda, y, u) := \Phi(y, u) - \psi F(y, u) - \lambda G(y, u)$$

of the vectors ψ, λ, trajectories y and controls u [the Lagrangean function of the problem (65)–(67)].

Theorem 9. *Let (y^0, u^0) be a maximum for the problem* (65)–(67). *Under Assumptions* (1)–(4) *there exist $\lambda^0 \geqq 0$ and ψ^0 (Lagrange multipliers) such that*

$$L_y(\psi^0, \lambda^0, y^0, u^0) = 0, \tag{69}$$

$$L(\psi^0, \lambda^0, y^0, u^0) = \max_{u \in U} L(\psi^0, \lambda^0, y^0, u), \tag{70}$$

$$\lambda^0 G(y^0, u^0) = 0. \quad \square \tag{71}$$

The proof of this result can be found, for example, in the book of Ioffe and Tichomirov [1], Section I.1.2. A more general result will be presented in §2.2.2. We show now how the statement of Theorem 8 may be concluded from Theorem 9.

$\square$ We have that

$$\lambda := \{\lambda_t\}_{t=0}^{N-1}, \qquad \psi := \{\psi_t\}_{t=1}^{N},$$

$$L(\psi, \lambda, y, u) := \sum_{t=0}^{N-1} \phi^t(y_t, u_t) + \sum_{t=0}^{N-1} \psi_t[y_{t+1} - f^{t+1}(y_t, u_t)]$$

$$- \sum_{t=0}^{N-1} \lambda_t g^t(y_t, u_t).$$

Using this we obtain from (69) the *conjugate* (backwards difference equation) system

$$\begin{aligned} 0 &= \left.\frac{\partial L}{\partial y}\right|_{y=\{y_t^0\}, u=\{u_t^0\}} \\ &= \phi_y^t - \psi_t^0 + \psi_{t+1}^0 f_y^{t+1,0} - \lambda_t^0 g_y^{t0} \\ &= -\psi_t^0 + \frac{\partial H^{t+1,0}}{\partial y}, \qquad t = 1, \ldots, N-1, \end{aligned}$$

$$\psi_N^0 = 0$$

in an obvious notation. From the inequality $L(\psi^0, \lambda^0, y^0, u^0) \geqq L(\psi^0, \lambda^0, y^0, u)$, with v in the form $u = (u_0^0, \ldots, u_{t-1}^0, u_t, u_{t+1}^0, \ldots, u_{N-1}^0)$, the maximization of the Hamiltonian in u_t, (62), is obtained. Finally, the complementary slackness condition (64) can be concluded directly from (71). □

3. The Gale Model and Optimal Control

We now show that the planning problem over a *finite* horizon in the Gale model may be considered to be a particular case of the general optimal control problem formulated in §7.1.

Suppose such a model is given with technology sets Q_t and utility functions F_t. Then the optimal plan of length N with initial vector y_0 is obtained from the following optimization problem:

$$\text{maximize} \quad \sum_{t=0}^{N-1} F_{t+1}(a_t, b_{t+1})$$

$$\text{subject to} \quad a_t \leqq y_t, \qquad y_{t+1} = b_{t+1}, \qquad (a_t, b_{t+1}) \in Q_{t+1},$$
$$t = 0, 1, \ldots, N-1.$$

This may be reduced to relations like (57)–(59) if we set $U_t := Q_{t+1}$ and, for $u := (a, b) \in U_t$,

$$\phi^t(y, u) := F_{t+1}(a, b),$$
$$f^{t+1}(y, u) := b,$$
$$g^t(y, u) := a - y.$$

Then Conditions 1° and 2° are obviously valid, and the validity of Condition 3° is established by the existence of sequences of controls for which $b_t > a_t$.

Let λ_t^0, ψ_t^0 be the vectors given by the application of the maximum principle to this model. The Hamiltonian of the problem is of the form

$$H^{t+1} := F_{t+1}(a, b) + \psi_{t+1}^0 b - \lambda_t^0(a - y).$$

By virtue of the conjugate system, we have that

$$\psi_t^0 = \partial H^{t+1,0}/\partial y = \lambda_t^0, \qquad \psi_N^0 = 0.$$

The maximum Hamiltonian condition (62) means that the total utility

$$G_{t+1}(a, b) = F_{t+1}(a, b) + \psi_{t+1}^0 b - \psi_t^0 a$$

achieves a maximum along an optimal programme $\{(a_t^0, b_{t+1}^0)\}$. The complementary slackness condition becomes $\psi_t^0(b_t^0 - a_t^0) = 0$. It follows that $\{\psi^0\}$ is the supporting price system.

4. A Model of the Dynamic Distribution of Resources

Suppose that the state of an economic system is characterized by some set of *industrial stocks* (or *productive factors*, e.g., labour, capital plant and energy) $y = (y_1, \ldots, y_n)$. Consider for simplicity that one *good* (e.g., monetary value) is produced and consumed. Let a *production function* $f(y_1, \ldots, y_n)$ be given, representing the amount of product which may be produced with the help of the available set of industrial stocks.

The dynamics of the model are described in the following way.

If at time t the set of industrial stocks applied to production in the current period is characterized by the vector $y_t = (y_{t1}, \ldots, y_{tn})$, then at time $t + 1$ product in the amount of $f^{t+1}(y_t) \geqq 0$ $(t = 0, 1, \ldots)$ is produced. Designate the control parameter u_{ti} as that part of the output produced at time $t + 1$ devoted to increasing industrial stocks of ith type. Then

$$y_{t+1,i} = y_{ti} + u_{ti} f^{t+1}(y_t), \qquad i = 1, \ldots, n. \tag{72}$$

A sequence of control parameter vectors

$$u := (u_0, \ldots, u_{N-1}), \qquad u_{ti} \geqq 0, \quad \sum_{i=1}^{n} u_{ti} = 1,$$

is called a *programme* (*for the distribution of available resources*). If an initial vector of industrial stocks y_0 and some programme u are given, then the equations (72) determine the *trajectory* $\{y_t\}$ of the system. The problem is to find a programme maximizing

$$\sum_{t=1}^{N-1} \phi^t(y_t)$$

(the planners' intertemporally additive *valuation function*).

Suppose that $f^{t+1}(y)$ and $\phi^t(y)(y \in \mathbb{R}^n)$ represent continuously differentiable (coordinatewise) nondecreasing functions of their arguments. Then the maximum principle may be applied to the present model, since Condition 2° holds in virtue of the linearity of the problem with respect to u and because the inequality constraints (58) are absent. We shall derive some consequences of the maximum principle which have an economic interpretation.

Consider the Hamiltonian for this model, which is given by

$$H^{t+1}(\psi_{t+1}^0, y_t^0, u) := \phi^t(y_t^0) + \psi_{t+1}^0[y_t^0 + uf^{t+1}(y_t^0)],$$

and let $\bar{\psi}_{t+1}^0 := \max_i \psi_{t+1,i}^0$. Under the assumption that $f^{t+1}(y_t^0) > 0$, it follows from the maximum Hamiltonian condition that

$$u_{ti}^0 = 0 \qquad \text{for} \quad \psi_{t+1,i}^0 < \bar{\psi}_{t+1}^0. \tag{73}$$

The ψ_{ti}^0 are usually interpreted as the *marginal resource values* (or *shadow prices*) for the various industrial stocks (productive factors). They may be interpreted as the increments of the optimal valuation resulting, respectively, from small (e.g., unit) increments of individual industrial stocks.

The marginal value $\bar{\psi}_t^0$ may be interpreted as the (*shadow*) price of the product produced at time t. Expression (73) implies that under an optimal programme resources are "sold" at the end of the production period $(t - 1,t]$ only to those stocks for which ψ_{ti}^0 coincides with $\bar{\psi}_t^0$.

Let us introduce the value $q_{t+1}(y) := \bar{\psi}_{t+1}^0 f^{t+1}(y)$, which may be interpreted as the *value of production*, expressed in terms of the prices $\bar{\psi}_{t+1}^0$, produced at time $t + 1$ from the application of the stocks y. The partial derivative $\partial q_{t+1}(y)/\partial y_i$ is called the *marginal return* to the ith industrial stock (factor) and may be interpreted as the growth of production (in value terms at optimal prices) per unit of growth of the ith industrial stock.

The conjugate system can be written

$$\psi_t^0 - \psi_{t+1}^0 = \partial q_{t+1}(y_t^0)/\partial y + \partial\phi^t(\psi_t^0)/\partial y, \qquad \psi_N^0 = 0. \tag{74}$$

The differences $\psi_{ti}^0 - \psi_{t+1,i}^0$ are termed *marginal resource value increments*.

Equation (74) thus says that an optimal vector of marginal resource value increments is the sum of the corresponding optimal vector of marginal returns and the current utility gradient. It should also be pointed out that the inequalities $\psi_t^0 \geqq 0$ and $\psi_t^0 \geqq \psi_{t+1}^0$ (i.e., falling marginal resource values) follow from the assumption of monotonicity for the functions f^{t+1} and ϕ^t and relation (74).

COMMENTS ON CHAPTER 1

The Gale model represents a development of the von Neumann [1] model; our presentation of it is based on Gale's [1, 2] work.

Prices in connection with optimization problems were initially investigated by Kantorovich [e.g., 1, 2].

Mathematical formulation of the economic planning problem over an infinite horizon is due to Ramsey [1]. For the model treated, the theorem stating the existence of an infinite optimal programme was initially proved by Gale [1]. We used the proof given by Brock [1].

The turnpike theorem originates in the work of Dorfman, Samuelson and Solow [1] (for detailed references, see, for example, Makarov and Rubinov [1]). The results of Sections 3 and 5 are based on ideas of Radner [1], Nikaido [1, 2], McKenzie [1], Tsukui [1], Romanovski [1] and Winter [1].

An extensive literature is devoted to the discrete version of the maximum principle (see, for example, Boltyanski [1] and Propoi [1], who give an annotated bibliography and describe the history of the problem).

The connection between the theory of optimal control and models of economic dynamics has been noticed by many authors (see, for example, the Ter-Krikorov [1] monograph and the article by Arrow [1]).

2 THE MAXIMUM PRINCIPLE FOR STOCHASTIC MODELS OF OPTIMAL CONTROL AND ECONOMIC DYNAMICS

1. STATEMENT OF THE OPTIMAL CONTROL PROBLEM AND FORMULATION OF THE STOCHASTIC MAXIMUM PRINCIPLE

1. The Optimal Control Problem

We formulate the *probabilistic* analogue of the deterministic *optimal control problem* discussed in §7 of Chapter 1. Let $\mathbf{s}_t$, $t = 0, 1, \ldots, N$, be an arbitrary *random* (or *stochastic*) *process*[0] with values *in* a *measurable space* $(S, \mathscr{E})$. Suppose that the probability measure P (on the σ-algebra $\mathscr{F} := \mathscr{E}^{N+1} := \times_{i=0}^{N} \mathscr{E}$ of subsets of S^{N+1}) corresponding to the process $\{\mathbf{s}_t\}$ is generated by an *initial distribution* given by $P_0(ds_0)$ and *transition probabilities* given by $P(s^t, ds_{t+1})$, where $\mathbf{s}^t := (\mathbf{s}_0, \mathbf{s}_1, \ldots, \mathbf{s}_t)$, $t = 0, 1, \ldots, N$ is the *history* of the process $\mathbf{s}_t$ up to time t, $N < \infty$ is the *horizon* and the space of sequences s^t is denoted S^t. A sequence of

[0] Boldface type will be used throughout the English edition of this book to denote random variables, vectors and functions (see the translators' preface for more details).

measurable functions $u_t : s^t \mapsto u_t(s^t)$, $t = 0, 1, \ldots, N-1$, with values in some complete separable metric space U is called a *control* (*process*).

We fix a measurable function $\mathbf{y}_0 := y_0(\mathbf{s}^0)$ with values in n-dimensional Euclidian space $\mathbb{R}^n$ (to be interpreted as the random initial *state* of the system). Each control $\mathbf{u}_t$, $t = 0, 1, \ldots$, with fixed initial condition $\mathbf{y}_0$ generates the *state* (or *controlled*) process (or trajectory) $\mathbf{y}_t := y_t(\mathbf{s}^t)$ corresponding to the system of stochastic difference equations:

$$\mathbf{y}_0 := y_0(\mathbf{s}^0), \quad \mathbf{y}_{t+1} = f^{t+1}(\mathbf{s}^{t+1}, \mathbf{y}_t, \mathbf{u}_t) \qquad \text{a.s.,} \quad t = 0, 1, \ldots, N-1. \tag{1}$$

Here $f^{t+1} : S^{t+1} \times \mathbb{R}^n \times U \to \mathbb{R}^n$ are given functions and the equations are required to hold *almost surely* (*a.s.*), i.e., with probability 1. A constraint

$$\mathbf{u}_t \in U_t(\mathbf{s}^t) \qquad \text{a.s.,} \tag{2}$$

is imposed on the choice of the control parameter u_t, where $U_t(s^t)$ are given subsets of the space U which depend on the parameters $s^t \in S^t$ and $t = 0, 1, \ldots, N-1$. In addition, a system of inequality *constraints*

$$g^t(\mathbf{s}^t, \mathbf{y}_t, \mathbf{u}_t) \leqq 0 \qquad \text{a.s.,} \tag{3}$$

defining a combined restriction on the processes $\mathbf{y}_t$ and $\mathbf{u}_t$, are assumed to hold for $N = 0, 1, \ldots, N-1$. Here $g^t : S^t \times \mathbb{R}^n \times U \to \mathbb{R}^k$. A control process $\{\mathbf{u}_t\}$ and state process $\{\mathbf{y}_t\}$ are called an *admissible* pair if they satisfy the constraints (1)–(3). It is required to find a pair $\{(\mathbf{y}_t^0, \mathbf{u}_t^0)\}_{t=0}^{N-1}$ in the class of admissible pairs $\{(\mathbf{y}_t, \mathbf{u}_t)\}_{t=0}^{N-1}$ which yields a *maximum* of the functional

$$E \sum_{t=0}^{N-1} \phi^t(\mathbf{s}^t, \mathbf{y}_t, \mathbf{u}_t). \tag{4}$$

Here the ϕ^t, $t = 0, 1, \ldots$, are scalar functions and $E(\cdot)$ denotes the *mathematical expectation* with respect to the process measure P on the measurable space of process trajectories $(\times_{t=0}^{N} S, \times_{t=0}^{N} \mathcal{F})$.

The problem defined by (1)–(4) includes a large class of models of economic dynamics. The control $u_t(s^t)$ is often interpreted as a choice of *technological processes* in the situation defined by s^t, and the state or controlled process $\{\mathbf{y}_t\}$ is interpreted as a random sequence of outputs corresponding to the chosen technological processes. We shall discuss in detail in the sequel some economic models permitting this interpretation. Next, however, we formulate assumptions required to obtain necessary optimality conditions for the problem (1)–(4).

2. Problem Assumptions

The conditions which we impose on the functions ϕ^t, f^t, g^t and the sets U_t may be broken down according to their rôle in ensuring the validity of the maximum principle.

(A) General conditions (which guarantee the well-posedness of, and the existence of variations for, the problem).

(A_1) *The functions given by* $\phi^t(s^t, y, u)$, $t = 0, 1, \ldots, N-1$, *are jointly measurable and the composition* $\phi^t(\cdot, y_t(\cdot), u_t(\cdot)) \in L_1(S^t)$ *for all admissible pairs* $\{(\mathbf{y}_t, \mathbf{u}_t)\}$. *At each point* (s^t, y, u) *the functions given by* $\phi^t(s^t, y, u)$ *are differentiable with respect to* y *and their derivatives* $\phi^t_y(s^t, y, u)$ *(gradients with respect to* y*) are continuous in* y *and satisfy the following condition:*

for any bounded set $C \subseteqq \mathbb{R}^n$ *there exists a function* $\rho^t_C \in L_1(S^t)$ *such that for all* $y \in C$

$$|\phi^t_y(s^t, y, u)| \leqq \rho^t_C(s^t).$$

(A_2) *The vector-valued functions given by* $f^{t+1}(s^{t+1}, y, u)$, $g^t(s^t, y, u)$, $t = 0, 1, \ldots, N-1$, *are jointly measurable. The set* $U_t(s^t)$ *depends measurably on the parameter* s^t, $t = 0, 1, \ldots, N-1$.

Hence, by the technique of *measurable selection* (see Appendix I) the control $u_t(s^t)$ may be chosen to depend measurably on s^t.

For any bounded set $C \subseteqq \mathbb{R}^n$ *there exists a constant* K_C *such that*

$$|f^{t+1}(\mathbf{s}^{t+1}, y, u(\mathbf{s}^t))| + |g^t(\mathbf{s}^t, y, u(\mathbf{s}^t))| \leqq K_C \qquad \text{a.s.}$$

for all $y \in C$ *and* $t = 0, 1, \ldots, N-1$. *The derivatives of the constraint functions* $f^{t+1}_y(s^{t+1}, y, u)$ *and* $g^t_y(s^t, y, u)$ *with respect to* y *exist and the constant* K_C *which corresponds to every bounded set* $C \subseteqq \mathbb{R}^n$ *has the further properties that*

$$|f^{t+1}_y(\mathbf{s}^{t+1}, y, u(\mathbf{s}^t))| + |g^t_y(\mathbf{s}^t, y, u(\mathbf{s}^t))| \leqq K_C \qquad \text{a.s.}$$

for all $y \in C$ *and* $t = 0, 1, \ldots, N-1$, *and*

$$\begin{aligned} &|f_y^{t+1}(\mathbf{s}^{t+1}, y_1, u(\mathbf{s}^t)) - f_y^{t+1}(\mathbf{s}^{t+1}, y_2, u(\mathbf{s}^t))| \\ &\quad + |g_y^t(\mathbf{s}^t, y_1, u(\mathbf{s}^t)) - g_y^t(\mathbf{s}^t, y_2, u(\mathbf{s}^t))| \\ &\leqq K_C|y_1 - y_2| \quad \text{a.s.} \end{aligned}$$

for all $y_1, y_2 \in C$ *and* $t = 0, \ldots, N-1$.

(B) Convexity condition. *For any set of parameters* $\sigma := (s^t, y, u', u'', \alpha)$, *where* $u', u'' \in U_t(s^t)$, $y \in \mathbb{R}^n$, $0 \leqq \alpha \leqq 1$ *and* $0 \leqq t \leqq N$, *an element* $u_\sigma \in U_t(s^t)$ *may be found such that the following relations hold:*

$$\begin{aligned} \phi^t(s^t, y, u_\sigma) &\geqq \alpha\phi^t(s^t, y, u') + (1-\alpha)\phi^t(s^t, y, u''), \\ f^{t+1}(s^{t+1}, y, u_\sigma) &= \alpha f^{t+1}(s^{t+1}, y, u') \\ &\quad + (1-\alpha) f^{t+1}(s^{t+1}, y, u'') \qquad \text{a.s. } [P(\cdot|s^t)], \\ g^t(s^t, y, u_\sigma) &\leqq \alpha g^t(s^t, y, u') + (1-\alpha) g^t(s^t, y, u''). \end{aligned}$$

Here the second expression must hold almost surely for *conditional* histories $\mathbf{s}^{t+1}$ of the process $\{\mathbf{s}_t\}$ of the form $(s^t, \mathbf{s}_{t+1})$ where s^t is an entry of σ.

(C) Regularity condition. *For each* t, $0 \leqq t \leqq N-1$, *one can find a control* $\tilde{\mathbf{u}}_t \in U_t(\mathbf{s}^t)$ *a.s. for which* $E|\phi^t(\mathbf{s}^t, \mathbf{y}_t^0, \tilde{\mathbf{u}}_t)| < \infty$ *and*

$$g^t(\mathbf{s}^t, \mathbf{y}_t^0, \tilde{\mathbf{u}}_t) < -\gamma 1 \qquad a.s.$$

for some constant vector $\gamma 1 := (\gamma, \gamma, \ldots, \gamma)$, $\gamma > 0$.[1]

3. Formulation of the Maximum Principle

Consider the *Hamiltonian*

$$H^{t+1}(s^{t+1}, \psi, \lambda, y, u) := \phi^t(s^t, y, u) + \psi f^{t+1}(s^{t+1}, y, u) - \lambda g^t(s^t, y, u)$$

for $t = 0, \ldots, N-1$, where $\psi \in \mathbb{R}^n$, $\lambda \in \mathbb{R}^k$ are termed *multipliers.*

Theorem 1. (Maximum principle.) *Let* $\{(\mathbf{y}_t^0, \mathbf{u}_t^0)\}_{t=0}^{N-1}$ *be a solution of the problem given by* (1)–(4), *and suppose Conditions* (A)–(C) *hold.*

[1] We remind the reader that the pairs $\{(y_t^0, u_t^0)\}_{t=0}^{N-1}$ satisfy the constraints (1)–(3) and yield the maximum of the functional (4).

Then there exist measurable functions given by $\psi_t^0 := \psi_t^0(s^t)$, *with values in* $\mathbb{R}^n$, *and* $\lambda_t^0 := \lambda_t^0(s^t)$, *with values in* $\mathbb{R}^k$, *such that* $\boldsymbol{\lambda}_t^0 \geqq 0$ *a.s.*, $E|\boldsymbol{\lambda}_t^0| < \infty$, $t = 0, \ldots, N-1$, *and* $E|\boldsymbol{\psi}_t^0| < \infty$, $t = 1, \ldots, N$. *Further, the conditional expected value of the Hamiltonian*

$$E[H^{t+1}(\mathbf{s}^{t+1}, \boldsymbol{\psi}_{t+1}^0, \boldsymbol{\lambda}_t^0, \mathbf{y}_t^0, u)|\mathbf{s}^t]$$

$$= \int_S H^{t+1}(\mathbf{s}^t, s_{t+1}, u)P(ds_{t+1}|\mathbf{s}^t) \qquad \text{a.s.}$$

considered as a function of the variable u achieves a maximum a.s. over $U_t(\mathbf{s}^t)$ *at* $u_t^0(\mathbf{s}^t)$; i.e.,

$$\max_{u \in U_t(\mathbf{s}^t)} E[H^{t+1}(\mathbf{s}^{t+1}, \boldsymbol{\psi}_{t+1}^0, \boldsymbol{\lambda}_t^0, \mathbf{y}_t^0, u)|\mathbf{s}^t]$$

$$= E[H^{t+1}(\mathbf{s}^{t+1}, \boldsymbol{\psi}_{t+1}^0, \boldsymbol{\lambda}_t^0, \mathbf{y}_t^0, \mathbf{u}_t^0)|\mathbf{s}^t] \qquad \text{a.s.} \tag{5}$$

for $t = 0, \ldots, N-1$. *The multiplier process* $\{\boldsymbol{\psi}_t^0\}$ *satisfies the following* conjugate *backwards difference system*:

$$\begin{aligned} \boldsymbol{\psi}_t^0 &= E[H_y^{t+1}(\mathbf{s}^{t+1}, \boldsymbol{\psi}_{t+1}^0, \boldsymbol{\lambda}_t^0, \mathbf{y}_t^0, \mathbf{u}_t^0)|\mathbf{s}^t] \qquad \text{a.s.,} \quad t = 1, \ldots, N-1, \\ \boldsymbol{\psi}_N^0 &= 0 \qquad \text{a.s.} \end{aligned} \tag{6}$$

The multiplier process $\{\boldsymbol{\lambda}_t^0\}$ *satisfies the* complementary slackness *condition*:

$$\boldsymbol{\lambda}_t^0 g^t(\mathbf{s}^t, \mathbf{y}_y^0, \mathbf{u}_t^0) = 0 \qquad \text{a.s.,} \quad t = 0, \ldots, N-1. \quad \square \tag{7}$$

4. Comments on the Problem Assumptions

We make a few comments about the conditions, stated above, under which the maximum principle will be proved.

1°. Condition (A_2) permits the consideration of the random vector $\mathbf{y}_t$ (measurable function y_t) as an element of the space $L_\infty^n(S^t)$ and the problem (1)–(4) as an optimization problem, in the space of random sequences $(\mathbf{y}_1, \mathbf{u}_0), \ldots, (\mathbf{y}_N, \mathbf{u}_{N-1})$ endowed with the topology defined by the L_∞ norm, as follows. Two sequences (y_t', u_{t-1}') and (y_t'', u_{t-1}''), $t = 1, \ldots, N$, are considered to be *close* if the normed differences $\| y_t' - y_t'' \|_\infty$, $t = 1, \ldots, N$, are *uniformly small* in t. The maximum principle as formulated is then a necessary condition for a *strong* local maximum. The convexity condition (B) is the natural probabilistic analogue of the corresponding condition in the deterministic case (cf.

Condition 2° in §1.7.2). The most restrictive condition seems to be the regularity condition (C) (cf. Condition 3° in §1.7.2). It is the analogue of *Slater's* condition in finite dimensional mathematical programming. Notice that if the inequality constraint (3) is absent, then the regularity condition holds automatically.

2°. Often problems of the form (1)–(4) are such that the problem functions given by

$$\phi^t(s^t, y, u), \qquad g^t(s^t, y, u), \qquad f^t(s^t, y, u)$$

are *jointly* differentiable in the variables (y, u). In that case the convexity condition (B) may be replaced by the requirement that $U_t(s^t)$ be convex. Such problems may be reduced by simple methods to problems of the form (1)–(4) in which the convexity condition (B) is automatically satisfied.

Indeed, consider a problem of the form (1)–(4) under the joint differentiability condition but for which the convexity condition is *not* assumed. Instead, let the set $U_t(s^t) \subseteqq \mathbb{R}^k$ be convex for each $s^t \in S^t$, $t = 0, \ldots, N-1$. We replace the old state variable by the new variable

$$x_{t+1} := y_t, \qquad t = 1, \ldots, N,$$

and we introduce the new state variable

$$z_{t+1} := u_t, \qquad t = 0, \ldots, N-1.$$

Finally, we define

$$\tilde{\phi}^{t+1}(s^t, y, u) := \phi^t(s^t, y, u),$$

$$\tilde{f}^{t+1}(s^t, y, u) := f^t(s^t, y, u),$$

$$\tilde{g}^{t+1}(s^t, y, u) := g^t(s^t, y, u).$$

Then in terms of the new variables the problem (1)–(4) becomes to

$$\text{maximize} \quad E \sum_{t=1}^{N} \tilde{\phi}^t(\mathbf{s}^{t-1}, \mathbf{x}_t, \mathbf{z}_t) \tag{1'}$$

$$\text{subject to} \quad \mathbf{x}_{t+1} = \tilde{f}^{t+1}(\mathbf{s}^t, \mathbf{x}_t, \mathbf{z}_t) \quad \text{a.s.,}\ t = 1, \ldots, N, \tag{2'}$$

$$\mathbf{x}_1 := \mathbf{y}_0 \quad \text{a.s.,}$$

$$\mathbf{z}_{t+1} = \mathbf{u}_t \quad \text{a.s.,}\ t = 0, \ldots, N-1,$$

$$\tilde{g}^t(\mathbf{s}^{t-1}, \mathbf{x}_t, \mathbf{z}_t) \leqq 0 \quad \text{a.s.,}\ t = 1, \ldots, N, \tag{3'}$$

$$\mathbf{u}_t \in U_t(\mathbf{s}^t) \quad \text{a.s.,}\ t = 0, \ldots, N-1. \tag{4'}$$

Obviously problem (1′)–(4′) is a special case of problem (1)–(4), and Condition (B) holds in this problem by virtue of the convexity of the sets $U_t(s^t)$.

If Theorem 1 is applied to the problem defined by (1′)–(4′), we obtain the maximum principle for the variables (x_t, z_t, u_t). Transforming back to the old variables (y_t, u_t) yields a necessary optimality condition for the original problem. However, it should be mentioned that although the maximum principle is obtained as a necessary condition for a *strong* local maximum in the space of the variables (x_t, z_t, u_t), on transforming back to the original problem we obtain only a necessary condition for a *weak* local maximum of the original problem (i.e., a maximum of the Hamiltonian *linearized* about the optimum) in virtue of the equation $\mathbf{z}_{t+1} = \mathbf{u}$, a.s. [Neighbourhoods in the space of random sequences $(\mathbf{y}_1, \mathbf{u}_0), \ldots, (\mathbf{y}_N, \mathbf{u}_{N-1})$ are defined in terms of the norms $\|y_t\|_\infty + \|u_{t-1}\|_\infty$.]

We illustrate the situation for the problem defined by (1), (2) and (4) (i.e., in the absence of the inequality constraint $g^t(\mathbf{s}^t, \mathbf{y}_t, \mathbf{u}_t) \leqq 0$ a.s.). Suppose that the functions given by $\phi^t(s^t, y, u)$ and $f^t(s^t, y, u)$ satisfy Condition (A) with the pair (y, u) playing the rôle of the variable y. Then the following theorem arises directly from Theorem 1 and the problem transformation discussed above:

Theorem 2. (Maximum principle in differential form.) *Let* $\{(\mathbf{y}_t^0, \mathbf{u}_t^0)\}_{t=0}^{N-1}$ *be the solution of the problem defined by* (1), (2) and (4) *and let* $H^{t+1}(s^{t+1}, \psi, y, u) := \phi^t(s^t, y, u) + \psi f^{t+1}(s^{t+1}, y, u)$ *be the Hamiltonian corresponding to the problem. Assume that the problem satisfies Condition* (A) *in the variables* (y, u) *and that* $U_t(s^t)$ *is almost surely convex for* $s^t \in S^t$, $t = 0, \ldots, N$. *Then there exists a multiplier process* $\{\boldsymbol{\psi}_t^0\}$ *satisfying the measurability and integrability conditions of Theorem 1 such that*

$$\max_{u \in U_t(\mathbf{s}^t)} (E[H_u^{t+1}(\mathbf{s}^{t+1}, \boldsymbol{\psi}_{t+1}^0, \mathbf{y}_t^0, \mathbf{u}_t^0) | \mathbf{s}^t])u$$
$$= (E[H_u^{t+1}(\mathbf{s}^{t+1}, \boldsymbol{\psi}_{t+1}^0, \mathbf{y}_t^0, u_t^0) | \mathbf{s}^t])\mathbf{u}_t^0 \qquad \text{a.s.}$$

The multiplier process $\{\boldsymbol{\psi}_t^0\}$ *is the solution of the following conjugate system of equations*

$$\boldsymbol{\psi}_t^0 = E[H_y^{t+1}(\mathbf{s}^{t+1}, \psi_{t+1}^0, y_t^0, u_t^0) | \mathbf{s}^t] \qquad \text{a.s.,} \quad t = 0, \ldots, N-1,$$

$$\boldsymbol{\psi}_N^0 = 0, \qquad \text{a.s.} \quad \square$$

Theorem 2 is sometimes called the *weak* or *differential* form of the maximum principle.

A proof of the maximum principle is given in §2 and 3. In §2 an abstract smoothly convex optimization problem with operator constraints is introduced to derive the necessary optimality conditions in the form of an *abstract* maximum principle. The proof of Theorem 1 by "decoding" the abstract maximum principle in terms of problem (1)–(4) is given in §3.

2. SMOOTHLY CONVEX OPTIMIZATION PROBLEMS WITH OPERATOR CONSTRAINTS

1. Description of the Problem and Definition of a Local Maximum

Let Y and Z be Banach spaces, U an arbitrary set, $(\Omega_i, \mathscr{F}_i, P_i)$ probability spaces and k_i natural numbers, $i = 1, 2, \ldots, l$. Given the mappings

$$\Phi: Y \times U \to \mathbb{R}, \qquad F: Y \times U \to Z,$$

$$G: Y \times U \to L_\infty^{k_1}(\Omega_1, \mathscr{F}_1, P_1) \times \cdots \times L_\infty^{k_l}(\Omega_l, \mathscr{F}_l, P_l) := H,$$

we consider the optimization problem

$$\text{maximize} \quad \Phi(y, u) \tag{8}$$

over all (y, u) satisfying the constraints

$$F(y, u) = 0, \tag{9}$$

$$G(y, u) \leqq 0, \tag{10}$$

$$u \in U, \tag{11}$$

where $\leqq$ denotes the partial order generated by the Cartesian product of the (closed convex) nonnegative orthants of $L_\infty^{k_i}(\Omega_i, \mathscr{F}_i, P_i)$, $i = 1, \ldots, l$, with nonempty (strong) interior in H.

We shall say that (y^0, u^0) is a *local maximum* for the problem (defined by) (8)–(11) if it satisfies the constraints (9)–(11) and if there exists a neighbourhood $W \subseteq Y$ of the point y^0 having the property that for any $y \in W$ and $u \in U$ satisfying the constraints (9)–(11) the inequality $\Phi(y, u) \leqq \Phi(y^0, u^0)$ holds.

2. Statement of the Main Result

Let $\lambda_0 \in \mathbb{R}$, $\psi \in Z^*$ and $\lambda \in H^*$. Here the symbol * denotes the *conjugate* (i.e., Banach dual) *space*. We define the *Lagrangian function* for the problem (8)–(11) as

$$L(\lambda_0, \psi, \lambda, y, u) := \lambda_0 \Phi - \langle \psi, F \rangle - \langle \lambda, G \rangle,$$

where $\langle \cdot, \cdot \rangle$ represents the usual bilinear pairing of conjugate Banach spaces, which is (strongly) continuous in the second (primal) argument.

Theorem 3. (Abstract maximum principle.) *Let* (y^0, u^0) *be a local maximum for the problem* (8)–(11). *Suppose that a neighbourhood* V *of the point* y^0 *exists such that the following properties hold:*

(a) *For each* $u \in U$ *the maps* $y \mapsto \Phi(y, u)$, $y \mapsto F(y, u)$, $y \mapsto G(y, u)$ *have Fréchet derivatives (denoted* Φ_y, F_y *and* G_y, *respectively) which are continuous at the point* y^0.

(b) *For each* $y \in V$, $u_1, u_2 \in U$, $0 \leqq \alpha \leqq 1$ *there exists* $u \in U$, *which satisfies the relations*

$$\Phi(y, u) \geqq \alpha \Phi(y, u_1) + (1 - \alpha)\Phi(y, u_2),$$

$$F(y, u) = \alpha F(y, u_1) + (1 - \alpha)F(y, u_2),$$

$$G(y, u) \leqq \alpha G(y, u_1) + (1 - \alpha)G(y, u_2).$$

Suppose also that the map $y \mapsto F(y, u^0)$ *is* regular *at the point* y^0; i.e., im $F_y(y^0, u^0) = Z$. *Under these assumptions, there exist* $\lambda_0^0 \in \mathbb{R}$, $\psi^0 \in Z^*$, $\lambda^0 \in H^*$ (*i.e.*, Lagrange multipliers) *not all zero, with* $\lambda_0^0 \geqq 0$, $\lambda^0 \geqq 0$, *satisfying*

$$L_y(\lambda_0^0, \psi^0, \lambda^0, y^0, u^0) = \lambda_0^0 \Phi_y(y^0, u^0) - F_y^*(y^0, u^0)\psi^0 - G_y^*(y^0, u^0)\lambda^0 = 0, \tag{12}$$

$$L(\lambda_0^0, \psi^0, \lambda^0, y^0, u^0) = \max_{u \in U} L(\lambda^0, \psi^0, \lambda^0, y^0, u), \tag{13}$$

$$\langle \lambda^0, G(y^0, u^0) \rangle = 0, \tag{14}$$

where F_y^* *and* G_y^* *denote the* conjugate (*i.e., Banach adjoint*) *operators to* F_y *and* G_y, *respectively.*

Suppose further that the following regularity condition *holds.*

There exist $\tilde{y} \in Y$, $\tilde{u} \in U$ *and a constant* $\delta > 0$ *such that*

$$F_y(y^0, u^0)\tilde{y} + F(y^0, \tilde{u}) = 0 \tag{15}$$

and for each $i = 1, \ldots, l, j = 1, \ldots, k_i$,

$$G_y^{ij}(y^0, u^0)\tilde{y} + G^{ij}(y^0, \tilde{u}) < -\delta$$

almost everywhere (a.e.) $[P_i]$ *on the set*

$$\{\omega_i : 0 \geqq G^{ij}(y^0, u^0)(\omega_i) \geqq -\delta\}.$$

(Here the jth *coordinate function of an element of the* ith *space* $L_\infty^{k_i}(\Omega_i)$ *is denoted by* G^{ij}*). Then* $\lambda_0 \neq 0$ *and may be taken to be unity.* □

We observe that relation (12) is the usual necessary condition for maximum of a smooth extremum problem. Expression (13) is the analogue for *convex* problems (compare with the Kuhn–Tucker theorem, §III.2). Condition (14) is often called the *complementary slackness* condition.

Now we turn to the proof of the theorem.

3. Preliminary Comments on the Proof

□ It is sufficient to prove the theorem for the case $l = 1$, $k_1 = 1$, because the vector-valued functions in $L_\infty^{k_1} \times \cdots \times L_\infty^{k_l}$ given by

$$\{(y^1(\omega_1), \ldots, y^{k_1}(\omega_1)), \ldots, (y^1(\omega_1), \ldots, y^{k_l}(\omega_1))\}$$

may be interpreted as scalar-valued functions

$$\tilde{\omega} := (i, j, \omega_i) \mapsto y(\tilde{\omega}) := y(i, j, \omega_i)$$

of the arguments

$$i \in \{1, \ldots, l\}, \qquad j \in \{1, \ldots, k_i\}, \qquad \omega_i \in \Omega_i. \tag{16}$$

This generates a natural isomorphism between H and $L_\infty(\tilde{\Omega}, \tilde{P})$, where $\tilde{\Omega}$ is the set of triples (i, j, ω) of the form (16), and $\tilde{P}$ is defined by

$$\tilde{P}(\{i\} \times \{j\} \times \Delta) := \frac{1}{k_1 + \cdots + k_1} P_i(\Delta), \qquad \Delta \in \mathscr{F}_i.$$

Under this isomorphism all conditions and assertions of Theorem 3 remain invariant, except that the second part of the regularity condition assumes the following simpler form:

$$G_y(y^0, u^0)\tilde{y} + G(y^0, \tilde{u}) < -\delta \qquad \text{a.e. } [\tilde{P}] \tag{17}$$

on the set

$$\{\tilde{\omega} : 0 \geqq G(y^0, u^0)(\tilde{\omega}) \geqq -\delta\}.$$

In the remainder of this section we denote the underlying probability space simply by $(\Omega, \mathscr{F}, P)$. We shall also suppress the arguments (y^0, u^0); the symbols Φ^0, F^0 and G^0 will denote $\Phi(y^0, u^0)$, $F(y^0, u^0)$ and $G(y^0, u^0)$, respectively, and the corresponding Fréchet derivatives with respect to y will similarly be denoted Φ_y^0, F_y^0 and G_y^0.

We outline next the plan of proof. Let

$$a(y, u) := -\langle \Phi_y^0, y\rangle - \Phi(y^0, u) + \Phi^0, \tag{18}$$

$$b(y, u) := F_y^0 y + F(y^0, u) \quad (= F_y^0 y + F(y^0, u) - F^0), \tag{19}$$

$$c(y, u) := G_y^0 y + G(y^0, u) - G^0 \qquad (y \in Y,\ u \in U) \tag{20}$$

and

$$\Omega_\delta := \{\omega : 0 \geqq G^0(\omega) \geqq -\delta\}.$$

Define the set

$$C := \{(a, b, c) \in \mathbb{R} \times Z \times L_\infty : y \in Y,\ u \in U \text{ s.t. } a \geqq a(y, u),$$
$$b = b(y, u),\ c \geqq c(y, u) \text{ a.e. } [\mathrm{P}]\}.$$

From Condition (b) of Theorem 3 it follows easily that the set C is is convex. It will be shown that

$$\operatorname{int} C \neq \varnothing \tag{21}$$

and

$$M \cap \operatorname{int} C = \varnothing, \tag{22}$$

where

$$M := \{(0, 0, c) : c \in L_\infty,\ 1_{\Omega\delta} c = 0 \text{ for some } \delta > 0\}$$

and 1_S denotes the *indicator* function of a set S. It follows from (21) and (22), by the separation theorem (see §III.1), that there exists a continuous linear functional $l^0 := (\lambda_0^0, \psi^0, \lambda^0) \neq 0$ on $\mathbb{R} \times Z \times L_\infty$ which separates M and C.

4. The Functional l^0 Defines the Required Lagrange Multipliers

□ Let l^0 *separate* M and C, i.e., let $l^0(m) \leqq l^0(c)$ for any $m \in M$, $c \in C$. Since M is a linear space, it follows that $l^0|_M = 0$, and hence $l^0|_C \geqq 0$.

This last relation yields the inequality

$$\lambda_0^0 a(y,u) + \langle \psi^0, b(y,u)\rangle + \langle \lambda^0, c(y,u)\rangle \geqq 0 \tag{23}$$

for all $y \in Y$, $u \in U$. In light of the definition of C, inequality (23) holds if $a(y,u)$ and $c(y,u)$ are replaced by any $a \geqq a(y,u)$ and $c \geqq c(y,u)$. From this it follows that $\lambda_0^0 \geqq 0$ and $\lambda^0 \geqq 0$. Setting $y = 0$ in (23) yields (13). Further, substituting $u = u^0$ in (23), we find that

$$-\lambda_0^0 \langle \Phi_y^0, y\rangle + \langle \psi^0, F_y^0 y\rangle + \langle \lambda^0, G_y^0 y\rangle \geqq 0 \tag{24}$$

for all $y \in Y$, but this is possible only if the linear form in the left-hand side of (24) is identically equal to zero, i.e., if (12) holds.

Finally, to establish (14) we use the property that $l^0|_M = 0$. This implies $\langle \lambda^0, c\rangle = 0$ provided $1_{\Omega_\delta} c = 0$ (for some $\delta > 0$). Thus by the definition of M, it follows that $\langle \lambda^0, c - 1_{\Omega_\delta} c\rangle = 0$ for all $c \in L_\infty$ and $\delta > 0$. Applying this relation with $c := G^0$, we obtain

$$0 \geqq \langle \lambda^0, G^0\rangle = \langle \lambda^0, 1_{\Omega_\delta} G^0\rangle \geqq -\delta\langle \lambda^0, 1\rangle$$

by virtue of the definition of Ω_δ and since $\lambda^0 \geqq 0$. Letting δ tend to 0, we obtain (14). □

Next we check (21) and (22).

5. The Set C Has Interior Points

□ Fix $u = u^0$ and let y range over the open sphere $E := \{y \in Y : \|y\| < 1\}$. Then $b(y, u^0) = F_y^0 y + F^0 = F_y^0 y$ ranges in some open set D in the space Z as a consequence of the Banach open mapping theorem, since from Condition (b) im $F_y^0 = Z$. Further, by virtue of the boundedness of the operators G_y^0 and Φ_y^0 there exists a constant $d > 0$ such that $\|G_y^0 y\|_\infty < d$ and $|\Phi_y^0 y| < d$ for all $y \in E$. From this we may conclude that C contains the open set $\{a \in \mathbb{R} : a > d\} \times F_y^0(E) \times \operatorname{int}\{c \in L_\infty : c \geqq d1\}$. □

6. The Interior of C Does Not Intersect the Set *M*

□ Suppose the interior of C *does* intersect M. Then we can find $\tilde{\delta} > 0$, $\tilde{y}$, $\tilde{u}$, $\tilde{c}$ such that

$$-\tilde{\delta} > a(\tilde{y},\tilde{u}), \qquad 0 = b(\tilde{y},\tilde{u}), \qquad \tilde{c} - \tilde{\delta} > c(\tilde{y},\tilde{u}), \tag{25}$$

and $\tilde{c}$ is equal to 0 on Ω_δ for some $\delta > 0$. Define mappings A, B and C by

$$A(y, \alpha) := (1 - \alpha)\Phi(y^0 + y, u^0) + \alpha\Phi(y^0 + y, \tilde{u}), \qquad y \in Y, \quad \alpha \in \mathbb{R}$$

and analogously for $B(y, \alpha)$ and $C(y, \alpha)$ (by replacing Φ by F and G, respectively). In light of the differentiability condition described in the statement of the theorem, these maps on $Y \times \mathbb{R}$ possess Fréchet derivatives A', B', C' in a neighbourhood of the point $(0, 0)$, which are given at $(0, 0)$ by

$$A'(0, 0)(y, \alpha) = \langle \Phi_y^0, y \rangle + [-\Phi^0 + \Phi(y^0, \tilde{u})]\alpha, \tag{26}$$

$$B'(0, 0)(y, \alpha) = F_y^0 y + [-F^0 + F(y^0, \tilde{u})]\alpha, \tag{27}$$

$$C'(0, 0)(y, \alpha) = G_y^0 y + [-G^0 + G(y^0, \tilde{u})]\alpha. \tag{28}$$

From these expressions and (25) we find that

$$A'(0, 0)(\tilde{y}, 1) = -a(\tilde{y}, \tilde{u}) > -\tilde{\delta}, \tag{29}$$

$$B'(0, 0)(\tilde{y}, 1) = b(\tilde{y}, \tilde{u}) = 0, \tag{30}$$

$$C'(0, 0)(\tilde{y}, 1) = c(\tilde{y}, \tilde{u}) < -\tilde{\delta} + \tilde{c}. \tag{31}$$

From (27) and the assumption that the map F is regular at y^0, i.e., that $\operatorname{im} F_y^0 = Z$, we conclude that the map B is regular at the point $(0, 0)$. Consequently, by Liusternik's theorem (see §III.3), (30) means that the vector $(\tilde{y}, 1)$ is a *tangent* to the set

$$\{(y, \alpha) \in Y \times \mathbb{R} : B(y, \alpha) = 0\}$$

at the point $(0, 0)$; i.e., there exist $\epsilon > 0$ and functions $\hat{y}(t)$ and $\hat{\alpha}(t)$ $(t \in [0, \epsilon])$ such that

$$\|\hat{y}(t)\| + |\alpha(t)| \to 0 \qquad \text{as} \quad t \to 0$$

and

$$B(y(t), \alpha(t)) = 0, \tag{32}$$

where

$$y(t) := t[\tilde{y} + \hat{y}(t)], \qquad \alpha(t) := t[1 + \hat{\alpha}(t)]. \tag{33}$$

Let us examine how the values of the maps $A(y, \alpha)$ and $C(y, \alpha)$ change along the curve $(y(t), \alpha(t))$ from the point $(0, 0)$. Using formulae (29) and (31) we can approximate the linear terms to find that

$$A(y(t), \alpha(t)) = \Phi^0 - a(\tilde{y}, \tilde{u})t + o(t) > \Phi^0 + \tilde{\delta}t + o(t),$$

$$C(y(t), \alpha(t)) = G^0 + c(\tilde{y}, \tilde{u})t + o(t),$$

where, by virtue of (31), the definition of Ω_δ and the fact that $\tilde{c} = 0$ on Ω_δ,

$$G^0 + c(\tilde{y}, \tilde{u})t + o(t) = \begin{cases} G^0 - \tilde{\delta}t + o(t) & \text{a.e. on } \Omega_\delta, \\ -\delta_1 + c(\tilde{y}, \tilde{u})t + \chi(t) & \text{a.e. on } \Omega \backslash \Omega_\delta, \end{cases}$$

and $\|\chi(t)\|_\infty = o(t)$. From this and (32) it follows that, for all sufficiently small t,

$$A(y(t), \alpha(t)) > \Phi^0, \qquad B(y(t), \alpha(t)) = 0, \qquad C(y(t), \alpha(t)) \leqq 0.$$

Now, by the definitions of A, B and C and the convexity condition (b) assumed in the statement of the theorem, for each such t we can find a $u(t) \in U$ satisfying the relations

$$A(y(t), \alpha(t)) = \Phi(y^0 + y(t), u(t)) > \Phi^0,$$

$$B(y(t), \alpha(t)) = F(y^0 + y(t), u(t)) = 0,$$

$$C(y(t), \alpha(t)) = G(y^0 + y(t), u(t)) \leqq 0,$$

which contradicts the assumption that (y^0, u^0) is a local maximum. □

7. The Regular Case

For some $\tilde{y} \in Y$, $\tilde{u} \in U$ and $\delta > 0$, suppose that (15) holds and inequality (17) is valid on the set Ω_δ. Then $\lambda_0^0 \neq 0$ and may be taken to be 1.

□ Suppose the contrary. Then, using (14), relations (12) and (13) may be rewritten as follows:

$$\langle \psi^0, F_y^0 y \rangle + \langle \lambda^0, G_y^0 y \rangle = 0 \qquad (y \in Y), \tag{34}$$

$$\langle \psi^0, F(y^0, u) \rangle + \langle \lambda^0, G(y^0, u) \rangle \geqq 0 \qquad (u \in U), \tag{35}$$

respectively.

Now $\lambda^0 \neq 0$. Indeed, if $\lambda^0 = 0$, then from (34) $\langle \psi^0, F_y^0 \rangle = 0$ for all $y \in Y$, so that $\psi^0 = 0$, because im $F_y^0 = z$. Consequently, λ_0^0, ψ^0 and λ^0 are all zero, which contradicts the fact that the separating functional

$$l^0 = (\lambda_0^0, \psi^0, \lambda^0) \neq 0.$$

Next we show that from the relations $\lambda^0 \geqq 0$, $\langle \lambda^0, G^0 \rangle = 0$ it follows that the equation $\langle \lambda^0, g1_{\{G^0 < -\delta\}} \rangle = 0$ holds for all $g \in L_\infty$.

□ Since

$$0 \leqq |\langle \lambda^0, g1_{\{G^0 < -\delta\}} \rangle| \leqq \|g\|_\infty \langle \lambda^0, 1_{\{G^0 < -\delta\}} \rangle,$$

we need only show that $0 = \langle \lambda^0, 1_{\{G^0 < -\delta\}} \rangle$. But this is so in light of the inequalities

$$0 = \langle \lambda^0, G^0 \rangle = \langle \lambda^0, G^0 1_{\{G^0 < -\delta\}} + G^0 1_{\Omega_\delta} \rangle$$
$$\leqq \langle \lambda^0, G^0 1_{\{G^0 < -\delta\}} \rangle \leqq -\delta \langle \lambda^0, 1_{\{G^0 < -\delta\}} \rangle \leqq 0. \quad \square$$

Note that we have just demonstrated that the optimal multiplier λ_0 has support 1_{Ω_δ} for $\Omega_\delta := \{\omega : 0 \geqq G^0(\omega) \geqq -\delta\}$ for all $\delta > 0$; in this sense it "lives" on the "boundary" subset $\{\omega : G^0(\omega) = 0\}$ of the "ground" set $\{\omega : G(\omega) \leqq 0\}$ [more generally, on the boundary subset of the ground set corresponding to constraints which hold as equations at the local maximum (y^0, u^0)].

Using the result just established and (17), with g set equal to $\tilde{g} := G_y^0 \tilde{y} + G(y^0, \tilde{u})$, we obtain the following relations:

$$\langle \lambda^0, \tilde{g} \rangle = \langle \lambda^0, \tilde{g} 1_\Omega \rangle < \langle \lambda^0, -\delta 1_\Omega \rangle = -\delta \langle \lambda^0, 1_\Omega \rangle \leqq 0.$$

Thus

$$\langle \lambda^0, \tilde{g} \rangle = \langle \lambda^0, G_y^0 \tilde{y} \rangle + \langle \lambda^0, G(y^0, \tilde{u}) \rangle < 0,$$

but, using (34) and (15), we have that

$$\langle \lambda^0, G_y^0 \tilde{y} \rangle = -\langle \psi^0, F_y^0 \tilde{y} \rangle = \langle \psi^0, F(y^0, \tilde{u}) \rangle,$$

and hence that

$$\langle \psi^0, F(y^0, \tilde{u}) \rangle + \langle \lambda^0, G(y^0, \tilde{u}) \rangle < 0,$$

which contradicts (35).

Finally, since $\lambda_0^0 > 0$, we may replace the separating functional $l^0 = (\lambda_0^0, \psi^0, \lambda^0)$ by $\bar{l}^0 := (1, \psi^0/\lambda_0^0, \lambda^0/\lambda_0^0)$ without loss of generality. $\square\square$

3. PROOF OF THE MAXIMUM PRINCIPLE

1. Reduction to a Smoothly Convex Problem

To prove the maximum principle we shall apply the results of the previous section. Hence we must first formulate the optimal control problem (1)–(4) in terms of the smoothly convex optimization problem (8)–(11).

Let $L^n_\infty(S^t) := L^n_\infty(S^t, \mathscr{F}^t, P^t)$, where $\mathscr{F}^t := \mathscr{E}^{t+1}$ is the σ-algebra of subsets of S^{t+1} generated by the history $\mathbf{s}^t$ of the process $\{\mathbf{s}_t\}$ and $P^t(E) := P(E \times S^{N-t})$ for $E \in \mathscr{F}^t$, $t = 0, \ldots, N$ ($\mathscr{F} := \mathscr{F}^N$), and define

$$Y := Z := \bigtimes_{t=1}^{N} L^n_\infty(S^t),$$

$$y = (y_1(s^1), \ldots, y_N(s^N)) \in Y,$$

$$z = (z_1(s^1), \ldots, z_N(s^N)) \in Z,$$

$$U := \{u : u = (u_0(s^0), \ldots, u_{N-1}(s^{N-1})),\ s^t \in S^t,$$

$$u_t(s^t) \in U_t(s^t) \text{ a.s. } [P],\ u_t \text{ measurable},\ t = 0, \ldots, N-1\},$$

$$\Phi(y, u) := E \sum_{t=0}^{N-1} \phi^t(\mathbf{s}^t, \mathbf{y}_t, \mathbf{u}_t),$$

$$F(y, u) := \{z_t := y_t - f^t(s^t, y_{t-1}, u_t)\}_{t=0}^{N-1},$$

$$G^t(y, u) := g^t(s^t, y_t, u_t), \qquad t = 0, 1, \ldots, N-1.$$

By Condition (A_2) of §1.2,

$$F(\cdot,\cdot): Y \times U \to Y, \qquad G^t(\cdot,\cdot): Y \times U \to L^k_\infty(S^t).$$

In the remainder of §3.1 we shall check that the functional Φ and the operators F, G^t satisfy the conditions of Theorem 2.

☐ We show first that these maps have continuous Fréchet derivatives with respect to y at each point $(y, u) \in Y \times U$, which are given by the formulae

$$\Phi_y(y, u)\bar{y} = E \sum_{t=0}^{N-1} \phi_y(\mathbf{s}^t, \mathbf{y}_t, \mathbf{u}_t)\bar{y}_t, \tag{36}$$

$$F_y(y, u)\bar{y} = \{\bar{y}_t - f^t_y(s^t, y_{t-1}, u_{t-1})\bar{y}_{t-1}\}_{t=1}^{N}, \tag{37}$$

$$G^t_y(y, u)\bar{y} = g^t_y(s^t, y_t, u_t)\bar{y}_t, \qquad t = 0, \ldots, N-1 \quad (\bar{y}_0 = 0). \tag{38}$$

Formula (36) is a direct consequence of the following lemma.

Lemma 1. *Let $(\Omega, \mathscr{F}, P)$ be a probability space, and suppose there is a real-valued function, given by $r(\omega, x)$ for $x \in \mathbb{R}^n$, which is jointly measurable (i.e., measurable with respect to the product σ-field of $\mathscr{F}$ and the Borel σ-field $\mathscr{B}$ of $\mathbb{R}^n$). At each point (ω, x), let r possess a continuous derivative with respect to x, $r_x(\omega, x)$, satisfying the following condition:*

For each bounded set $C \subseteqq \mathbb{R}^n$ *there exists a function* $\rho_C \in L_1(\Omega)$ *such that*

$$|r_x(\omega, x)| \leqq \rho_C(\omega) \qquad \text{for all} \quad x \in C. \tag{39}$$

For each function $x(\cdot) \in L^n_\infty(\Omega)$ *define the functional* $R: L^n_\infty(\Omega) \to \mathbb{R}$ *by*

$$R(x(\cdot)) := \mathbf{E}\mathbf{r}(\mathbf{x}) := \int_\Omega r(\omega, x(\omega))P(d\omega). \tag{40}$$

Then at each point $x(\cdot)$ *the functional* R *possesses a continuous Fréchet derivative given by the formula*

$$R_x(x(\cdot))\bar{x}(\cdot) = \mathbf{E}\mathbf{r}_x(\mathbf{x})\bar{\mathbf{x}} := \int_\Omega r_x(\omega, x(\omega))\bar{x}(\omega)P(d\omega). \tag{41}$$

□ We show first that $\mathbf{E}\mathbf{r}_x(\mathbf{x})\bar{\mathbf{x}}$ is the (linear) Gateaux derivative of the functional (40). It is sufficient to check that

$$\lim_{\epsilon \to 0} \int \left| \frac{r(\omega, x(\omega) + \bar{\epsilon}x(\omega)) - r(\omega, x(\omega))}{\epsilon} - r_x(\omega, x(\omega))\bar{x}(\omega) \right| P(d\omega) = 0 \tag{42}$$

for any fixed elements $x, \bar{x} \in L^n_\infty(\Omega)$. For each ω we use the mean value formula

$$r(\omega, x(\omega) + \epsilon\bar{x}(\omega)) - r(\omega, x(\omega)) = r_x(\omega, x(\omega) + \epsilon\Theta(\omega)\bar{x}(\omega))\epsilon\bar{x}(\omega), \tag{43}$$

where $0 \leqq \Theta(\omega) \leqq 1$.

We observe that the function given by $r_x(\omega, x(\omega) + \epsilon\Theta(\omega)\bar{x}(\omega))$ is measurable with respect to ω, since the left-hand side of (43) is measurable under our assumptions. Now (42) may be rewritten

$$\lim_{\epsilon \to 0} \int_\Omega |[r_x(\omega, x(\omega) + \epsilon\Theta(\omega)\bar{x}(\omega)) - r_x(\omega, x(\omega))]\bar{x}(\omega)| P(d\omega) = 0. \tag{44}$$

The truth of (44) follows from the continuity of the function $r_x(\omega, x)$ and, by condition (39), from the possibility of passing to the limit x under the integral sign (using the Lebesgue dominated convergence theorem). To prove the existence of the Fréchet derivative it is sufficient to prove the continuity of the Gateaux derivative. In other words, we must check that

$$\sup_{\|\bar{x}\|_\infty \leq 1} \int_\Omega |[r_x(\omega, x(\omega) + x_n(\omega)) - r_x(\omega, x(\omega))]\bar{x}(\omega)| P(d\omega) \to 0 \tag{45}$$

as $\| x_n \|_\infty \to 0$.

The proof of this statement is exactly analogous to the justification of the interchange of limit and integration in (44). Note that from (45) the continuity of the Fréchet derivative follows immediately. ☐

Formulae (37) and (38) are valid as a consequence of the following lemma:

Lemma 2. *Let an* $\mathscr{F} \times \mathscr{B}$ *measurable function be given by* $q(\omega, x)$ *for* $x \in \mathbb{R}^n$, *and suppose that at each point* (ω, x) *derivatives* $q_x(\omega, x)$ *with respect to* x *exist. Suppose further that for any bounded set* $C \subseteqq \mathbb{R}^n$ *there exists a constant* K_C *such that*

$$|q(\omega, x)| + |q_x(\omega, x)| \leqq K_C \qquad \text{for all} \quad x \in C,$$
$$|q_x(\omega, x_1) - q_x(\omega, x_2)| \leqq K_C|x_1 - x_2| \qquad \text{for all} \quad x_1, x_2 \in C$$

(*i.e.,* a local Lipschitz *condition on* q_x). *Then the mapping* $Q(x(\cdot)) := q(\cdot, x(\cdot))$ *maps* $L^n_\infty(\Omega)$ *to* $L_\infty(\Omega)$ *and has a continuous Frechet derivative with respect to* $x(\cdot)$ *given a.e.* $[P]$ *by*

$$Q'(x(\cdot))\bar{x}(\cdot)(\omega) = q_x(\omega, x(\omega))\bar{x}(\omega). \tag{46}$$

☐ The first part of the statement follows directly from the conditions of the lemma. We calculate the Fréchet derivative by showing that the right-hand side of (46) defines the Gateaux derivative. We have that

$$\begin{aligned} &\left\| \frac{q(\omega, x(\omega) + \epsilon\bar{x}(\omega)) - q(\omega, x(\omega))}{\epsilon} - q_x(\omega, x(\omega))\bar{x}(\omega) \right\|_\infty \\ &\quad = \|[q_x(\omega, x(\omega) + \epsilon\Theta(\omega)\bar{x}(\omega)) - q_x(\omega, x(\omega))]\bar{x}(\omega)\|_\infty \\ &\quad \leqq \epsilon K\|\bar{x}\|^2_\infty \to 0 \end{aligned}$$

as $\epsilon \to 0$.

The first equality holds by the mean value theorem, and the inequality follows from the local Lipschitz condition. The continuity of the Gateaux derivative is proved analogously, from which it may be concluded that (46) defines the Fréchet derivative, which is continuous at each point $x(\cdot)$. ☐

It follows from the lemma and (37) that the range of the operator $F_y(y^0, u^0)$ coincides with Z.

Next we check that the functional $\Phi(y, u)$ and the mappings $F(y, u)$

and $G^t(y, u)$ satisfy the convexity condition (b) of Theorem 3 with the neighbourhood V of y_0 taken to be Y.

□ We fix a sequence $\mathbf{y}_t$, $t = 1, \ldots, N$, in Y, a number $\alpha \in [0, 1]$ and two control sequences $\mathbf{u}_t', \mathbf{u}_t'' \in U_t(\mathbf{s}^t)$ a.s., $t = 0, \ldots, N-1$. It is enough to show that there exists a control sequence $\mathbf{u}_t \in U_t(\mathbf{s}^t)$ a.s. such that the following relations hold:

$$\begin{aligned}
&\alpha\phi^t(\mathbf{s}^t, \mathbf{y}_t, \mathbf{u}_t') + (1-\alpha)\phi^t(\mathbf{s}^t, \mathbf{y}_t, \mathbf{u}_t'') \\
&\qquad \leqq \phi^t(\mathbf{s}^t, \mathbf{y}_t, \mathbf{u}_t) \qquad \text{a.s.}, \\
&\alpha f^{t+1}(\mathbf{s}^{t+1}, \mathbf{y}_t, \mathbf{u}_t') + (1-\alpha) f^{t+1}(\mathbf{s}^{t+1}, \mathbf{y}_t, \mathbf{u}_t'') \\
&\qquad = f^{t+1}(\mathbf{s}^{t+1}, \mathbf{y}_t, \mathbf{u}_t) \qquad \text{a.s. } [P(\cdot|s^t)], \\
&\alpha g^t(\mathbf{s}^t, \mathbf{y}_t, \mathbf{u}_t') + (1-\alpha) g^t(\mathbf{s}^t, \mathbf{y}_t, \mathbf{u}_t'') \\
&\qquad \geqq g_t(\mathbf{s}^t, \mathbf{y}_t, \mathbf{u}_t) \qquad \text{a.s.}
\end{aligned} \tag{47}$$

To prove these relations, we note that by the convexity condition (B) of Theorem 1, for almost every s^t we may find an element $u \in U_t(s^t)$ such that they hold almost surely with respect to $P(\cdot|s^t)$. But, because the left-hand sides of these relations are measurable functions of s^t, by virtue of Fillipov's lemma (Corollary I.4) there exists a measurable function $u_t(\cdot)$ such that $u_t(\mathbf{s}^t) \in U_t(\mathbf{s}^t)$ a.s. satisfying (47) for $t = 0, \ldots, N-1$. □

Thus all conditions have been verified for the application of Theorem 3. □

2. The Maximum Principle with Respect to Functionals in L_∞^*

Consider the Lagrangian for the problem (1)–(4):

$$\begin{aligned}
L(\{\mathbf{y}_t\}, \{\mathbf{u}_t\}, \lambda_0, \{\boldsymbol{\psi}_t\}, \{\boldsymbol{\lambda}_t\}) := \lambda_0 E \sum_{t=0}^{N-1} \phi^t(\mathbf{s}^t, \mathbf{y}_t, \mathbf{u}_t) \\
- \sum_{t=0}^{N-1} \langle \psi_{t+1}, y_{t+1} - f^{t+1}(\cdot, y_t, u_t)\rangle \\
- \sum_{t=0}^{N-1} \langle \lambda_t, g^t(\cdot, y_t, u_t)\rangle.
\end{aligned}$$

If $\{\mathbf{y}_t^0\}_{t=0}^N$, $\{\mathbf{u}_t^0\}_{t=0}^{N-1}$ are a solution of problem (1)–(4), then according to Theorem 3 there exist a constant $\lambda^0 \geqq 0$ and sequences $\{\psi_t^0\}_{t=1}^N$, $\{\lambda_t^0\}_{t=0}^{N-1}$, $\psi_t^0 \in L_\infty^{n*}$, $0 \leqq \lambda_t^0 \in L_\infty^{k*}$, not all zero, such that [cf. (13)]

$$\sum_{t=0}^{N-1} [\lambda_0^0 E(\phi^t(\mathbf{s}^t, \mathbf{y}_t^0, \mathbf{u}_t^0) - \phi^t(\mathbf{s}^t, \mathbf{y}_t^0, \mathbf{u}_t))$$
$$+ \langle \psi_{t+1}^0, f^{t+1}(\cdot, y_t^0, u_t^0) - f^{t+1}(\cdot, y_t^0, u_t)\rangle$$
$$- \langle \lambda_t^0, g^t(\cdot, y_t^0, u_t^0) - g^t(\cdot, y_t^0, u_t)\rangle] \geqq 0$$

for any sequence of measurable functions $u_t(\mathbf{s}^t) \in U_t(\mathbf{s}^t)$ a.s.

Setting sequentially $u_s = u_s^0$ at $s \neq t$, $s = 0, \ldots, N-1$, in this equality, we obtain

$$\lambda_0^0 E\phi^t(\mathbf{s}^t, \mathbf{y}_t^0, \mathbf{u}_t^0) + \langle \psi_{t+1}^0, f^{t+1}(\cdot, y_t^0, u_t^0)\rangle - \langle \lambda_t^0, g^t(\cdot, y_t^0, u_t^0)\rangle$$
$$\geqq \lambda_0^0 E\phi^t(\mathbf{s}^t, \mathbf{y}_t^0, \mathbf{u}_t) + \langle \psi_{t+1}^0, f^{t+1}(\cdot, y_t^0, u_t)\rangle$$
$$- \langle \lambda_t^0, g^t(\cdot, y_t^0, u_t)\rangle \tag{48}$$

for any measurable function u_t such that $u_t(\mathbf{s}^t) \in U_t(\mathbf{s}^t)$ a.s., $t = 0, \ldots, N-1$. Applying the remaining conclusions of Theorem 3, we have first [cf. (12)]

$$\sum_{t=0}^{N-1} [\lambda_0^0 E\phi_y^t(\mathbf{s}^t, \mathbf{y}_t^0, \mathbf{u}_t^0)\bar{y}_t - \langle \psi_{t+1}^0, \bar{y}_{t+1} - f_y^{t+1}(\cdot, y_t^0, u_t^0)\bar{y}_t\rangle$$
$$- \langle \lambda_t^0, g_y^t(\cdot, y_t^0, u_t^0)\bar{y}_t\rangle] = 0$$

for any sequence

$$\bar{y}_t \in L_\infty^n(S^t), \qquad t = 1, \ldots, N-1, \quad \bar{y}_0 = 0.$$

In this equation, set sequentially $\bar{y}_s = 0$, $s \neq t$, $s = 1, \ldots, N-1$. Then, after simple manipulation, we obtain the conjugate backwards difference system

$$\langle \psi_t^0, \bar{y}_t\rangle = \lambda_0^0 E\phi_y^t(s^t, y_t^0, u_t^0)\bar{y}_t + \langle \psi_{t+1}^0, f_y^{t+1}(\cdot, y_t^0, u_t^0)\bar{y}_t\rangle$$
$$- \langle \lambda_t^0, g_y^t(\cdot, y_t^0, u_t^0)\bar{y}_t\rangle \tag{49}$$

for any $\bar{y}_t \in L_\infty(S^t)$, $t = 1, \ldots, N-1$; $\langle \psi_N^0, \bar{y}_N\rangle = 0$ for any $\bar{y}_N \in L_\infty^n(S^N)$. The complementary slackness conditions (14) take the form

$$\langle \lambda_t^0, g^t(\cdot, y_t^0, u_t^0)\rangle = 0. \tag{50}$$

Relations (48)–(50) constitute the maximum principle for the problem (1)–(4) with respect to functionals in L_∞^*.

Note that we did not use the regularity condition (C) in deriving this version of the maximum principle.

3. The Integral Form of the Maximum Principle

□ The regularity condition (C) plays a main rôle in the establishment of the integral form of the maximum principle.

We show first that $\lambda_0^0 > 0$ (and hence without loss of generality we may take $\lambda_0^0 = 1$).

□ Suppose the contrary, i.e., $\lambda_0^0 = 0$. We shall show by induction that all the functionals ψ_t^0, λ_t^0 are then zero. To this end suppose that $\psi_{t+1}^0 = \cdots = \psi_N^0 = 0$ and $\lambda_{t+1}^0 = \cdots = \lambda_N^0 = 0$. We shall show that $\psi_t^0 = 0$ and $\lambda_t^0 = 0$.

From (48) and (50) we have

$$0 \geqq -\langle \lambda_t^0, g^t(\cdot, y_t^0, \tilde{u}_t)\rangle \geqq \langle \lambda_t^0, \gamma 1\rangle \geqq 0,$$

where $\tilde{u}_t$ and $\gamma 1$ are as in Condition (C). Thus $\lambda_t^0 = 0$, and from (49) we see that $\psi_t^0 = 0$.

By induction we can therefore conclude that $\lambda_0^0 = 0$, $\psi_t^0 = \lambda_t^0 = 0$ for all t, which is a contradiction (see §3.2). □

By the Yosida–Hewitt theorem (see §III.6) the functionals λ_t^0 and ψ_t^0 in relations (48)–(50) are represented, respectively, by the sum of absolutely continuous functionals $\lambda_t^{\mathrm{a}}, \psi_t^{\mathrm{a}}$ and singular functionals $\lambda_t^{\mathrm{s}}, \psi_t^{\mathrm{s}}$. By the nonnegativity of the functional λ_t^0 and the nonpositivity of the function given by $g^t(s^t, y_t^0, u_t^0)$, it follows immediately from (50) that

$$\langle \lambda_t^{\mathrm{a}}, g^t(\cdot, y_t^0, u_t^0)\rangle = 0. \tag{51}$$

We shall show now that the functionals λ_t^0 and ψ_t^0 are actually absolutely continuous; i.e., $\lambda_t^{\mathrm{s}} = \psi_t^{\mathrm{s}} = 0$.

□ The proof of this is also by induction. Suppose, therefore, that

$$\psi_{t+1}^{\mathrm{s}} = \cdots = \psi_N^{\mathrm{s}} = 0, \qquad \lambda_t^{\mathrm{s}} = \cdots = \lambda_{N-1}^{\mathrm{s}} = 0.$$

We shall show that $\psi_t^{\mathrm{s}} = 0$ and $\lambda_{t-1}^{\mathrm{s}} = 0$.

To this end, consider first equation (49). By induction, the right-hand side of this equation is the result of the action of absolutely continuous functionals on linear transformations of an element $\bar{y}_t$.

But because (49) holds for *all* $\bar{y}_t \in L^n_\infty(S^t)$, the functional ψ^0_t must therefore be absolutely continuous; i.e., $\psi^s_t = 0$.

We show next that $\lambda^s_{t-1} = 0$.

□ Suppose the contrary. Then to the singular functional λ^s_{t-1} there corresponds a sequence of measurable sets $\{E_m\}$, $E_{m+1} \subseteqq E_m \subseteqq S^t$, $P(E_m) \to 0$ with the property that $\langle \lambda^s_{t-1}, (1 - 1_{E_m})g \rangle = 0$ for any element $g \in L^k_\infty(S^t)$ [see Property (a) in the definition of a singular functional in §III.6]. Here $1_{E_m}(\cdot)$ is the indicator function of the set E_m. Let the element $\hat{u}_{t-1}$ satisfy the regularity condition (C) of §1 and suppose that

$$u^m_{t-1} := u^0_{t-1} \qquad \text{outside } E_m$$

and

$$u^m_{t-1} := \hat{u}_{t-1} \qquad \text{on } E_m. \tag{52}$$

Obviously, $\mathbf{u}^m_{t-1} \in U_{t-1}(\mathbf{s}^{t-1})$ a.s. Our next aim is to assess the value

$$\mu_m := \langle \lambda^s_{t-1}, g^{t-1}(\cdot, y^0_{t-1}, u^m_{t-1}) \rangle.$$

We have

$$\mu_m = \langle \lambda^s_{t-1}, (1 - 1_{E_m})g^{t-1}(\cdot, y^0_{t-1}, u^0_{t-1}) \rangle + \langle \lambda^s_{t-1}, 1_{E_m} g^{t-1}(\cdot, y_{t-1}, \hat{u}_{t-1}) \rangle.$$

By definition the sequence $\{E_m\}$ is such that for any m

$$\langle \lambda^s_{t-1}, (1 - 1_{E_m})g^{t-1}(\cdot, y^0_{t-1}, u^0_{t-1}) \rangle = 0.$$

Therefore

$$\begin{aligned} \mu_m &= \langle \lambda^s_{t-1}, 1_{E_m} g^{t-1}(\cdot, y^0_{t-1}, \hat{u}_{t-1}) \rangle \\ &= \langle \lambda^s_{t-1}, g^{t-1}(\cdot, y^0_{t-1}, \hat{u}_{t-1}) \rangle - \langle \lambda^s_{t-1}, (1 - 1_{E_m})g^{t-1}(\cdot, y^0_{t-1}, \hat{u}_{t-1}) \\ &= \langle \lambda^s_{t-1}, g^{t-1}(\cdot, y^0_{t-1}, \hat{u}_{t-1}) \rangle. \end{aligned}$$

Thus, μ_m is not dependent on m; i.e. $\mu_m \equiv \mu$. From Condition (C), for some constant $\gamma > 0$, $g^{t-1}(\mathbf{s}^{t-1}, \mathbf{y}^0_{t-1}, \hat{\mathbf{u}}_{t-1}) \leqq -\gamma 1 < 0$ a.s. Therefore, by the nonnegativity of the functional λ^s_{t-1} and from the hypothesis that $\lambda^s_{t-1} \neq 0$ if follows immediately that

$$\mu \leqq -\gamma \langle \lambda^s_{t-1}, 1 \rangle < 0. \tag{53}$$

Consider next the inequality (48) (replacing t by $t - 1$), which holds for any measurable function u_{t-1} such that $u_{t-1}(\mathbf{s}^{t-1}) \in U_{t-1}(\mathbf{s}^{t-1})$ a.s., and in particular for the function u_{t-1}^m. Thus, replacing u_{t-1} by u_{t-1}^m in (48), in light of the absolute continuity of ψ_t^0 and relations (50) and (51), we have that

$$\begin{aligned} &E\phi^{t-1}(\mathbf{s}^{t-1}, \mathbf{y}_{t-1}^0, \mathbf{u}_{t-1}^0) + E\boldsymbol{\psi}_t^{\mathrm{a}} f^t(\mathbf{s}^t, \mathbf{y}_{t-1}^0, \mathbf{u}_{t-1}^0) \\ &\qquad - E\boldsymbol{\lambda}_{t-1}^{\mathrm{a}} g^{t-1}(\mathbf{s}^{t-1}, \mathbf{y}_{t-1}^0, \mathbf{u}_{t-1}^0) \\ &\qquad \geqq E\phi^{t-1}(\mathbf{s}^{t-1}, \mathbf{y}_{t-1}^0, \mathbf{u}_{t-1}^m) + E\boldsymbol{\psi}_t^{\mathrm{a}} f^t(\mathbf{s}^t, \mathbf{y}_{t-1}^0, \mathbf{u}_{t-1}^m) \\ &\qquad\quad - E\boldsymbol{\lambda}_{t-1}^{\mathrm{a}} g^{t-1}(\mathbf{s}^{t-1}, \mathbf{y}_{t-1}^0, \mathbf{u}_{t-1}^m) - \langle \lambda_{t-1}^{\mathrm{s}}, g^{t-1}(\cdot, y_{t-1}^0, u_{t-1}^m) \rangle, \end{aligned}$$

where $\boldsymbol{\psi}_t^{\mathrm{a}} := \psi_t^{\mathrm{a}}(\mathbf{s}^t)$ and $\boldsymbol{\lambda}_{t-1}^{\mathrm{a}} := \lambda_{t-1}^{\mathrm{a}}(\mathbf{s}^{t-1})$ are (norm) *summable* (i.e., finitely integrable) vector-valued functions (interpreted here as random vectors) defining the absolutely continuous components of the functionals $\psi_t^0, \lambda_{t-1}^0$.

Now we move all terms to the right-hand side of the above inequality, split each term into 1_{E_m} and $1 - 1_{E_m}$ parts and take limits as $m \to \infty$. By the summability of the functions $\phi^{t-1}(\cdot, y_{t-1}^0, u_{t-1}^0)$, $\phi^{t-1}(\cdot, y_{t-1}^0, \hat{u}_{t-1})$ and the boundedness of the functions $f^t(\cdot, y_{t-1}^0, u_{t-1})$, $g^{t-1}(\cdot, y_{t-1}^0, u_{t-1})$ for admissible u_{t-1}, the expression

$$\begin{aligned} &E1_{E_m}\{[\phi^{t-1}(\mathbf{s}^{t-1}, \mathbf{y}_{t-1}^0, \hat{\mathbf{u}}_{t-1}) - \phi^{t-1}(\mathbf{s}^{t-1}, \mathbf{y}_{t-1}^0, \mathbf{u}_{t-1}^0)] \\ &\qquad + \boldsymbol{\psi}_t^{\mathrm{a}}[f^t(\mathbf{s}^t, \mathbf{y}_{t-1}^0, \hat{\mathbf{u}}_{t-1}) - f^t(\mathbf{s}^t, \mathbf{y}_{t-1}^0, \mathbf{u}_{t-1}^0)] \\ &\qquad + \boldsymbol{\lambda}_{t-1}^{\mathrm{a}}[g^{t-1}(\mathbf{s}^{t-1}, \mathbf{y}_{t-1}^0, \hat{\mathbf{u}}_{t-1}) - g^{t-1}(\mathbf{s}^{t-1}, \mathbf{y}_{t-1}^0, \mathbf{u}_{t-1}^0)]\} \end{aligned}$$

converges to zero as $m \to \infty$. The corresponding expression involving $1 - 1_{E_m}$ is identically zero by the definition of u_{t-1}^m. On passing to the limit we therefore have that

$$\lim_{m \to \infty} \langle \lambda_{t-1}^{\mathrm{s}}, g^{t-1}(\cdot, y_{t-1}^0, u_{t-1}^m) \rangle = \mu \geqq 0.$$

This inequality contradicts (53). Therefore, $\lambda_{t-1}^{\mathrm{s}} = 0$. □

The general induction step is proven. The initial step ($t = N$) is established similarly. For example, it follows immediately from the fact that $\langle \psi_N^0, \bar{y}_N \rangle = 0$ for any $\bar{y}_N \in L_\infty^n(S^N)$ [cf. (49)] that $\psi_N^{\mathrm{s}} = 0$. □

Now the inequality (48) may be rewritten

$$\begin{aligned} &E[\phi^t(\mathbf{s}^t, \mathbf{y}_t^0, \mathbf{u}_t^0) + \boldsymbol{\psi}_{t+1}^0 f^{t+1}(\mathbf{s}^{t+1}, \mathbf{y}_t^0, \mathbf{u}_t^0) - \boldsymbol{\lambda}_t^0 g^t(\mathbf{s}^t, \mathbf{y}_t^0, \mathbf{u}_t^0)] \\ &\qquad \geqq E[\phi^t(\mathbf{s}^t, \mathbf{y}_t^0, \mathbf{u}_t) + \boldsymbol{\psi}_{t+1}^0 f^{t+1}(\mathbf{s}^{t+1}, \mathbf{y}_t^0, \mathbf{u}_t) - \boldsymbol{\lambda}_t^0 g^t(\mathbf{s}^t, \mathbf{y}_t^0, \mathbf{u}_t)], \quad (54) \end{aligned}$$

which holds for any measurable function u_t such that $\mathbf{u}_t \in U_t(\mathbf{s}^t)$ a.s.,

$t = 0, \ldots, N-1$. The conjugate backwards difference system (49) takes the form

$$E\boldsymbol{\psi}_t^0\bar{y}_t = E[\phi_y^t(\mathbf{s}^t, \mathbf{y}_t^0, \mathbf{u}_t^0) + \boldsymbol{\psi}_{t+1}^0 f_y^{t+1}(\mathbf{s}^{t+1}, \mathbf{y}_t^0, \mathbf{u}_t^0)\bar{\mathbf{y}}_t - \boldsymbol{\lambda}_t^0 g_y^t(\mathbf{s}^t, \mathbf{y}_t^0, \mathbf{u}_t^0)\bar{\mathbf{y}}_t] \tag{55}$$

and $E\boldsymbol{\psi}_N\bar{\mathbf{y}}_N = 0$ for any functions $\bar{y}_t \in L_\infty^n(S^t)$, $t = 1, \ldots, N$. The complementary slackness condition (50) in integral form is

$$E\boldsymbol{\lambda}_t^0 g^t(\mathbf{s}^t, \mathbf{y}_t^0, \mathbf{u}_t^0) = 0, \qquad t = 0, \ldots, N-1. \tag{56}$$

Relations (54)–(56) constitute the *integral form of the maximum principle* for the problem (1)–(4). □

If we use the definition of the Hamiltonian introduced in §1.3, then inequality (54) can be rewritten in the form

$$EH^{t+1}(\mathbf{s}^{t+1}, \boldsymbol{\lambda}_t^0, \boldsymbol{\psi}_{t+1}^0, \mathbf{y}_t^0, \mathbf{u}_t^0) \geqq EH^{t+1}(\mathbf{s}^{t+1}, \boldsymbol{\lambda}_t^0, \boldsymbol{\psi}_{t+1}^0, \mathbf{y}_t^0, \mathbf{u}_t) \tag{57}$$

for any measurable function u_t such that $\mathbf{u}_t \in U_t(\mathbf{s}^t)$ a.s., $t = 0, \ldots, N-1$. The conjugate system becomes

$$E\boldsymbol{\psi}_t^0\bar{\mathbf{y}}_t = EH_y^{t+1}(\mathbf{s}^{t+1}, \boldsymbol{\lambda}_t^0 \boldsymbol{\Upsilon} \boldsymbol{\psi}_{t+1}^0, \mathbf{y}_t^0, \mathbf{u}_t^0)\bar{\mathbf{y}}_t, \qquad E\boldsymbol{\psi}_N^0\bar{\mathbf{y}}_N = 0 \tag{58}$$

for any functions $\bar{y}_t \in L_\infty^n(S^t)$, $t = 1, \ldots, N$.

4. Reduction to the Pointwise Maximum Principle

□ Consider the function

$$\mathscr{H}^t(\mathbf{s}^t, \mathbf{u}) := E[H^{t+1}(\mathbf{s}^{t+1}, \boldsymbol{\lambda}_t^0, \boldsymbol{\psi}_{t+1}^0, \mathbf{y}_t^0, \mathbf{u}) \mid \mathbf{s}^t] \qquad \text{a.s.} \tag{59}$$

Note that by the measurability of $H^{t+1}(s^{t+1}, u)$ and the existence of conditional probabilities $P(ds_{t+1} \mid \mathbf{s}^t)$ it is possible to choose a version of conditional expectation in (59) such that the function $H^t(s^t, u)$ will be jointly measurable (cf. §II.1).

Our aim is to show first that

$$\max_{u \in U_t(\mathbf{s}^t)} \mathscr{H}^t(\mathbf{s}^t, u) = \mathscr{H}^t(\mathbf{s}^t, \mathbf{u}_t^0) \qquad \text{a.s.,} \tag{60}$$

i.e., statement (5) of Theorem 1.

□ Consider the set

$$A := \{(s^t, u) \colon \mathscr{H}^t(s^t, u) > \mathscr{H}^t(s^t, u_t^0(s^t)),\ u \in U_t(s^t)\}.$$

This set is measurable with respect to the product σ-field $\mathscr{F}^t \times \mathscr{B}(U)$

on the product space $S^t \times U$. [Here $\mathscr{F}^t$ denotes the σ-field generated by the history $\mathbf{s}^t$ of the process to time t, and $\mathscr{B}(U)$ denotes the Borel σ-field on the complete separable metric space U.] Let B be the projection of set A on the space S^t. By the projection theorem (see §I.5, Corollary 1) the set B is universally measurable. If $P(B) = 0$, (60) is proven. So suppose $P(B) > 0$ and note that a measurable set $C \subseteq B$ such that $P(C) = P(B)$ exists. We construct a multifunction by associating with each point $s^t \in C$ the set $\{u: \mathscr{H}^t(s^t, u) > \mathscr{H}^t(s^t, u_t^0(s^t)), u \in U_t(s^t)\}$. This multifunction is easily seen to satisfy all conditions of Aumann's measurable choice theorem (see §I.5, Corollary 3). Let $\bar{u}_t$ be any measurable selector of this multifunction and define

$$\tilde{u}_t := \begin{cases} \bar{u}_t & \text{on } C, \\ u_t^0 & \text{on } S^t \backslash C. \end{cases}$$

Obviously, $\tilde{u}_t \in U_t(\mathbf{s}_t)$ a.s. and

$$\mathscr{H}^t(\mathbf{s}^t, \tilde{\mathbf{u}}_t) > \mathscr{H}^t(\mathbf{s}^t, \mathbf{u}_t^0) \qquad \text{a.s.}$$

Taking expectations on both sides of this inequality, noting the definition of the function $\mathscr{H}^t(s^t, u)$ and using the fundamental property of conditional expectation, we obtain a contradiction to the inequality (57) of the integral maximum principle. □

To obtain the conjugate system (6) of Theorem 1 it is sufficient to rewrite (58) in the form

$$E\psi_t^0 \bar{\mathbf{y}}_t = E(E[H_y^{t+1}(\mathbf{s}^{t+1}, \boldsymbol{\lambda}_t^0, \boldsymbol{\psi}_{t+1}^0, \mathbf{y}_t^0, \mathbf{u}_t^0) | \mathbf{s}^t] \bar{\mathbf{y}}_t)$$

and note that equality holds in this expression for all $\bar{y}_t \in L_\infty^n(S^t)$. The complementary slackness condition in pointwise form, (7), follows from the integral form, (56), on taking into account the nonnegativity of the function λ_t^0 and the nonpositivity of the function given by $g^t(s^t, y_t^0(s^t), u_t^0(s^t))$. □□

4. STOCHASTIC ANALOGUES OF THE GALE MODEL

1. Technology, Objective Functionals and Programmes

We begin with the description of a model which is a direct stochastic generalization of the Gale model. Some versions of the scheme described below are included as particular cases of the general problem of optimal control already discussed.

Suppose one is given a random *data process* $\mathbf{s}_0, \mathbf{s}_1, \ldots, \mathbf{s}_N$ *in* some measurable space $(S, \mathscr{E})$ (the values $\mathbf{s}_t$ may be interpreted, for example, as environmental conditions at time t).

A *technological process* is defined by pairs of measurable functions[2] x_{t-1}, y_t such that

$$(x_{t-1}(\mathbf{s}^{t-1}), y_t(\mathbf{s}^t)) \geqq 0 \qquad \text{a.s.,} \quad t = 1, \ldots, N,$$

where $\mathbf{s}^t$ is the *history* of process $\{\mathbf{s}_t\}$ up to time t (the random situation at time t); i.e., $\mathbf{s}^t := (\mathbf{s}_0, \ldots, \mathbf{s}_t)$. The function value $x_{t-1}(s^{t-1})$ is interpreted as the *input* to the technological process made at time $t - 1$ on the realization of the random situation $\mathbf{s}^{t-1} = s^{t-1}$, and $y_t(s^t)$ is its *output* at time t in situation s^t.

We emphasize that the output $y_t(\mathbf{s}^t)$ depends on the random parameters $\mathbf{s}_0, \mathbf{s}_1, \ldots, \mathbf{s}_{t-1}$ that influence input and also on the random parameter $\mathbf{s}_t$ which is *unknown* at the time of input. Consequently it may be said that this type of model allows for uncertainty during the technological processing of inputs into outputs.

Production possibilities are given (as in Chapter 1) by the *technology sets* Q_t, which are formally defined to be the collection of feasible technological processes in the time interval $(t - 1, t]$. For each t a real-valued *objective functional* F_t, which characterizes the (expected) "utility" of feasible technological processes, is supposed defined on the set Q_t. It is further assumed that the sets Q_t are convex and the functionals F_t are concave. The following condition is also assumed to hold for all t:

If the random vector $\mathbf{z} := (x(\mathbf{s}^{t-1}), y(\mathbf{s}^t))$ *belongs to* Q_t *and* $\mathbf{z}' := (x'(\mathbf{s}^{t-1}), y'(\mathbf{s}^t))$ *coincides with* $\mathbf{z}$ *almost surely, i.e., with probability* 1, *then* $\mathbf{z}' \in Q_t$ *and* $F_t(\mathbf{z}') = F_t(\mathbf{z})$.[3]

Sequences of technological processes $\zeta := \{\mathbf{z}_t\} = \{(\mathbf{x}_{t-1}, \mathbf{y}_t)\}$,

[2] For the economic models in this book, it will be assumed throughout that all vector functions of the random parameters $\mathbf{s}_t$ considered are measurable; this assumption will not be mentioned further in the sequel. Usually such functions will be interpreted as random vectors of the appropriate dimension.

[3] As an example of such a Q_t, we can consider

$$Q_t := \{(x(\mathbf{s}^{t-1}), y(\mathbf{s}^t)) : (x(\mathbf{s}^{t-1}), y(\mathbf{s}^t)) \in G_t(\mathbf{s}^t) \text{ a.s.}\},$$

where $G_t(\mathbf{s}^t)$ is a subset of $\mathbb{R}^{2n}$. However, there are important technologies that are not covered by this example (see §4.7).

$t = 1, \ldots, N$, which satisfy the constraints

$$\mathbf{z}_t \in Q_t, \qquad t = 1, \ldots, N,$$

$$\mathbf{y}_t \geqq \mathbf{x}_t \qquad \text{a.s.,} \quad t = 0, \ldots, N-1$$

are termed *programmes*. *Optimal programmes* maximize

$$F(\zeta) = F_1(\mathbf{z}_1) + \cdots + F_N(\mathbf{z}_N)$$

amongst all programmes $\zeta := \{(\mathbf{x}_{t-1}, \mathbf{y}_t)\} := \{\mathbf{z}_t\}$ with $\mathbf{x}_0 \leqq \mathbf{y}_0$ a.s. [i.e., amongst programmes with *initial vector* (*i.v.*) $\mathbf{y}_0$].

To distinguish the stochastic nature of the Gale model proposed above from that to be described in §4.7, we shall say that the present model is described in *functional form*.

2. The Existence of Optimal Programmes

Let $0 \leqq y_0 \in L^n_\infty(S^0)$, where S^0 denotes the set of all possible initial data s_0, be fixed, and suppose that at least one programme exists with i.v. $\mathbf{y}_0$.

Theorem 4. (Existence of an optimal programme over a finite horizon.) *The following conditions are sufficient for the existence of optimal programmes:*

(I) *The sets Q_t are closed relative to a.s. convergence and bounded in the L_1 norm (i.e., there exists a constant C such that $E|z(\mathbf{s}^t)| \leqq C$ for all $\mathbf{z} \in Q_t$).*

(II) *The functionals F_t are upper semicontinuous relative to a.s. convergence.*[4]

□ We shall use Theorem III.5. For this purpose the programme $\zeta = \{(\mathbf{x}_0, \mathbf{y}_1), \ldots, (\mathbf{x}_{N-1}, \mathbf{y}_N)\}$ will be interpreted as an element of the space $L_1(S^0) \times L_1(S^1) \times \cdots \times L_1(S^N)$, where S^t denotes the set of all sequences s^t.

Notice first that the set Π of all programmes with i.v. $\mathbf{y}_0$ is closed with respect to a.s. convergence. This follows from (I) and the fact that inequality $\mathbf{y}_t \geqq \mathbf{x}_t$ holds a.s. for the limit of a sequence from Π.

[4] We consider convergence with respect to sequences (rather than nets) throughout.

From (I) and (II) it is easily seen that Π and F satisfy all the requirements of Theorem III.5 and, therefore, that F achieves a maximum on Π. $\square$

3. Supporting Prices

The following condition will also be assumed to hold in the sequel.

(III) *There exists a constant C such that, for all $\mathbf{z} \in Q_t$, $|z(\mathbf{s}^t)| \leqq C$ a.s. for all t.*

This condition permits us to consider the functions (x_{t-1}, y_t), determining the technological processes as elements of the space $D_{t-1} \times D_t$ where $D_t := L_\infty(S^t, \mathbb{R}^n)$.

A *price system* (or simply *prices*) is defined to be a sequence of coordinatewise nonnegative integrable functions $\{p_t(\mathbf{s}^t)\}$ (interpreted as random vectors) with values in $\mathbb{R}^n$. The ith coordinate of the random vector $\mathbf{p}_t := p_t(\mathbf{s}^t)$ is interpreted as the price of the ith good, and the scalar product $p_t(\mathbf{s}^t)x = \sum_{i=1}^n p_{ti}(\mathbf{s}^t)x_i$ is the random *cost* of the set of products x (at time t in the random situation $\mathbf{s}^t$).

Similar to the case for deterministic models, in the probabilistic theory prices play a main rôle.

The prices $\{\mathbf{p}_t\}$, $t = 0, \ldots, N$, *support* the programme $\zeta = \{(\mathbf{x}_{t-1}, \mathbf{y}_t)\} := \{\mathbf{z}_t\}$, $t = 1, \ldots, N$, with i.v. $\mathbf{y}_0$, if the following conditions hold:

A. *For all $t \geqq 1$ and for $\mathbf{z}' \in Q_t$*

$$G_t(\mathbf{z}') \leqq G_t(\mathbf{z}_t), \tag{61}$$

where

$$G_t(\mathbf{x}, \mathbf{y}) := F_t(\mathbf{x}, \mathbf{y}) + E\mathbf{p}_t\mathbf{y} - E\mathbf{p}_{t-1}\mathbf{x}.^5 \tag{62}$$

B. $E\mathbf{p}_t(\mathbf{y}_t - \mathbf{x}_t) = 0$, $t = 0, \ldots, N-1$.

The functional G_t of expression (62) is called the *reduced utility* of the technological process $(\mathbf{x}, \mathbf{y})$. Its value is calculated from the (expected) utility F_t of the process $(\mathbf{x}, \mathbf{y})$ and its expected production *profit* $E(\mathbf{p}_t\mathbf{y} - \mathbf{p}_{t-1}\mathbf{x})$ (the difference between the expectations of the value of output and the cost of input).

[5] The reader will have noticed that here, and wherever possible, we omit the arguments $\mathbf{s}^t$, denoting, for example, $z_t(\mathbf{s}^t)$ simply by $\mathbf{z}_t$.

Condition B states that the expected cost of the unused resources $\mathbf{y}_t - \mathbf{x}_t$ of the programme ζ is equal to zero. Note that, since $\mathbf{p}_t \geqq 0$ a.s. and $\mathbf{y}_t \geqq \mathbf{x}_t$ a.s., Condition B is equivalent to the following condition:

B′. $\mathbf{p}_t(\mathbf{y}_t - \mathbf{x}_t) = 0$ a.s., $t = 0, \ldots, N - 1$.

It is worth mentioning by way of analogy with the optimal control problem that G_t is the analogue of the Hamiltonian function, and Condition B is a version of the complementary slackness condition. For more details on the connections of this model with optimal control, see §4.9.

Prices as defined above are a direct generalization of the similar concept introduced in Chapter 1 for the deterministic model (see §1.1.4). The discussion in §1.1.5 of the economic meaning of prices carries over to the stochastic case, provided we are interested only in the expected (i.e., average) values of the corresponding economic parameters (input cost, production profit, etc.).

Next we investigate conditions for the existence of supporting prices. For this purpose we shall need the following concept.

1. Generalized Prices

Let us say that a sequence $\{\boldsymbol{\pi}_t\}$, $t = 0, \ldots, N$, is a system of *generalized prices* if π_t is a nonnegative continuous linear functional on D_t for each t. *Ordinary prices* $\mathbf{p}_t$ generate generalized prices if we define the corresponding integral functional as $\boldsymbol{\pi}_t(\mathbf{x}) := E\mathbf{p}_t\mathbf{x}$. In this regard, ordinary prices are also called prices of *integral type*.

Obviously, Conditions A and B have meaning *mutatis mutandis* for generalized prices, and we may speak about generalized *supporting* prices.

Let us introduce the following assumption:

(IV) *There exists a programme* $\tilde{\zeta} = \{(\tilde{\mathbf{x}}_{t-1}, \tilde{\mathbf{y}}_t\}$ *with i.v.* $\tilde{\mathbf{y}}_0$ *and a (nonrandom) vector* $\delta 1 < 0$ *such that* $\tilde{\mathbf{y}}_t \geqq \tilde{\mathbf{x}}_t + \delta 1$ *a.s.*, $t = 0, \ldots, N - 1$.

Mathematically, Condition (IV) plays the rôle of the Slater condition for the optimal economic planning problem (see §III.2).

Fix $\mathbf{y}_0 \in D_0$, $\mathbf{y}_0 \geqq 0$ a.s. and suppose that at least one optimal programme exists with i.v. $\mathbf{y}_0$.

Theorem 5. (Existence of generalized supporting prices.) *If* (III) *and* (IV) *hold and* $\mathbf{y}_0 \geqq \tilde{\mathbf{y}}_0$ *a.s., then there exists a system of generalized prices which support the family of optimal programmes with i.v.* $\mathbf{y}_0$.

□ The proof of Theorem 5 follows the same scheme as the proof of Theorem 1 in §1.2.1. We treat the programmes $\zeta := \{(\mathbf{x}_0, \mathbf{y}_1), \ldots, (\mathbf{x}_{N-1}, \mathbf{y}_N)\}$ analytically as the elements of space $H := D_0 \times D_1 \times D_1 \times \cdots \times D_N$. Denote by Q the set of all sequences $\zeta = \{\mathbf{z}_t\}$ such that $\mathbf{z}_t \in Q_t$ and consider the mapping g which transforms $\zeta = \{(\mathbf{x}_{t-1}, \mathbf{y}_t)\}$ into the element $g(\zeta) := \{\mathbf{y}_0 - \mathbf{x}_0, \mathbf{y}_1 - \mathbf{x}_1, \ldots, \mathbf{y}_{N-1} - \mathbf{x}_{N-1}\}$ of the space $D := D_0 \times D_1 \times \cdots \times D_{N-1}$. By (IV), $g(\tilde{\zeta}) \geqq \delta 1$ a.s. for some $\tilde{\zeta}$; i.e., $g(\tilde{\zeta})$ belongs to the interior of the nonnegative cone in D. By the Kuhn–Tucker theorem (see Appendix III) this is sufficient for the existence of a functional $\pi^0 := (\pi_0^0, \ldots, \pi_{N-1}^0) \in D^*$ such that $\pi^0 \geqq 0$ and

$$F(\zeta) + \pi^0(g(\zeta)) \leqq F(\zeta^0) \qquad (\zeta \in Q), \tag{63}$$

where ζ^0 is an optimal programme. "Decoding" the notation in (63), we see that the functionals $\pi_0^0, \ldots, \pi_{N-1}^0$ have the following property:

C. *For any sequence* $\{\mathbf{z}_t\} = \{(\mathbf{x}_{t-1}, \mathbf{y}_t)\}$ *such that* $\mathbf{z}_t \in Q_t$,

$$\sum_{t=1}^{N} F_t(\mathbf{z}_t) + \sum_{t=0}^{N-1} \pi_t^0(\mathbf{y}_t - \mathbf{x}_t) \leqq \sum_{t=1}^{N} F_t(\mathbf{z}_t^0). \tag{64}$$

Let $\pi_N^0 := 0$. Theorem 5 follows from the next lemma.

Lemma 3. *Condition* B *holds if the prices* $\pi_0^0, \ldots, \pi_N^0$ *support the family of optimal programmes with i.v.* $\mathbf{y}_0$.

□ This statement is proved in a similar manner to Lemma 1 of §1.2.1 (replacing p with π). □□

5. Construction of Prices of Integral Type

In the previous subsection, we found generalized prices which support the family of optimal programmes. Now, by introducing additional hypotheses, we shall construct ordinary prices with similar properties. Such prices are measurable functions $\mathbf{p}_t$, interpreted as random vectors, which generate the absolutely continuous components of the functionals π_t^0 (by integration with respect to the appropriate probability measure; see §III.6).

Let us introduce the following conditions:

(V) $(0, 0) \in Q_t$.

(VI) *For any* $\mathbf{z} \in Q_t$ *and any sequence* $\{\mathbf{z}_k\} \subseteqq Q_t$ *such that* $P\{\mathbf{z}_k \neq \mathbf{z}\} \to 0$, *we have* $F_t(\mathbf{z}_k) \to F_t(\mathbf{z})$.

(VII) *If* $\mathbf{z} \in Q_t$ *and* θ *is a (measurable) function of* s^{t-1} *which takes only the two values* 0 *and* 1, *then* $\boldsymbol{\theta}\mathbf{z} \in Q_t$.

Condition (V) has a technical character (the possibility of zero input and zero output). Condition (VI) holds, for example, if the functionals F_t are continuous relative to convergence in measure.[6] As a consequence of (VII) it is possible to choose between a technological process $\mathbf{z}$ and (0, 0) depending on the random situation $\mathbf{s}^{t-1}$. (Economically, this corresponds to the possibility of feasibly ceasing economic production—and consumption—temporarily if certain circumstances are realized.)

Under hypotheses (V)–(VII) we have the following:

Theorem 6. (Existence of ordinary supporting prices.) *Suppose the prices* π_t^0, $t = 0, \ldots, N$, $\pi_N^0 = 0$, *support the nonempty family of optimal programmes of length N with i.v.* $\mathbf{y}_0$. *Let Conditions (V)–(VII) hold, and suppose* $\mathbf{p}_t^0$ *are the functions in* $L_1(S^t)$ *corresponding to the absolutely continuous components* π_t^a *of the functionals* π_t^0 *so that* $\pi_t^a(\mathbf{x}) = E\mathbf{p}_t^0\mathbf{x}$ *for* $\mathbf{x} \in L_1(S^t)$. *Then the prices* $\mathbf{p}_t^0$ *support the same family of optimal programmes.*

□ Fix $\zeta = \{(\mathbf{x}_{t-1}, \mathbf{y}_t)\} \in Q$ and consider the inequality

$$F(\zeta) + \sum_{t=0}^{N-1} \pi_t^a(\mathbf{y}_t - \mathbf{x}_t) + \sum_{t=0}^{m} \pi_t^s(\mathbf{y}_t - \mathbf{x}_t) \leqq F(\zeta^0). \tag{65}$$

For $m = N - 1$ this inequality is the same as (64) and, therefore, is true. Our purpose is to prove by induction that the inequality holds at $m = -1$, i.e., when all terms involving singular functionals are removed. Suppose therefore that (65) holds at some m; we shall show that (65) is true for $m - 1$.

[6] Or, equivalently, are continuous relative to convergence almost surely. Continuity with respect to these two types of convergence is identical, since any sequence which converges a.s. converges in measure, and it is possible to choose a subsequence which converges a.s. from a sequence which converges in measure.

For this purpose consider the sequence of sets $\Gamma_k \subseteq S^m$ on which the functional π_m^s is "concentrated" (see §III.6), and let

$$(\mathbf{x}_m^k, \mathbf{y}_{m+1}^k) := \mathbf{z}_{m+1}^k := \begin{cases} (0,0) & \text{for } \{s^m \in \Gamma_k\}, \\ \mathbf{z}_{m+1} & \text{for } \{s^m \notin \Gamma_k\}, \end{cases}$$

$$\zeta^k := \{\mathbf{z}_1, \ldots, \mathbf{z}_m, \mathbf{z}_{m+1}^k, \mathbf{z}_{m+2}, \ldots, \mathbf{z}_N\}.$$

By Condition (VII), $\mathbf{z}_{m+1}^k \in Q_{m+1}$ when $\mathbf{z}_{m+1} \in Q_{m+1}$. It follows that $\zeta^k \in Q$, and by (65)

$$F(\zeta^k) + \pi^a(g(\zeta^k)) + \sum_{t=0}^{m-1} \pi_t^s(\mathbf{y}_t - \mathbf{x}_t) + \pi_m^s(\mathbf{y}_m - \mathbf{x}_m^k) \leqq F(\zeta^0), \quad (66)$$

where $g(\cdot)$ was defined in the proof of Theorem 5. In this inequality, $\pi_m^s(\mathbf{y}_m) \geqq 0$, since $\pi_m^s \geqq 0$ and $\mathbf{y}_m \geqq 0$. Further, $\pi_m^s(\mathbf{x}_m^k) = 0$ by definition of the sets Γ_k. Indeed, the function x_m^k takes the value 0 on Γ_k, and thus the functional π_m^s has a zero value at it.

Therefore the last term on the left-hand side of (66) is nonnegative and we can ignore it, and so

$$F(\zeta^k) + \pi^a(g(\zeta^k)) + \sum_{t=0}^{m-1} \pi_t^s(\mathbf{y}_t - \mathbf{x}_t) \leqq F(\zeta^0). \quad (67)$$

Taking limits as $k \to \infty$, we obtain $P(\Gamma_k) \to 0$ and $P\{\mathbf{z}_{m+1}^k \neq \mathbf{z}_{m+1}\} \to 0$, so that, by virtue of (VI), $F_{m+1}(\mathbf{z}_{m+1}^k) \to F_{m+1}(\mathbf{z}_{m+1})$. It also follows from $P(\Gamma_k) \to 0$ that the random value $g(\zeta^k)$ tends to $g(\zeta)$ in probability. As a consequence of (III), the function g is bounded and therefore $\pi^a(g(\zeta^k)) \to \pi^a(g(\zeta))$ by Lebesque's bounded convergence theorem. So, as $k \to \infty$ in (67) we obtain (65) with $m - 1$ replacing m.

The argument used to establish the induction step is valid for $m = 0$, resulting in the removal of all singular functionals from (65), the desired result. □

6. When Prices of Integral Type Do Not Exist

We give the simplest possible example. Consider a single-good ($n = 1$), single-step ($N = 1$) model described as follows:

(a) $S := [0, 1]$.

(b) $\mathbf{s}_0$ has a distribution given by Lebesque measure m on S, and independently $\mathbf{s}_1$ is an arbitrary random variable taking values in S.

(c) Q_1 consists of functions which are equal a.s. to constants (x, y), where $0 \leqq x \leqq a$, $0 \leqq y \leqq \phi(x)$ and ϕ is a continuous concave nonnegative function on $[0, a]$.

(d) $F_1(x, y) := x$.

Let us consider the optimal planning problem with i.v. $y_0(\mathbf{s}_0)$ where the function y_0 is continuous, has a single minimum on S and takes values in the interval $[\gamma, \delta]$, where $0 < \gamma < \delta < a$.

The problem of finding the optimal programme (x^0, y^0) reduces to the following:

$$\begin{aligned} &\text{Maximize} \quad x \\ &\text{subject to} \quad x \leqq y_0(s_0) \quad \forall s_0,^{7} \\ &\qquad\qquad\quad x \in [0, a]. \end{aligned} \tag{68}$$

The optimal value x^0 of x is found from this problem, and then y^0 may be taken to be any vector which satisfies the inequalities $0 \leqq y^0 \leqq \phi(x^0)$.

Obviously, the maximum value x^0 equals $y_0(b)$, where b is the minimum of the function y_0 on S. Moreover, Conditions (I)–(VI) clearly hold [but (VII) does not!]. Therefore generalized prices exist which support the optimal programme.

Suppose that these supporting prices are of integral type. By virtue of Lemma 3, this implies the existence of an integrable function given by $p^0(s_0) \geqq 0$ such that $x + Ep^0(\mathbf{s}_0)[y_0(\mathbf{s}_0) - x] \leqq x^0$ $(0 \leqq x \leqq a)$. [In the sequel we mostly omit the sub- and superscripts 0 and write, for example, $y(\mathbf{s})$ instead of $y_0(\mathbf{s}_0)$.] Setting $x = x^0$ in the left-hand side of this inequality, we obtain the equation

$$Ep(\mathbf{s})[y(\mathbf{s}) - x^0] = 0, \tag{69}$$

so that for $0 \leqq x \leqq a$

$$x + Ep(\mathbf{s})[y(\mathbf{s}) - x] \leqq x^0 + Ep(\mathbf{s})[y(\mathbf{s}) - x^0].$$

Thus $x[1 - Ep(\mathbf{s})] \leqq x^0[1 - Ep(\mathbf{s})]$. Since $x^0 = y(b) \in [\gamma, \delta] \subseteq (0, a)$,

[7] In general, the inequality (68) should be written "a.s." However, in our case, the function y_0 is continuous, and therefore here the inequality holding surely is equivalent to the inequality holding almost surely.

this is possible only if

$$Ep(\mathbf{s}) := \int_0^1 p(s)m(ds) = 1. \tag{70}$$

Moreover, from this and (69) we may conclude that

$$x^0 = \int_0^1 p(s)y(s)m(ds), \tag{71}$$

but this is impossible, since the right-hand side of (71) is always greater than the left-hand side. Indeed,

$$\int_0^1 p(s)y(s)m(ds) - x^0 = \int_0^1 p(s)[y(s) - x^0]m(ds) > 0,$$

since the function $y(s) - x^0$ is positive almost everywhere $[m]$ (actually, everywhere except at the point b) and the function p is positive on a set of positive measure. Hence, we are led to a contradiction, and so [owing to the failure of Condition (VII) in this example] integral prices do not exist!

7. Model Definition in Parametric Form

In this subsection we describe a model in which the technology set is generated by parameters in some complete separable metric space (cf. §1.1.8). Such a parametric representation permits the consideration of the resulting model as a special case of the general problem of optimal control.

Let U be a complete separable metric space (the control space). Suppose that for each $t = 0, \ldots, N - 1$ we are given measurable multifunctions $s^t \mapsto U_t(s^t) \subseteq U$ and nonnegative $\mathbb{R}^n$-valued functions given by $a^t(s^t, u)$, $b^{t+1}(s^{t+1}, u)$ for $u \in U$. The set $U_t(s^t)$ is interpreted as the class of *admissible controls* (or *production techniques*) at time t in situation s^t. The random function values $a^t(\mathbf{s}^t, u)$ and $b^{t+1}(\mathbf{s}^{t+1}, u)$ are interpreted as random *inputs* and *outputs* with production technique u.

The *technology set* Q_{t+1}, $t = 0, \ldots, N - 1$, is defined as the set of all pairs of functions given by $(x(s^t), y(s^{t+1}))$ represented in the form

$$x(\mathbf{s}^t) = a^t(\mathbf{s}^t, u(\mathbf{s}^t)),\ y(\mathbf{s}^{t+1}) = b^{t+1}(\mathbf{s}^{t+1}, u(\mathbf{s}^t)) \qquad \text{a.s.},$$

where the function u satisfies the relation

$$u(\mathbf{s}^t) \in U_t(\mathbf{s}^t) \qquad \text{a.s.} \tag{72}$$

We say that u is a *control function* giving rise to the *technological process* (x, y).

For each t, *utility functionals* are defined on the technological processes $(\mathbf{x}, \mathbf{y})$ by means of *utility functions* given by $f_t(s^t, c)$ as follows:

$$F_t(\mathbf{x}, \mathbf{y}) := Ef_t(\mathbf{s}^t, x(\mathbf{s}^{t-1}), y(\mathbf{s}^t)). \tag{73}$$

Let us suppose that the following conditions hold

(M_1) *The functions given by $a^t(s^t, u)$ and $b^t(s^t, u)$ are jointly measurable and bounded in both arguments.*
(M_2) *The sets $U_t(s^t)$ depend measurably on s^t.*
(M_3) *For each t the function given by $f_t(s^t, c)$ is defined and concave on the closed convex set $A_t(s^t)$ which contains all images $(a^{t-1}(s^{t-1}, u), b^t(s^t, u))$ for $u \in U_{t-1}(s^{t-1})$.*
(M_4) *The function given by $\Phi_t(s^t, c)$, which equals ∞ for $c \notin A_t(s^t)$ and $f_t(s^t, c)$ for $c \in A_t(s^t)$, is jointly measurable in (s^t, c).*
(M_5) *There exists a function given by $q(s^t)$ such that $E\mathbf{q} < \infty$ and $|f_t(s^t, c)| \leqq q(s^t)$ for $c \in A_t(s^t)$ for all s^t.*
(M_6) *There exists a conditional distribution $P(\cdot|s^t)$ for the parameter $\mathbf{s}_{t+1}$ given $\mathbf{s}^t = s^t$.*
(M_7) *For any s^t, any $u_1, u_2 \in U_t(s^t)$ and any number $\alpha \in [0, 1]$, we can find a $u \in U_t(s^t)$ such that*

$$c^{t+1}(s^{t+1}, u) = \alpha c^{t+1}(s^{t+1}, u_1) + (1 - \alpha)c^{t+1}(s^{t+1}, u_2) \qquad \text{a.s. } [P(\cdot|s^t)],$$

where

$$c^{t+1}(s^{t+1}, u) := (a^t(s^t, u), b^{t+1}(s^{t+1}, u)).$$

Note first of all that these hypotheses imply that the utility functionals F_t are well defined in the form (73); the expectations have meaning and are finite.

8. The Relations between Parametric and Functional Conditions

We now show that the conditions of §4.7, together with three others, imply the conditions which were introduced in §§4.1–4.5. This allows the application of the functional model results to the model given in parametric form.

The first additional hypothesis is the following.

(M_8) *The functions given by* $a^t(s^t, u)$ *and* $b^t(s^t, u)$ *are continuous with respect to* u, *the sets* $U_t(s^t)$ *are compact and the functions given by* $f_t(s^t, c)$ *are upper semicontinuous with respect to* c.

We show first that

(I) *and* (III) *follow from* (M_1), (M_2) *and* (M_8).

□ For simplicity of notation, s replaces s^{t-1}, σ *replaces* s_t and the index t is omitted. Let $z_k := (x_k(s), y_k(s, \sigma))$ be a sequence of functions in Q which converges to $(x(s), y(s, \sigma))$ a.s., where x and y are measurable functions. We show that $(x, y) \in Q$.

We have that

$$x_k(\mathbf{s}) = a(\mathbf{s}, u_k(\mathbf{s})), \qquad y_k(\mathbf{s}, \boldsymbol{\sigma}) = b(\mathbf{s}, \boldsymbol{\sigma}, u_k(\mathbf{s})) \qquad \text{a.s.,}$$

where $u_k(\mathbf{s}) \in U(\mathbf{s})$ a.s. Consider for each s the set $\tilde{U}(s)$ of limit points of the sequence $u_k(s)$. The set $\tilde{U}(s)$ is almost surely nonempty, since $U(s)$ is compact. The graph of the multifunction $s \mapsto \tilde{U}(s)$ is measurable since its complement may be represented as

$$\{(u, s): \forall m, \exists j \text{ s.t. } \forall i \geqq j, \rho(u_i(s), u) \geqq 1/m\}$$
$$= \bigcap_{m=1}^{\infty} \bigcup_{j=1}^{\infty} \bigcap_{i \geqq j}^{\infty} \{(u, s): \rho(u_i(s), u) \geqq 1/m\},$$

where ρ is the metric in the space U. Since the multifunction $s \mapsto \tilde{U}(s)$ is measurable, by virtue of Aumann's theorem (Corollary I.3) there exists a measurable function given by $u(s)$ such that $u(\mathbf{s}) \in \tilde{U}(\mathbf{s}) \subseteq U(\mathbf{s})$ a.s. It follows that for almost all s we can find a sequence $k_i := k_i(s)$ such that $u_{k_i}(s) \to u(s)$. But then for such s

$$x_{k_i}(s) := a(s, u_{k_i}(s)) \quad \to a(s, u(s)),$$
$$y_k(s, \sigma) := b(s, \sigma, u_{k_i}(\sigma)) \to b(s, \sigma, u(s))$$

by virtue of the continuity of a and b in u. Therefore, $x(s) = a(\mathbf{s}, u(\mathbf{s}))$ a. s., and $y(\mathbf{s}, \boldsymbol{\sigma}) = b(\mathbf{s}, \boldsymbol{\sigma}, u(\mathbf{s}))$ a.s., so Q_t is closed with respect to a.s. convergence.

Boundedness in the L_1 norm follows from Condition (III), which in turn follows from (M_1). □

Conditions (M_4), (M_5) *and* (M_8) *imply that* F_t *is well defined and satisfies* (II).

□ Let $\mathbf{z}_k \to \mathbf{z}$ a.s. and $\mathbf{z}_k, \mathbf{z} \in Q$. Then (omitting the s, σ arguments)

$$\overline{\lim}\, E\mathbf{f}(\mathbf{z}_k) \leqq E\, \overline{\lim}\, \mathbf{f}(\mathbf{z}_k) \leqq E\mathbf{f}(\mathbf{z}),$$

where the first inequality follows from (M_5) and Fatou's lemma, the second from the fact that $f(s^t, c)$ is upper semicontinuous in c. □

Condition (VI) *follows from* (M_5).

□ Let Δ_k denote the set of (s, σ) where $z_k \neq z$. We have that $P(\Delta_k) \to 0$ and hence

$$|F(\mathbf{z}_k) - F(\mathbf{z})| = |E[\mathbf{f}(\mathbf{z}_k) - \mathbf{f}(\mathbf{z})]| = |E\mathbf{1}_{\Delta_k}[\mathbf{f}(\mathbf{z}_k) - \mathbf{f}(\mathbf{z})]|$$

$$\leqq E\mathbf{1}_{\Delta_k} 2\mathbf{q} \to 0,$$

since $E\mathbf{q} < \infty$. □

The following condition will also be needed.

(M_9) *There exists a* $u_t^*(\mathbf{s}^t)$ *such that* $u_t^*(\mathbf{s}^t) \in U_t(\mathbf{s}^t)$ *a.s. with the property that*

$$a^t(\mathbf{s}^t, u_t^*(\mathbf{s}^t)) = 0 \quad \text{a.s.} \qquad \text{and} \qquad b^{t+1}(\mathbf{s}^t, u_t^*(\mathbf{s}^t)) = 0 \quad \text{a.s.}$$

Clearly (M_9) implies (V) for the model in parametric form. Moreover,

Condition (M_9) *implies* (VII).

□ We show that the following condition, which together with (M_9) obviously implies (VII), is a property of the model in parametric form by the definition of a control function.

For any $z, z' \in Q$ *and any measurable function given by* $\lambda(s)$ *which takes only the values* 0 *and* 1, *the function* $z'' := \lambda z + (1 - \lambda)z'$ *belongs to* Q.

Define $\lambda(s) := 1_\Gamma(s)$, where Γ is some measurable set. Then if $z(s, \sigma)$ [resp. $z'(s, \sigma)$] is generated by a control function $u(s)$ [resp. $u'(s)$], then z'' is generated by the control function u'', which equals u for $s \in \Gamma$ and u' for $s \notin \Gamma$. □

Hence the set of conditions (M_1)–(M_9) guarantees the validity of (I)–(III) and (V)–(VII). We shall give a condition which implies (IV) for the model in parametric form in §4.9 [see (M*)].

Note also that the concavity of F_t follows obviously from the concavity of f_t, and the convexity of Q_t is obtained from (M_7) by means of Filippov's lemma (§I.5, Corollary 4).

9. Reduction to the General Problem of Optimal Control

Introducing the auxiliary random variables $y_t, t = 1, \ldots, N$, we may write the optimization problem for the parametric economic model as follows:

$$\text{Maximize} \quad \sum_{t=0}^{N-1} Ef_{t+1}(\mathbf{s}^{t+1}, a^t(\mathbf{s}^t, \mathbf{u}_t), b^{t+1}(\mathbf{s}^{t+1}, \mathbf{u}_t)) \tag{74}$$

$$\text{subject to} \quad y_{t+1}(\mathbf{s}^{t+1}) = b^{t+1}(\mathbf{s}^{t+1}, \mathbf{u}_t) \quad \text{a.s.,} \tag{75}$$

$$a^t(\mathbf{s}^t, \mathbf{u}_t) \leqq y_t(\mathbf{s}^t) \quad \text{a.s.,} \tag{76}$$

$$u_t(\mathbf{s}^t) \in U_t(\mathbf{s}^t) \quad \text{a.s.,} \ t = 0, \ldots, N-1. \tag{77}$$

A sequence $\mathbf{u}_t^0$, $t = 0, \ldots, N - 1$, yielding the maximum of the functional (74) defines an optimal programme of length N with fixed i.v. $\mathbf{y}_0$. Define

$$\phi^t(s^t, u) := \int_S f_{t+1}(s^{t+1}, a^t(s^t, u), b^{t+1}(s^{t+1}, u))P(ds_{t+1} \mid s^t).$$

By virtue of (M_5) the integral is well defined,

$$|\phi^t(\mathbf{s}^t, u)| \leqq q'(\mathbf{s}^t) \qquad \text{for} \quad u \in U_t(\mathbf{s}^t) \ \text{a.s.}, \ q' \in L_1(S^t), \tag{78}$$

and (74) coincides with

$$\sum_{t=1}^{N-1} E\phi^t(\mathbf{s}^t, \mathbf{u}_t).$$

Now letting

$$f^{t+1}(s^{t+1}, u) := b^{t+1}(s^{t+1}, u), \qquad g^t(s^t, u, y) := a^t(s^t, u) - y,$$

we have converted the problem (74)–(77) to the form (1)–(4).

Notice that ϕ^t and f^{t+1} do not depend on y, and the dependence of g^t on y is simple. Owing to this and by virtue of (M_1)–(M_7), using (78), it is easy to check that Conditions (A) and (B) of §1 hold. To apply the maximum principle we must reformulate Condition (C) in the terminology of the economic planning model.

(M*) *For each* $t = 0, \ldots, N - 1$, *there exists a constant* $\gamma > 0$ *and a control* $\mathbf{u}_t$ *such that*

$$\mathbf{y}_t^0 - a^t(\mathbf{s}^t, \mathbf{u}_t) > \gamma 1 \qquad \text{a.s.} \tag{79}$$

(There exists an input vector a.s. strictly less than the optimal output.)

So, if the conditions (M_1)–(M_7) and (M*) hold, then the maximum principle may be applied.

The optimal Hamiltonian function for this problem is given by

$$^0H^{t+1} := \phi^t(s^t, u) + \psi_{t+1}^0(s^{t+1})b^{t+1}(s^{t+1}, u) - \lambda_t^0(s^t)[a^t(s^t, u) - y_t^0(s^t)].$$

Moreover,

$$\boldsymbol{\psi}_t^0 = E[{}^0\mathbf{H}_y^{t+1} | \mathbf{s}^t] = \boldsymbol{\lambda}_t^0 \qquad \text{a.s.} \tag{80}$$

where

$$E[{}^0\mathbf{H}^{t+1} | \mathbf{s}^t] = \phi(\mathbf{s}^t, u) + \int_S \lambda_{t+1}^0(\mathbf{s}^t, s_{t+1}) \times b^{t+1}(\mathbf{s}^t, s_{t+1}, u) P(ds_{t+1} | \mathbf{s}^t) - \lambda_t^0(\mathbf{s}^t)[a^t(\mathbf{s}^t, u) - y_t^0(\mathbf{s}^t)] \qquad \text{a.s.}$$

Therefore the maximum principle gives the prices $\{\boldsymbol{\lambda}_t^0\}$ for which $\mathbf{u}_t^0$ maximizes (80) and further [by virtue of (7)]

$$\boldsymbol{\lambda}_t^0(\mathbf{y}_t^0 - a^t(\mathbf{s}^t, \mathbf{u}_t^0)) = 0 \qquad \text{a.s.} \tag{81}$$

($\mathbf{y}_0^0 := \mathbf{y}_0$). Taking the expectations in (80) and (81), we find that the prices $\{\boldsymbol{\lambda}_t^0\}$ support the optimal programme.

Note that in many studies *pointwise* conditions of the type (80) and (81) (these conditions are stronger than ours of supporting on average) are taken as the basis for the definition of supporting prices.

10. Models Described in Terms of Elementary Technological Processes

We make brief mention of one "intermediate" (between the functional and the parametric) method of constructing a stochastic version of the Gale model. A pair $(x, y(\cdot))$ is called an *elementary technological process* (e.t.p.) if x is a nonnegative n-dimensional vector and $y(s)$ defines a nonnegative $\mathbb{R}^n$-valued function on S. The vector x is interpreted as *inputs* and $y(\mathbf{s})$ as *outputs* depending on a random parameter $\mathbf{s}$.

Suppose one is given for each s^t a set $V_t(s^t)$ whose elements are e.t.p.s. Define the technology sets Q_{t+1}, $t = 0, 1, 2, \ldots$, as those classes of technological processes $(x(s^t), y(s^{t+1}))$ such that for almost all s_t

$$(x(s^t),\ y(s^t, \cdot)) \in V_t(s^t). \tag{82}$$

Expression (82) must be understood in the following way. Each pair of functions given by $(x(s^t), y(s^{t+1}))$ defines a mapping taking s^t to the e.t.p. $(x(s^t), y(s^t, \cdot))$, and it is required that for almost all s^t this e.t.p. belongs to the given set $V_t(s^t)$. (This set is naturally called the *elementary technology set.*)

This method of model description, with the technology as described above and utility functionals of the form $F_{t+1}(x, y) := Ef_t(\mathbf{s}^t, x(\mathbf{s}^t), y(\mathbf{s}^t, \cdot))$, where $f_t(s^t, x, y(\cdot))$ is a given functional of e.t.p.s, is of independent interest.[8]

COMMENTS ON CHAPTER 2

The results in this chapter concerning the stochastic maximum principle were obtained by Arkin and Krechetov [1, 2].

The optimization problem with operator constraints considered in §2 is of some independent interest. It is the functional analytic part of the proof of maximum principle. Such problems, without the operator constraints of inequality type, were studied by Pshenichni and Nenachov [1] and Ioffe and Tichomirov [1]. The proof in §2 is a development of the method of Ioffe and Tichomirov [1] and follows basically that given by Arkin and Krechetov [2].

The establishment of a stochastic maximum principle for the continuous time case requires considerable modification of the methods presented here (see Arkin and Saksonov [1,2]).

Different stochastic analogues of Gale's model of optimal economic

[8] See Evstigneev and Kuznetsov [1].

growth were formulated by Dynkin [1], Radner [3, 4], Jeanjean [1] and Dana [1], whose results on the existence of supporting prices are presented in one form or another. Radner [2] proposed the probabilistic version of von Neumann's model [1]. One sector probabilistic models were considered as early as 1962 by Phelps [1]. More refined questions connected with such models were studied by Brock and Mirman [1, 2]. The parametric model described in §4.7 was proposed by Arkin and Krechetov [2]; it is a natural extension of von Neumann's model [1]. The model described in functional form and the results concerning it are due to Evstigneev [4, 7].

The proof of the stochastic maximum principle rests, and the construction of supporting prices of integral type arc based on the Yosida–Hewitt [1] theorem. The work of Dubovitski and Milyutin [1] begin the wide application of this theorem in optimization theory. This method has been applied to economic equilibrium models by Bewley [1].

Finally, we mention the work on stochastic optimization problems closely related to the material of this chapter by Rockafellar and Wets [1–3] and Evstigneev [8].

3 MARKOV CONTROL: THE MAXIMUM PRINCIPLE AND DYNAMIC PROGRAMMING

1. THE SUFFICIENCY OF MARKOV CONTROL

1. Markov Optimal Control

Consider the following optimal control problem:

$$\text{Maximize} \quad \sum_{t=0}^{N-1} E\phi^t(\mathbf{s}_t, \mathbf{y}_t, \mathbf{u}_t) \tag{1}$$

$$\text{subject to} \quad \mathbf{y}_{t+1} = f^{t+1}(\mathbf{s}_t, \mathbf{s}_{t+1}, \mathbf{y}_t, \mathbf{u}_t) \quad \text{a.s.,} \tag{2}$$

$$\mathbf{u}_t := u_t(\mathbf{s}^t) \in U_t(\mathbf{s}_t) \quad \text{a.s.,} \tag{3}$$

$$g^t(\mathbf{s}_t, \mathbf{y}_t, \mathbf{u}_t) \leqq 0 \quad \text{a.s.,} \tag{4}$$

and $\mathbf{u}_t$ can be represented as

$$\mathbf{u}_t = v_t(\mathbf{s}_t, \mathbf{y}_t) \quad \text{a.s.,} \ t = 0, \ldots, N-1, \tag{5}$$

for some v_t, $t = 0, \ldots, N-1$, which are jointly measurable functions of s and y. Here $\{\mathbf{s}_t\}$ is a *Markov process* with values in the measurable space $(S, \mathscr{E})$ with initial distribution $P_0(ds_0)$ and a transition probability measure given by $P_t(s_t, ds_{t+1})$.

In order to satisfy the constraints (5) there must exist for any t a jointly measurable function given by $v_t(s, y)$ on $S \times \mathbb{R}^n$, called a *feedback (control) function*, such that $\mathbf{u}_t = v_t(\mathbf{s}_t, \mathbf{y}_t)$ a.s., where $\mathbf{y}_t$ is the trajectory corresponding to $\mathbf{u}_t$. Controls $\mathbf{u}_t$ possessing this property are called *Markovian*. In order to distinguish such controls from controls which depend *arbitrarily* on previous states of the system, we shall term the latter *nonanticipative*. Except where already explicitly stated to the contrary, the detailed structure of the problem (1)–(5) is assumed to be the same as the problem (2.1)–(2.4), treated in Chapter 2.

In fact, problem (2.1)–(2.4) is a particular case of the present problem (1)–(5) for the following reasons. First, we treat here the additional variables and constraints of (5), which express the Markov character of admissible controls. Second, the special nature of the dependency of ϕ^t, f^t, g^t, and U_t on the process $\{s_t\}$ and the Markovian assumption for this process do not *formally* restrict the generality at all. Indeed, we can transform to a Markov process from an arbitrary process by considering the new process $\boldsymbol{\sigma}_t = \mathbf{s}^t$. With this substitution the problem (2.1)–(2.4) reduces to (1)–(5).[1]

The optimal control model described by (1)–(5) is the principal object of study in this chapter. Necessary optimality conditions are stated for the problem (1)–(5) in the form of a maximum principle. The main tool is a theorem which shows the sufficiency of Markov controls by demonstrating that the extension of the problem through the admission of non-Markov controls of general type does not increase the maximum value of the utility functional. Further, we shall trace the connection between the maximum principle and the dynamic programming approach. Effective methods are also given for constructing Markov controls in problems with some additional convexity properties. Finally, in the last section, the Markov maximum principle is applied to some models of economic dynamics.

In this chapter it is assumed that

the mappings ϕ^t, f^t, U_t, g^t *are measurable and the functional* (1) *is finite for any pairs* $\{(\mathbf{y}_t, \mathbf{u}_t)\}$ *satisfying constraints* (2)–(4).

We begin with a lemma which shows that the feedback function for Markov control can be chosen in a particular way:

[1] It should be mentioned, however, that, no matter how the state space of the new process $\{\boldsymbol{\sigma}_t\}$ is technically implemented, knowledge of the process $\{\mathbf{s}_t\}$ up to time t is equivalent to knowledge of the process $\{\boldsymbol{\sigma}_t\}$ up to time t (i.e., the σ-algebras $\mathscr{F}_{\mathbf{s}}t$ and $\mathscr{F}_{\boldsymbol{\sigma}}t$ are identifiable).

Lemma 1. *If $u_t(\mathbf{s}^t) \in U_t(\mathbf{s}_t)$ a.s., then the feedback control function given by $v_t(s, y)$ can always be modified so that*

$$P\{\forall y \in \mathbb{R}^n,\ v_t(\mathbf{s}_t, y) \in U_t(\mathbf{s}_t)\} = 1.$$

If the feedback function possesses this additional property, we say that control is given by a *Markov strategy*.

□ Consider the distribution Q of the random element $(\mathbf{s}_t, \mathbf{y}_t)$ in the space $S \times \mathbb{R}^n$ and let $D := \{(s, y): v_t(s, y) \in U_t(s)\}$. The set D is measurable, since $D = \{(s, y): (s, v_t(s, y)) \in \operatorname{gr} U_t\}$, and $Q(D) = 1$. Therefore the projection of D on the space S is universally measurable (see Corollary I.1) and $Q_S(\operatorname{pr}_S D) = 1$, where Q_S is the projection of the measure Q on S. By Aumann's theorem (Corollary I.3) there exists a measurable function $\hat{u}$ such that $\hat{u}(s) \in U_t(s)$ a.s. $[Q_S]$. The function given by

$$v_t'(s, y) := \begin{cases} v_t(s, y) & \text{if } (s, y) \in D, \\ \hat{u}(s) & \text{if } (s, y) \notin D \end{cases}$$

possesses the required properties. □

Theorem 1. (Sufficiency of Markov controls.) *Let $\{\tilde{\mathbf{u}}_t\}_{t=0}^{N-1}$ be a control and $\{\tilde{\mathbf{y}}_t\}_{t=0}^{N}(\tilde{\mathbf{y}}_0 := \mathbf{y}_0)$ a trajectory which satisfy the constraints* (2)–(4). *Then there exists a Markov control $\{\mathbf{u}_t\}_{t=0}^{N-1}$ and a trajectory $\{\mathbf{y}_t\}_{t=0}^{N}$ which satisfy* (2)–(4) *and for which*

$$E \sum_{t=0}^{N-1} \phi^t(\mathbf{s}_t, \mathbf{y}_t, \mathbf{u}_t) \geqq E \sum_{t=0}^{N-1} \phi^t(\mathbf{s}_t, \tilde{\mathbf{y}}_t, \tilde{\mathbf{u}}_t). \tag{6}$$

Moreover, this control is given by a Markov strategy satisfying (5). □

It follows immediately from this theorem that to find the optimal solution of the problem (1)–(4) it is sufficient to restrict search to controls of Markov type.

2. The Basic Lemma

Lemma 2. *Let $(\Omega, \mathscr{F}, P)$ be a probability space, $\mathscr{F}_0$ a sub-σ-algebra of $\mathscr{F}$ and U a Polish space with Borel σ-algebra $\mathscr{B}$. Further, suppose one is given a real-valued function which is measurable with respect to the σ-algebra $\mathscr{F}_0 \times \mathscr{B}$, given by $\Phi(\omega, u)$, an $\mathscr{F}_0$-measurable multifunction $\omega \mapsto \Gamma(\omega) \subseteqq U$ and an $\mathscr{F}$-measurable function u such that $u(\omega) \in \Gamma(\omega)$*

a.s. and $E|\Phi(\boldsymbol{\omega}, u(\boldsymbol{\omega}))| < \infty$. *Then there exists an* $\mathscr{F}_0$*-measurable function* v *for which* $v(\boldsymbol{\omega}) \in \Gamma(\boldsymbol{\omega})$ a.s. and $E\Phi(\boldsymbol{\omega}, v(\boldsymbol{\omega})) \geqq E\Phi(\boldsymbol{\omega}, u(\boldsymbol{\omega}))$.

□ Define

$$\Psi(\omega) := E[\Phi(\omega, u(\omega)) | \mathscr{F}_0](\omega),$$

$$A := \{(\omega, u) : \Phi(\omega, u) \geqq \Psi(\omega),\ u \in \Gamma(\omega)\}.$$

The set A belongs to $F_0 \times \mathscr{B}$ and its projection $\mathrm{pr}_\Omega A \in \bar{\mathscr{F}}_0$, where $\bar{\mathscr{F}}_0$ denotes the universal completion of $\mathscr{F}_0$ (see Corollary I.1).

We shall show that $P(\mathrm{pr}_\Omega A) = 1$. Suppose, to the contrary, that the set

$$B := \Omega \backslash \mathrm{pr}_\Omega A = \{\omega : \Phi(\omega, u) < \Psi(\omega),\ u \in \Gamma(\omega)\}$$

has positive measure. Since $\Phi(\omega, u(\omega)) < \Psi(\omega)$ for $\omega \in B$, then $E1_B(\boldsymbol{\omega})\Phi(\boldsymbol{\omega}, u(\boldsymbol{\omega})) < E1_B(\boldsymbol{\omega})\Psi(\boldsymbol{\omega})$, which contradicts the definition of Ψ. Therefore $P(\mathrm{pr}_\Omega A) = 1$.

By Aumann's theorem (Corollary I.3), there exists an $\mathscr{F}_0$-measurable function v such that $(\boldsymbol{\omega}, v(\boldsymbol{\omega})) \in A$ a.s.; i.e.,

$$v(\boldsymbol{\omega}) \in \Gamma(\boldsymbol{\omega}) \quad \text{a.s.} \qquad \text{and} \qquad \Phi(\boldsymbol{\omega}, v(\boldsymbol{\omega})) \geqq \Psi(\boldsymbol{\omega}) \quad \text{a.s.}$$

The latter inequality yields $E\Phi(\boldsymbol{\omega}, v(\boldsymbol{\omega})) \geqq E\Psi(\boldsymbol{\omega}) = E\Phi(\boldsymbol{\omega}, u(\boldsymbol{\omega}))$. □

3. The Induction Hypothesis for the Proof of the Sufficiency Theorem

□ We prove Theorem 1 by induction.

Let us assume given random vectors $\mathbf{y}_{k+1}^k, \ldots, \mathbf{y}_N^k$ and measurable functions given by $v_k(s, y), \ldots, v_{N-1}(s, y)$ with the following properties:

(a) $P\{\forall y \in \mathbb{R}^n,\ v_t(\mathbf{s}_t, y) \subseteqq U_t(\mathbf{s}_t)\} = 1, \qquad t = k, \ldots, N-1.$

(b) $\mathbf{y}_t^k = f^t(\mathbf{s}_{t-1}, \mathbf{s}_t, \mathbf{y}_{t-1}^k, v_{t-1}(\mathbf{y}_{t-1}^k, \mathbf{s}_{t-1}))$ a.s., $t = k+1, \ldots, N$, and $\mathbf{y}_k^k = \tilde{\mathbf{y}}_k$.

(c) $g^t(\mathbf{s}_t, \mathbf{y}_t^k, v_t(\mathbf{y}_t^k, \mathbf{s}_t)) \leqq 0$ a.s., $t = k, \ldots, N-1$.

(d) $E\sum_{t=k}^{N-1} \phi^t(\mathbf{s}_t, \mathbf{y}_t^k, v_t(\mathbf{s}_t, \mathbf{y}_t^k)) \geqq E\sum_{t=k}^{N-1} \phi^t(\mathbf{s}_t, \tilde{\mathbf{y}}_t, \tilde{\mathbf{u}}_t)$.

The theorem will be proven if we show that k may be replaced by $k-1$ (the general induction step) in (a)–(d). The initial step ($k := N-1$) is obtained similarly.

We prove the general induction step using the basic lemma (Lemma 2).

4. Preparation for the Application of the Basic Lemma

Consider a sequence of random variables $\mathbf{Y}_t(u)$, $t = k, \ldots, N$, depending on a parameter $u \in U$ and defined by the recurrence relation

$$\mathbf{Y}_k(u) := f^k(\mathbf{s}_{k-1}, \mathbf{s}_k, \tilde{\mathbf{y}}_{k-1}, u)$$

$$\mathbf{Y}_t(u) := f^t(\mathbf{s}_{t-1}, \mathbf{s}_t, \mathbf{Y}_{t-1}(u), v_{t-1}(\mathbf{s}_{t-1}, \mathbf{Y}_{t-1}(u))), \qquad t = k+1, \ldots, N.$$

From these formulae it follows directly that the function $Y_t(\cdot, \cdot)$ is measurable with respect to the σ-algebra $\mathscr{F}_{\mathbf{s}_{k-1}, \ldots, \mathbf{s}_t, \tilde{\mathbf{y}}_{k-1}} \times \mathscr{B}$ and $\mathbf{Y}_t(\tilde{\mathbf{u}}_{k-1}) = \mathbf{y}_t^k$ a.s., $t = k, \ldots, N-1$.[2]

Define functions G^t by

$$G^t(\mathbf{s}_{k-1}, \mathbf{s}_k, \ldots, \mathbf{s}_t, \hat{\mathbf{y}}_{k-1}, u) := g^t(\mathbf{s}_t, \mathbf{Y}_t(u), v_t(\mathbf{s}_t, \mathbf{Y}_t(u))),$$
$$t = k-1, \ldots, N-1.$$

The functions G^t are measurable with respect to the same σ-algebras as the functions Y_t (as compositions of suitably measurable functions).

Consider the sets

$$\Gamma^{k-1} := \{(\omega, u) : G^{k-1}(s_{k-1}, \tilde{y}_{k-1}, u) \leqq 0\}$$

$$\Gamma^t := \{(\omega, u) : G^t(s_{k-1}, s_k, \ldots, s_t, \tilde{y}_{k-1}, u) \leqq 0 \text{ a.s.}$$
$$[\pi(s_{k-1}, ds_k, \ldots, ds_t)]\}, \qquad t = k, \ldots, N-1,$$

where $\pi(ds_k, \ldots, ds_t | s_{k-1})$ denotes the conditional distribution of the random parameters $\mathbf{s}_k, \ldots, \mathbf{s}_t$ for fixed s_{k-1};

$$\pi(ds_k, \ldots, ds_t | s_{k-1}) := P_{k-1}(s_{k-1}, ds_k \times \cdots \times P_{t-1}(ds_{t-1}, ds_t).$$

Obviously, $\Gamma^{k-1} \in \mathscr{F}_{\mathbf{s}_{k-1}, \tilde{\mathbf{y}}_{k-1}} \times \mathscr{B}$. That Γ^t belongs to this σ-algebra

[2] Throughout this book, we consider the *states* $\mathbf{s}_t$ of the stochastic process $\{\mathbf{s}_t\}$ as the *coordinate functions* $s_t := s_t(\omega)$ of the *elementary events* $\omega := (s_0, \ldots, s_N) \in \Omega := S^{N+1}$ of the *canonical representation* of the process. If $\xi(\omega)$ defines a function of an elementary event ω taking values in a measurable space—e.g., $\mathbb{R}^n$ equipped with the Borel σ-algebra (generated by open sets)—then we denote by $\mathscr{F}_\xi$ the σ-algebra of subsets of Ω generated by ξ through taking inverse images of Borel sets. We usually find it convenient to denote the values of an $\mathscr{F}_{\mathbf{s}^t}$-measurable function ξ by $\xi(s^t)$ rather than the more proper $\xi(\omega)$. Our practice may be justified as follows. Let η denote a function taking values $\eta(\omega)$ in some measurable space. Then we note that the function given by $\eta(\omega)$ is measurable with respect to $\mathscr{F}_\xi$ if and only if it can be represented in the form $\eta(\omega) = g(\xi(\omega))$, where $g(\cdot)$ is a measurable mapping. Throughout this chapter, $\mathscr{B}$ denotes the σ-algebra of Borel subsets of U.

follows from the representation of Γ^t as the inverse image of a Borel set in the form

$$\Gamma^t = \left\{(\omega, u): \int_{S^{t-k+1}} G^t_+(s_{k-1}, s_k, \ldots, s_t, \tilde{\mathbf{y}}_{k-1}, u)\pi(ds_k, \ldots, ds_t | s_{k-1}) = 0\right\},$$

where $G^t_+ := \max\{G^t, 0\}$ and the maximum is taken for each coordinate of the vector-valued function G^t (see Corollary III.1). Let us define

$$\Gamma := \bigcap_{t=k-1}^{N-1} \Gamma^t \cap \{(\omega, u): u \in U_{k-1}(s_{k-1})\} \quad (7)$$

$$F(\mathbf{s}_{k-1}, \ldots, \mathbf{s}_{N-1}, \tilde{\mathbf{y}}_{k-1}, u) := \phi^{k-1}(\mathbf{s}_{k-1}, \tilde{\mathbf{y}}_{k-1}, u) + \sum_{t=k}^{N-1} \phi^t(\mathbf{s}_t, \mathbf{Y}_t(u), v_t(\mathbf{s}_t, \mathbf{Y}_t(u))) \quad (8)$$

$$\Phi(\mathbf{s}_{k-1}, \tilde{\mathbf{y}}_{k-1}, u) := \int_{S^{N-k}} F(\mathbf{s}_{k-1}, s_k, \ldots, s_{N-1}, \tilde{\mathbf{y}}_{k-1}, u) \times \pi(ds_k, \ldots, ds_{N-1} | \mathbf{s}_{k-1}). \quad (9)$$

5. Application of the Basic Lemma

Apply Lemma 2 to the set $\Gamma(\omega) := \{u: (\omega, u) \in \Gamma\}$, where Γ is defined by (7) and the function Φ is defined by (9), putting $\mathscr{F}_0 := \mathscr{F}_{\mathbf{s}_{k-1}, \tilde{\mathbf{y}}_{k-1}}$. This yields the existence of an $\mathscr{F}_{\mathbf{s}_{k-1}, \tilde{\mathbf{y}}_{k-1}}$-measurable function given by $v(s, y)$ such that

$$E\Phi(\mathbf{s}_{k-1}, \tilde{\mathbf{y}}_{k-1}, v(\mathbf{s}_{k-1}, \tilde{\mathbf{y}}_{k-1})) \geqq E\Phi(\mathbf{s}_{k-1}, \tilde{\mathbf{y}}_{k-1}, \tilde{\mathbf{u}}_{k-1}), \quad (10)$$

and, with probability one,

$$v(\mathbf{s}_{k-1}, \tilde{\mathbf{y}}_{k-1}) \in U_{k-1}(\mathbf{s}_{k-1}), \quad (11)$$

$$G^{k-1}(\mathbf{s}_{k-1}, \tilde{\mathbf{y}}_{k-1}, v(\mathbf{s}_{k-1}, \tilde{\mathbf{y}}_{k-1})) \leqq 0, \quad (12)$$

$$G^t(\mathbf{s}_{k-1}, \mathbf{s}_k, \ldots, \mathbf{s}_t, \tilde{\mathbf{y}}_{k-1}, v(\mathbf{s}_{k-1}, \tilde{\mathbf{y}}_{k-1})) \leqq 0 \quad \text{a.s. } [\pi(ds_k, \ldots, ds_t | \mathbf{s}_{k-1})], \qquad t = k, \ldots, N-1.$$

The latter relations are equivalent to

$$G^t(\mathbf{s}_{k-1}, \ldots, \mathbf{s}_t, \tilde{\mathbf{y}}_{k-1}, v(\mathbf{s}_{k-1}, \tilde{\mathbf{y}}_{k-1})) \leqq 0 \quad \text{a.s.}, \quad t = k, \ldots, N-1. \quad (13)$$

6. Completion of the Proof of Theorem 1

By Lemma 1 there exists a jointly measurable function given by $v_{k-1}(s, y)$ such that $v(\mathbf{s}_{k-1}, \tilde{\mathbf{y}}_{k-1}) = v_{k-1}(\mathbf{s}_{k-1}, \mathbf{y}_{k-1})$ a.s. and $P\{\forall y \in \mathbb{R}^n, v_{k-1}(\mathbf{s}_{k-1}, y) \in U_{k-1}(\mathbf{s}_{k-1})\} = 1$. Clearly, the relations (10)–(13) hold with v replaced by v_{k-1}. Define

$$\mathbf{y}_{k-1}^{k-1} = \tilde{\mathbf{y}}_{k-1},$$

$$\mathbf{y}_t^{k-1} = f^t(\mathbf{s}_{t-1}, \mathbf{s}_t, \mathbf{y}_{t-1}^{k-1}, v_{t-1}(\mathbf{s}_{t-1}, \mathbf{y}_{t-1}^{k-1})), \qquad t = k, \ldots, N-1,$$

and note that $\mathbf{Y}_t(v_{k-1}(\mathbf{s}_{k-1}, \tilde{\mathbf{y}}_{k-1})) = \mathbf{y}_t^{k-1}$ a.s., $t = k, \ldots, N-1$. It follows, using the definition of G^t, (12) and (13), that

$$g^t(\mathbf{s}_t, \mathbf{y}_t^{k-1}, v_t(\mathbf{s}_t, \mathbf{y}_t^{k-1})) = G^t(\mathbf{s}_{k-1}, \ldots, \mathbf{s}_t, \tilde{\mathbf{y}}_{k-1}, v_{k-1}(\mathbf{s}_{k-1}, \tilde{\mathbf{y}}_{k-1}))$$
$$\leqq 0 \qquad \text{a.s.,} \quad t = k-1, \ldots, N-1,$$

and, by virtue of (8),

$$E \sum_{t=k-1}^{N-1} \phi^t(\mathbf{s}_t, \mathbf{y}_t^{k-1}, v_t(\mathbf{s}_t, \mathbf{y}_t^{k-1}))$$
$$= EF(\mathbf{s}_{k-1}, \ldots, \mathbf{s}_{N-1}, \tilde{\mathbf{y}}_{k-1}, v_{k-1}(\mathbf{s}_{k-1}, \tilde{\mathbf{y}}_{k-1}))$$
$$= E\Phi(\mathbf{s}_{k-1}, \tilde{\mathbf{y}}_{k-1}, v_{k-1}(\mathbf{s}_{k-1}, \tilde{\mathbf{y}}_{k-1})) \geqq E\Phi(\mathbf{s}_{k-1}, \tilde{\mathbf{y}}_{k-1}, \tilde{\mathbf{u}}_{k-1})$$
$$= E\phi^{k-1}(\mathbf{s}_{k-1}, \tilde{\mathbf{y}}_{k-1}, \tilde{\mathbf{u}}_{k-1}) + E \sum_{t=k}^{N-1} \phi^t(\mathbf{s}_t, \mathbf{y}_t^k, v_t(\mathbf{s}_t, \mathbf{y}_t^k))$$
$$\geqq E \sum_{t=k-1}^{N-1} \phi^t(\mathbf{s}_t, \tilde{\mathbf{y}}_t, \tilde{\mathbf{u}}_t)$$

by the induction hypothesis. □

7. The Case of a Process of Independent Random Variables

Suppose that the random variables $\mathbf{s}_t, t = 0, \ldots, N-1$, are independent and the maps $\phi^t, f^{t+1}, U_t, g^t$ in expressions (1)–(4) do not depend on $\mathbf{s}_t$. In this situation we may choose for each nonanticipative control a not worse Markov control of special type which depends *only* on the value of the controlled process $\{\mathbf{y}_t\}$.

This gives the following result, whose proof we leave to the reader:

Theorem 1′. *Under the conditions of Theorem 1, and if, further,* $\{\mathbf{s}_t\}$ *is a process of independent random variables and* ϕ^t, f^{t+1}, U_t *and* g^t *are functionally independent of* $\mathbf{s}_t$, *then there exists a Markov control* $\{\mathbf{u}_t\}_{t=0}^{N-1}$, *generated by a sequence of measurable functions* $\{v_t(\cdot)\}_{t=0}^{N-1}$ *and a trajectory* $\{\mathbf{y}_t\}_{t=0}^{N}$ *such that* $\mathbf{u}_t = v_t(\mathbf{y}_t)$, *satisfying the constraints* (2)–(4) *and for which the inequality* (6) *holds.* □

2. THE MAXIMUM PRINCIPLE FOR MARKOV CONTROLS

1. Statement of the Maximum Principle

In this section a stochastic maximum principle satisfied by optimal Markov controls will be obtained for the problem (1)–(5). The main idea in the derivation of this maximum principle consists in the extension of the admissible control class so as to use the results of Chapter 2. Instead of Markov controls we therefore consider arbitrary nonanticipative controls. By the sufficiency theorem of §1, the optimal Markov control is also optimal for the class of all nonanticipative controls.

Consider the *Hamiltonian* function corresponding to problem (1)–(5). It is given by

$$H^{t+1}(s_t, s_{t+1}, \psi, \lambda, y, u) := \phi^t(s_t, y, u) + \psi f^{t+1}(s_t, s_{t+1}, y, u) - \lambda g^t(s_t, y, u), \qquad t = 0, \ldots, N-1, \quad (14)$$

where $\psi \in \mathbb{R}^n$, $\lambda \in \mathbb{R}^k$. If in the problem (1)–(5) all hypotheses of Theorem 2.1 hold, then a solution of this problem $\{(\mathbf{y}_t^0, \mathbf{u}_t^0)\}$ satisfies the maximum principle in the class of all nonanticipative controls. In the sequel we shall assume the existence of multipliers $\{\psi_t^0\}$, $\{\lambda_t^0\}$ with the properties encountered in Theorem 2.1 for the Hamiltonian in the form (14).

We fix a sequence of σ-algebras $\mathscr{G}^t$, $t = 1, 2, \ldots, N-1$, satisfying[3]

$$\mathscr{F}_{\mathbf{s}_t, \mathbf{y}_t^0} \subseteq \mathscr{G}^t \subseteq \mathscr{G}^{t-1} \vee \mathscr{F}_t. \quad (15)$$

Here $\mathscr{F}_t := \mathscr{F}_{\mathbf{s}_t}$, $\mathscr{G}^0 := \mathscr{F}_0$, and $\mathscr{G}^{t-1} \vee \mathscr{F}_t$ denotes the minimal σ-algebra which contains $\mathscr{G}^{t-1}$ and $\mathscr{F}_t$.

[3] For example $\mathscr{G}^t$ may be the σ-algebra

$$\mathscr{G}^t := \begin{cases} \mathscr{F}^t := \mathscr{F}_{\mathbf{s}^t} & \text{for } t = 1, \ldots, k, \\ \mathscr{F}_{\mathbf{s}_{t-k}, \ldots, \mathbf{s}_t, \mathbf{y}_t^0} & \text{for } t = k+1, \ldots, N-1, \end{cases}$$

Theorem 2. (The Markov form of the maximum principle.) *Let* $\{(\mathbf{y}_t^0, \mathbf{u}_t^0)\}_{t=0}^{N-1}$ *be a solution of problem* (1)–(5) *with associated multipliers* $\{\psi_t^0\}$ and $\{\lambda_t^0\}$. *Then for each sequence of σ-algebras* $\mathscr{G}^t$ *satisfying condition* (15) *there exist* $\mathbb{R}^n$*-valued* $\mathscr{G}^{t-1} \times \mathscr{S}$*-measurable functions given by* $\Psi_t^0(\omega, s_t)$ *and* $\mathbb{R}^k$*-valued* $\mathscr{G}^t$*-measurable functions given by* $\Lambda_t^0(\omega)$ *such that* $E|\Psi_t^0(\boldsymbol{\omega}, \mathbf{s}_t)| < \infty, t = 1, \ldots, N$, $E|\Lambda_t^0(\boldsymbol{\omega})| < \infty, t = 0, \ldots, N-1$, *and the conditional expected value of the Hamiltonian*

$$E[H^{t+1}(\mathbf{s}_t, \mathbf{s}_{t+1}, \Psi_{t+1}^0(\boldsymbol{\omega}, \mathbf{s}_{t+1}), \Lambda_t^0(\boldsymbol{\omega}), \mathbf{y}_t^0, u) | \mathscr{G}^t]$$
$$:= \int_S H^{t+1}(\mathbf{s}_t, \sigma, \Psi_{t+1}^0(\mathbf{s}^t, \sigma), \Lambda_t^0(\mathbf{s}^t), \mathbf{y}_t^0, u) P_t(s_t, d\sigma),$$

considered as a function of the variable u, achieves a maximum a.s. over $U_t(\mathbf{s}_t)$ *at* $\mathbf{u}_t^0$; i.e.,

$$\max_{u \in U_t(\mathbf{s}_t)} E[H^{t+1}(\mathbf{s}_t, \mathbf{s}_{t+1}, \Psi_{t+1}^0(\boldsymbol{\omega}, \mathbf{s}_{t+1}), \Lambda_t^0(\boldsymbol{\omega}), \mathbf{y}_t^0, u) | \mathscr{G}^t]$$
$$= E[H^{t+1}(\mathbf{s}_t, \mathbf{s}_{t+1}, \Psi_{t+1}^0(\boldsymbol{\omega}, \mathbf{s}_{t+1}), \Lambda_t(\boldsymbol{\omega}), \mathbf{y}_t^0, \mathbf{u}_t^0) | \mathscr{G}^t] \qquad a.s., \quad (16)$$

for $t = 0, \ldots, N-1$. *Moreover, the multiplier processes* $\{\Psi_t^0(\boldsymbol{\omega}, \mathbf{s}_{t+1})\}$ *and* $\{\Lambda_t^0(\boldsymbol{\omega})\}$ *satisfy the conjugate system*

$$E[\Psi_t^0(\boldsymbol{\omega}, \mathbf{s}_t) | \mathscr{G}^t]$$
$$= E[H^{t+1}(\mathbf{s}_t, \mathbf{s}_{t+1}, \qquad (\boldsymbol{\omega}, \mathbf{s}_{t+1}), \Lambda_t(\boldsymbol{\omega}), \mathbf{y}_t^0, \mathbf{u}_t^0 | \mathscr{G}^t] \qquad a.s.,$$
$$E[\Psi_N^0(\boldsymbol{\omega}, \mathbf{s}_t) | \mathscr{G}^t] \qquad (17)$$
$$= 0 \qquad a.s.$$

and the complementary slackness condition

$$\Lambda_t^0(\boldsymbol{\omega}) g^t(\mathbf{s}_t, \mathbf{y}_t^0, \mathbf{u}_t^0) = 0 \qquad a.s.$$

for $t = 1, \ldots, N-1$. □

The idea of this theorem is that in the Markov case the multiplier processes $\{\psi_t^0\}$ and $\{\lambda_t^0\}$ may be shown to depend on the past in a particular way. For example, if $\mathscr{G}^t$ is taken to be the σ-algebra $\mathscr{F}_{\mathbf{s}_t, \mathbf{y}_t^0}$

---

where k $(1 \leq k \leq N-1)$ is a fixed integer. It is easy to show recursively that $\mathscr{G}^t \subseteq \mathscr{F}^{t-1} \vee \mathscr{F}_t = \mathscr{F}^t$, $t = 1, \ldots, N-1$. Since by the structure of the problem $\mathscr{F}_{\mathbf{y}_{t+1}^0} \subseteq \mathscr{F}_{\mathbf{s}_t, \mathbf{s}_{t+1}, \mathbf{y}_t^0}$, it follows similarly that $\mathscr{F}_{\mathbf{y}_t^0} \subseteq \mathscr{F}^t$, and hence $\mathscr{F}_t \subseteq \mathscr{F}_{\mathbf{s}_t, \mathbf{y}_t^0} \subseteq \mathscr{G}^t \subseteq \mathscr{G}^{t-1} \vee \mathscr{F}_t \subseteq \mathscr{F}^t \subseteq \mathscr{F}$, $t = 0, \ldots, N-1$.

[which obviously satisfies Condition (15)], then the random vectors $\Psi_t^0(\mathbf{s}_{t-1}, \mathbf{y}_{t-1}^0, \mathbf{s}_t)$ and $\Lambda_t^0(\mathbf{s}_t, \mathbf{y}_t^0)$ play the rôle of multipliers.

2. Auxiliary Results

Before proving Theorem 2, we establish two results which will be useful in the remainder of this chapter.

Proposition 1. *Let $(\Omega, \mathscr{F}, P)$ be a probability space and ξ_1, ξ_2, ξ_3 random variables with values in the measurable spaces A_1, A_2, A_3, respectively. Suppose further that*

1. *the σ-algebras $\mathscr{F}_{\xi_1}$ and $\mathscr{F}_{\xi_3}$ are conditionally independent with respect to $\mathscr{F}_{\xi_2}$;*
2. $\mathscr{F}_{\xi_1} \subseteqq \mathscr{F}_{\xi_2}$;
3. *there exists a conditional distribution given by $\pi(da_3|a_2)$ for the random variable ξ_3, given ξ_2.*

Then for any measurable scalar function given by $\phi(a_1, a_3)$ such that $\phi(\xi_1, \xi_3)$ is in $L_1(\Omega)$,

$$E[\phi(\xi_1, \xi_3)|\xi_1] = \int_{A_3} \phi(\xi_1, a_3)\pi(da_3|\xi_2) \qquad \text{a.s.} \tag{18}$$

□ Suppose that $\phi(a_1, a_3)$ is bounded. We first show that (18) holds for a function ϕ given by

$$\phi(a_1, a_3) = \phi_1(a_1)\phi_3(a_3),$$

where ϕ_1 and ϕ_3 are bounded measurable functions. We have

$$\begin{aligned} E[\phi_1(\xi_1)\phi_3(\xi_3)|\xi_1] &= \phi_1(\xi_1)E[\phi_3(\xi_3)|\xi_1] \\ &= \phi_1(\xi_1)E[\phi_3(\xi_3)|\xi_1, \xi_2] \\ &= \phi_1(\xi_1)E[\phi_3(\xi_3)|\xi_2] \\ &= \phi_1(\xi_1)\int_{A_3} \phi_3(a_3)\pi(da_3|\xi_2) \\ &= \int_{A_3} \phi(\xi_1)\phi_3(a_3)\pi(da_3|\xi_2) \qquad \text{a.s.} \end{aligned}$$

Here $E[\cdot|\xi_1, \xi_2] := E[\cdot|\mathscr{F}_{\xi_1} \vee \mathscr{F}_{\xi_2}]$, so the second equality holds by Condition 2. The third equality holds, since for all $E \in \mathscr{F}_{\xi_1}$

$$\int_E \phi_3(\xi_3(\omega))P(d\omega) = \int_E E[\phi_3(\xi_3)|\xi_1](\omega)P(d\omega)$$
$$= \int_E E[\phi_3(\xi_3)|\xi_1, \xi_2](\omega)P(d\omega)$$
$$= \int_E E[\phi_3(\xi_3)|\xi_2](\omega)P(d\omega),$$

where the last equation is a consequence of Condition 1 and the fact that conditional expectation with respect to an independent random variable is ordinary expectation.

Next, taking ϕ to be an arbitrary bounded function, we can approximate it as the limit of a monotone increasing sequence of simple functions each of whose terms have the form of the previous case and satisfy (18). It is easy to check that such a sequence satisfies (18) and all conditions of the monotone class theorem (Theorem III.8). By virtue of that theorem, (18) is true for any bounded measurable function.

The general case of $\phi(\xi_1, \xi_3)$ in $L_1(\Omega)$ follows from Lebesque's monotone convergence theorem, with use of a monotone increasing sequence of bounded functions satisfying (18). □

Proposition 2. *Let $(\Omega, \mathscr{F}, P)$ be a probability space, and let $(X, \mathscr{B}(X))$ and $(Z, \mathscr{B}(Z))$ be Polish spaces equipped with their Borel σ-algebras. Suppose also that a measurable mapping*

$$\gamma := (\Omega \times X, \mathscr{F} \times \mathscr{B}(X)) \to (Z, \mathscr{B}(Z)),$$

is given, as well as a multifunction $\omega \mapsto G(\omega) \neq \varnothing \subseteq X$ with graph $G \in \mathscr{F} \times \mathscr{B}(X)$ and a multifunction $\omega \mapsto \Gamma(\omega) \neq \varnothing \subseteq Z$ with graph $\Gamma \in \mathscr{F} \times \mathscr{B}(Z)$. Suppose further that, for any $\mathscr{F}$-measurable function such that $x(\boldsymbol{\omega}) \in G(\boldsymbol{\omega})$ a.s., $\gamma(\boldsymbol{\omega}, x(\boldsymbol{\omega})) \in \Gamma(\boldsymbol{\omega})$ a.s. Then

$$P\{\forall x \in G(\boldsymbol{\omega}), \gamma(\boldsymbol{\omega}, x) \in \Gamma(\boldsymbol{\omega})\} = 1. \tag{19}$$

□ Consider the mapping $\alpha: (\Omega \times X, \mathscr{F} \times \mathscr{B}(X)) \to (\Omega \times Z \times X, \mathscr{F} \times \mathscr{B}(Z) \times \mathscr{B}(X))$ defined by $\alpha(\omega, x) := (\omega, \gamma(\omega, x), x)$. Obviously, α is measurable. Let Γ^c denote the complement of the set Γ. The set $A := \{(\omega, x): \alpha(\omega, x) \in \Gamma^c \times X\} \cap G$ belongs to $\mathscr{F} \times \mathscr{B}(X)$, and its projection $E := \mathrm{pr}_\Omega A$ is universally measurable (by Corollary I.1). It is not difficult to see that $E = \{\omega : \exists x \in G(\omega), \gamma(\omega, x) \notin \Gamma(\omega)\}$. Since the conclusion of the proposition is equivalent to $P(E) = 0$, suppose the contrary; i.e., suppose that $P(E) > 0$.

Then there exists an $\mathscr{F}$-measurable set $E' \subseteqq E$ such that $P(E') = P(E)$. Let $\mathscr{F}'$ be the restriction of the σ-algebra $\mathscr{F}$ to E', and let P' be the restriction of the measure P to $\mathscr{F}'$. Denote by $A(\omega)$ the section of the set A at the point ω. Consider the measurable multifunction on $(E', \mathscr{F}', P')$ defined by $A'(\omega) := A(\omega)$, $\omega \in E'$. Its graph $A' \in \mathscr{F}' \times \mathscr{B}(X)$. By Aumann's theorem (Corollary I.3) there exists an $\mathscr{F}'$-measurable function x' such that $x'(\omega) \in A'(\omega)$ a.s. $[P']$. Let x be an arbitrary measurable function such that $\mathbf{x}(\omega) \in \mathbf{G}(\omega)$ a.s., and define

$$\hat{x}(\omega) = \begin{cases} x'(\omega), & \omega \in E', \\ x(\omega), & \omega \in \Omega \backslash E'. \end{cases}$$

The function $\hat{x}$ is $\mathscr{F}$-measurable, and $\hat{x}(\boldsymbol{\omega}) \in G(\boldsymbol{\omega})$ a.s. It follows that $\gamma(\omega, \hat{x})) \notin \Gamma(\omega)$ for all $\omega \in E'$, but, since $P(E') > 0$, this is a contradiction to the assumption of the proposition. Therefore, $P(E) = 0$, as required. □

Corollary 1. *Let a scalar measurable function be given by $\phi(\omega, x)$. Then if $\gamma(\boldsymbol{\omega}, x(\boldsymbol{\omega})) \geqq 0$ a.s. for any measurable function x such that $x(\boldsymbol{\omega}) \in G(\boldsymbol{\omega})$ a.s.,*

$$\inf_{x \in G(\boldsymbol{\omega})} \gamma(\boldsymbol{\omega}, x) \geqq 0 \qquad \text{a.s.} \quad \square$$

3. Proof of Theorem 2

□ Since by Theorem 1 we may take $\mathbf{u}_t^0$ to be a Markov control optimal in the class of all nonanticipative controls, then according to Theorem 2.1 there exist $\mathscr{F}^t$-measurable functions ψ_t^0, with range in $\mathbb{R}^n$, and $\lambda_t^0 \geqq 0$, with range in $\mathbb{R}^k$, such that $E|\boldsymbol{\lambda}_t^0| < \infty$, $t = 0, \ldots, N-1$, $E|\boldsymbol{\psi}_t^0| < \infty$, $t = 1, \ldots, N$, and

$$\begin{aligned} &E[H^{t+1}(\mathbf{s}_t, \mathbf{s}_{t+1}, \boldsymbol{\psi}_{t+1}^0, \boldsymbol{\lambda}_t^0, \mathbf{y}_t^0, \mathbf{u}_t) | \mathscr{F}^t] \\ &\quad \leqq E(H^{t+1}(\mathbf{s}_t, \mathbf{s}_{t+1}, \boldsymbol{\psi}_{t+1}^0, \boldsymbol{\lambda}_t^0, \mathbf{y}_t^0, \mathbf{u}_t^0) | \mathscr{F}^t] \qquad \text{a.s.} \end{aligned} \tag{20}$$

for any $\mathscr{F}^t$-measurable function u_t such that $\mathbf{u}_t \in U_t(\mathbf{s}_t)$ a.s. Putting an arbitrary $\mathscr{G}^t$-measurable function u_t such that $\mathbf{u}_t \in U_t(\mathbf{s}_t)$ a.s. ($\mathscr{G}^t \subseteqq \mathscr{F}^t$)

in the left-hand side of this inequality, taking the conditional expectation with respect to the σ-algebra $\mathscr{G}^t$ of both sides and using the linearity of the Hamiltonian H^{t+1} in λ [cf. (14)], we obtain

$$E[H^{t+1}(\mathbf{s}_t, \mathbf{s}_{t+1}, {}^{0}_{t+1}, {}^{0}_{t}, \mathbf{y}_t^0, \mathbf{u}_t) | \mathscr{G}^t]$$
$$\leqq E[H^{t+1}(\mathbf{s}_t, \mathbf{s}_{t+1}, {}^{0}_{t+1}, {}^{0}_{t}, \mathbf{y}_t^0, \mathbf{u}_t^0) | \mathscr{G}^t] \qquad \text{a.s.,} \qquad (21)$$

where ${}^{0}_{t} := E[\boldsymbol{\lambda}_t^0 | \mathscr{G}^t]$. Obviously $\boldsymbol{\Lambda}_t^0$ is $\mathscr{G}^t$-measurable, with range in $\mathbb{R}^k$, ${}_t \geqq 0$ and $E| \;\, {}_t| < \infty$, $t = 0, \dots, N-1$. Inequality (21) may be written

$$E[E[H^{t+1}(\mathbf{s}_t, \mathbf{s}_{t+1}, \boldsymbol{\psi}_{t+1}^0, \boldsymbol{\Lambda}_t^0, \mathbf{y}_t^0, \mathbf{u}_t) | \mathscr{G}^t \vee \mathscr{F}_{t+1}] | \mathscr{G}^t]$$
$$\leqq E[E[H^{t+1}(\mathbf{s}_t, \mathbf{s}_{t+1}, \boldsymbol{\psi}_{t+1}^0, \boldsymbol{\Lambda}_t^0, \mathbf{y}_t^0, \mathbf{u}_t^0) | \mathscr{G}^t \vee \mathscr{F}_{t+1}] | \mathscr{G}^t] \qquad \text{a.s.}$$

Now using the linearity of the Hamiltonian H^{t+1} in ψ, we have

$$E[H^{t+1}(\mathbf{s}_t, \mathbf{s}_{t+1}, \Psi_{t+1}^0(\boldsymbol{\omega}, \mathbf{s}_{t+1}), \Lambda_t^0(\boldsymbol{\omega}), \mathbf{y}_t^0, \mathbf{u}_t) | \mathscr{G}^t]$$
$$\leqq E[H^{t+1}(\mathbf{s}_t, \mathbf{s}_{t+1}, \Psi_{t+1}^0(\boldsymbol{\omega}, \mathbf{s}_{t+1}), \Lambda_t^0(\boldsymbol{\omega}), \mathbf{y}_t^0, \mathbf{u}_t^0) | \mathscr{G}^t] \qquad \text{a.s.,} \quad (22)$$

where $\Psi_{t+1}^0(\omega, s)$ denotes a $\mathscr{G}^t \times \mathscr{E}_{t+1}$-measurable function with range in $\mathbb{R}^n$ such that (see footnote 2)

$$\Psi_{t+1}^0(\omega, s_{t+1}) := E[\;{}^{0}_{t} | \mathscr{G}^t \vee \mathscr{F}_{t+1}](\omega). \qquad (23)$$

By Proposition 1 (with $\mathscr{F}_{\xi_1} := \mathscr{G}^t$, $\mathscr{F}_{\xi_2} := \mathscr{F}_t$, $\mathscr{F}_{\xi_3} := \mathscr{F}_{t+1}$ and use of the Markov property) the inequality (22) may be rewritten

$$\int_S H^{t+1}(\mathbf{s}_t, \sigma, \Psi_{t+1}^0(\boldsymbol{\omega}^t, \sigma), \boldsymbol{\Lambda}_t^0, \mathbf{y}_t^0, \mathbf{u}_t) P_t(\mathbf{s}_t, d\sigma)$$
$$\leqq \int_S H^{t+1}(\mathbf{s}_t, \sigma, \Psi_{t+1}^0(\boldsymbol{\omega}^t, \sigma), \boldsymbol{\Lambda}_t^0, \mathbf{y}_t^0, \mathbf{u}_t^0) P_t(\mathbf{s}_t, d\sigma) \qquad \text{a.s.,} \quad (24)$$

which is true for any $\mathscr{G}^t$-measurable function u_t such that $\mathbf{u}_t \in U_t(\mathbf{s}_t)$ a.s. Next define the real-valued function γ by the formula

$$\gamma(\omega, u) := \int_S H^{t+1}(s_t, \sigma, \Psi_{t+1}^0(s^t, \sigma), \Lambda_t^0, y_t^0, u) P_t(\mathbf{s}_t, d\sigma).$$

This function is $\mathscr{G}^t \times \mathscr{B}(U)$-measurable and, by virtue of (24), $\gamma(\boldsymbol{\omega}, \mathbf{u}_t) \leq \gamma(\boldsymbol{\omega}, \mathbf{u}_t^0)$ a.s. for any $\mathscr{G}^t$-measurable function u_t such that $\mathbf{u}_t \in U_t(\mathbf{s}_t)$ a.s. From this we obtain, using Proposition 2,

$$P\{\forall u \in U_t(\mathbf{s}_t), \gamma(\boldsymbol{\omega}, u) \leq \gamma(\boldsymbol{\omega}, \mathbf{u}_t^0)\} = 1.$$

Therefore

$$\max_{u \in U_t(\mathbf{s}_t)} \gamma(\boldsymbol{\omega}, u) = \gamma(\boldsymbol{\omega}, \mathbf{u}_t^0) \qquad \text{a.s.,} \tag{25}$$

but by the definition of the function γ this is equivalent to the assertion (16), as required.

We turn next to the conjugate (backwards difference equation) system. By assumption

$$\boldsymbol{\psi}_t^0 = E[H_y^{t+1}(\mathbf{s}_t, \mathbf{s}_{t+1}, \boldsymbol{\psi}_{t+1}^0, \boldsymbol{\lambda}_t^0, \mathbf{y}_t^0, \mathbf{u}_t^0) | \mathscr{F}^t] \qquad \text{a.s.,} \quad t = 1, \ldots, N-1. \tag{26}$$

For each $t = 1, \ldots, N-1$ we take the conditional expectation with respect to $\mathscr{G}^t$ on both sides of this equation. Further, using the obvious relation $\mathscr{G}^t \subseteqq \mathscr{G}^t \vee \mathscr{F}_{t+1}$, the condition $\mathscr{G}^t \subseteqq \mathscr{G}^{t-1} \vee \mathscr{F}_t$ and the linearity of the Hamiltonian H^{t+1} with respect to ψ^0 and λ^0, we rewrite the resulting expression

$$E[E[\boldsymbol{\psi}_t^0 | \mathscr{G}^{t-1} \vee \mathscr{F}_t] | \mathscr{G}^t]$$
$$= E[H_y^{t+1}(\mathbf{s}_t, \mathbf{s}_{t+1}, E[\boldsymbol{\psi}_{t+1}^0 | \mathscr{G}^t \vee \mathscr{F}_{t+1}], E[\boldsymbol{\lambda}_t^0 | \mathscr{G}^t], \mathbf{y}_t^0, \mathbf{u}_t^0) | \mathscr{G}^t].$$

Since $E[\boldsymbol{\psi}_N^0 | \mathscr{G}^{N-1} \vee \mathscr{F}_N] = 0$, we obtain the conjugate system (17).

The complementary slackness conditions are obtained directly from the relations $\boldsymbol{\lambda}_t g^t(\mathbf{s}_t, \mathbf{y}_t^0, \mathbf{u}_t^0) = 0$ a.s. by taking the conditional expectation with respect to the σ-algebra $\mathscr{G}^t$ on both sides of the equations. □

4. A Simple Problem of Optimal Control

Consider the problem defined by (1)–(3) and (5) [i.e., *without* the *mixed constraints* $g^t(\mathbf{s}_t, \mathbf{y}_t, \mathbf{u}_t) \leqq 0$ a.s.]. In this case, the conclusions of Theorem 2 may be strengthened.

Define the Hamiltonian function for the problem (1)–(3), (5) as

$$H^{t+1}(s_t, s_{t+1}, \psi, y, u) := \phi^t(s_t, y, u) + \psi f^{t+1}(s_t, s_{t+1}, y, u). \tag{27}$$

Theorem 3. *Let* $\{(\mathbf{y}_t^0, \mathbf{u}_t^0)\}_{t=0}^{N-1}$ *be a solution of the problem* (1)–(3), (5) *satisfying conditions* (A) *and* (B) *of* §2.1.2. *Then there exists an* $\mathbb{R}^n$-*valued* $\mathscr{E} \times \mathscr{B}(\mathbb{R}^n)$-*measurable function* ψ_t^0 *such that* $E|\psi_t(\mathbf{s}_t, \mathbf{y}_t^0)| < \infty$,

$t = 1, 2, \ldots, N$, and the conditional expected value of the Hamiltonian

$$E[H^{t+1}(\mathbf{s}_t, \mathbf{s}_{t+1}, \psi^0_{t+1}(\mathbf{s}_{t+1}, \mathbf{y}^0_{t+1}), \mathbf{y}^0_t) | s_t, y^0_t, u] = \int_S H^{t+1} P_t(\mathbf{s}_t, ds_{t+1}),$$

considered as a function of the variable u, achieves a maximum a.s. over $U_t(\mathbf{s}_t)$ at $\mathbf{u}^0_t$; i.e.,

$$\max_{u \in U_t(\mathbf{s}_t)} E[H^{t+1}(\mathbf{s}_t, \mathbf{s}_{t+1}, \psi^0_{t+1}(\mathbf{s}_{t+1}, \mathbf{y}^0_{t+1}), \mathbf{y}^0_t, u) | \mathbf{s}_t, \mathbf{y}^0_t]$$

$$= E[H^{t+1}(\mathbf{s}_t, \mathbf{s}_{t+1}, \psi^0_{t+1}(\mathbf{s}_{t+1}, \mathbf{y}^0_{t+1}), \mathbf{y}^0_t, \mathbf{u}^0_t) | \mathbf{s}_t, \mathbf{y}^0_t] \quad \text{a.s.} \quad (28)$$

for $t = 0, \ldots, N-1$. Moreover, the multiplier process $\{\psi^0_t(\mathbf{s}_t, \mathbf{y}^0_t)\}$ satisfies the conjugate system (for $t = 1, \ldots, N-1$)

$$\psi^0_t(\mathbf{s}_t, \mathbf{y}^0_t)$$

$$= E[H^{t+1}_y(\mathbf{s}_t, \mathbf{s}_{t+1}, \psi^0_{t+1}(\mathbf{s}_{t+1}, \mathbf{y}^0_{t+1}), \mathbf{y}^0_t, \mathbf{u}^0_t) | \mathbf{s}_t, \mathbf{y}^0_t] \quad \text{a.s.} \quad (29)$$

$$\psi^0_N(\mathbf{s}_N, \mathbf{y}^0_N) = 0 \qquad \text{a.s.}$$

Theorem 3 strengthens Theorem 2 for the problem (1)–(3), (5) in that the multipliers ψ^0_t depend not on the "past" but only on the "present."

□ By virtue of Theorem 1 the Markov pair $\{(\mathbf{y}^0_t, \mathbf{u}^0_t)\}$ satisfies the maximum principle of Theorem 2.1 with Hamiltonian (27) relative to the class of controls depending on all the past. The corresponding conjugate system is therefore

$$\begin{aligned} \boldsymbol{\psi}^0_t &= E[H^{t+1}_y(\mathbf{s}_t, \mathbf{s}_{t+1}, \boldsymbol{\psi}^0_{t+1}, \mathbf{y}^0_t, \mathbf{u}^0_t) | \mathscr{F}^t] \quad \text{a.s.,} \quad t = 0, \ldots, N-1, \\ \boldsymbol{\psi}^0_N &= 0 \qquad \text{a.s.} \end{aligned} \quad (30)$$

By induction, the random vectors $\boldsymbol{\psi}^0_t$ are $\mathscr{F}_{\mathbf{s}_t, \mathbf{y}^0_t}$-measurable. Indeed, for $\boldsymbol{\psi}^0_N$ this statement is true. Suppose it is also true for $\boldsymbol{\psi}^0_{t+1}, \boldsymbol{\psi}^0_{t+2}, \ldots$. Then the function given by $H^{t+1}_y(s_t, s_{t+1}, \psi^0_{t+1}, y^0_t, u^0_t)$ is measurable with respect to the σ-algebra $\mathscr{F}_{\mathbf{s}_t, \mathbf{s}_{t+1}, \mathbf{y}^0_t}$ since ψ^0_{t+1} is $\mathscr{F}_{\mathbf{s}_{t+1}, \mathbf{y}^0_{t+1}}$-measurable by assumption and $\mathscr{F}_{\mathbf{y}^0_{t+1}} \subseteq \mathscr{F}_{\mathbf{s}_t, \mathbf{s}_{t+1}, \mathbf{y}^0_t}$. By the Markov nature of the process $\{\mathbf{s}_t\}$, the σ-algebras $\mathscr{F}^t$ and $\mathscr{F}_{t+1}$ are conditionally independent with respect to the σ-algebra $\mathscr{F}_{\mathbf{s}_t, \mathbf{y}^0_t} \subseteq \mathscr{F}^t$. Therefore

$$\begin{aligned} \boldsymbol{\psi}^0_t &= E[H^{t+1}_y(\mathbf{s}_t, \mathbf{s}_{t+1}, \boldsymbol{\psi}^0_{t+1}, \mathbf{y}^0_t, \mathbf{u}^0_t) | \mathbf{s}^t] \\ &= E[H^{t+1}_y(\mathbf{s}_t, \mathbf{s}_{t+1}, \boldsymbol{\psi}^0_{t+1}, \mathbf{y}^0_t, \mathbf{u}^0_t) | \mathbf{s}_t, \mathbf{y}^0_t, \mathbf{s}^t] \\ &= E[H^{t+1}_y(\mathbf{s}_t, \mathbf{s}_{t+1}, \boldsymbol{\psi}^0_{t+1}, \mathbf{y}^0_t, \mathbf{u}^0_t) | \mathbf{s}_t, \mathbf{y}^0_t] \qquad \text{a.s.} \end{aligned}$$

From this the $\mathscr{F}_{\mathbf{s}_t, \mathbf{y}_t^0}$-measurability of the function ψ_t^0 follows immediately, and therefore relation (29) is proven.

We now prove (28). Define

$$\gamma(\omega, u) := H^{t+1}(s_t, s_{t+1}, \psi_{t+1}^0(s_{t+1}, y_{t+1}^0), y_t^0, u).$$

The corresponding real-valued function γ is measurable with respect to the σ-algebra $\mathscr{F}_{\mathbf{s}_t, \mathbf{s}_{t+1}, \mathbf{y}_t^0} \times \mathscr{B}(U)$. From the maximum principle (2.5) we have that

$$E[\gamma(\boldsymbol{\omega}, \mathbf{u}_t) | \mathscr{F}^t] \leqq E[\gamma(\boldsymbol{\omega}, \mathbf{u}_t^0) | \mathscr{F}^t] \qquad \text{a.s.}$$

for all $\mathscr{F}_{\mathbf{s}_t, \mathbf{y}_t^0}$-measurable functions u_t such that $\mathbf{u}_t \in U_t(\mathbf{s}_t)$ a.s. Since $\{\mathbf{s}_t\}$ is a Markov process, it follows that

$$E[\gamma(\boldsymbol{\omega}, \mathbf{u}_t) | \mathscr{F}_{\mathbf{s}_t, \mathbf{y}_t^0}] \leqq E[\gamma(\boldsymbol{\omega}, \mathbf{u}_t^0) | \mathscr{F}_{\mathbf{s}_t, \mathbf{y}_t^0}] \qquad \text{a.s.} \tag{31}$$

Using Proposition 1, (31) may be rewritten (redefining γ to involve the relevant truncation of ω) as the inequality

$$\int_S \gamma(\mathbf{s}^{t+1}, \mathbf{u}_t) P_t(\mathbf{s}_t, ds_{t+1}) \leqq \int_S \gamma(\mathbf{s}^{t+1}, \mathbf{u}_t^0) P_t(\mathbf{s}_t, ds_{t+1}) \qquad \text{a.s.,}$$

which holds for any $\mathscr{F}_{\mathbf{s}_t, \mathbf{y}_t^0}$-measurable function u_t such that $\mathbf{u}_t \in U_t(\mathbf{s}_t)$ a.s. From Proposition 2 it follows that

$$\max_{u \in U_t(\mathbf{s}_t)} \int_S \gamma(\mathbf{s}^{t+1}, u) P_t(\mathbf{s}_t, ds_{t+1}) = \int_S \gamma(\mathbf{s}^{t+1}, \mathbf{u}_t^0) P_t(\mathbf{s}_t, ds_{t+1}) \qquad \text{a.s.}$$

By the definition of the function γ this is equivalent to (28). □

Next we state the Markov analogue of Theorem 2.2.

Theorem 3′. (The differential form of the maximum principle.) *Let* $\{(\mathbf{y}_t^0, \mathbf{u}_t^0)\}_{t=0}^{N-1}$ *be a solution of the problem* (1)–(3), (5) *satisfying the conditions of Theorem* 2. *Then there exists a multiplier process* $\{\psi_t^0(\mathbf{s}_t, \mathbf{y}_t^0)\}$ *with the properties listed in Theorem* 3 *and such that*

$$\max_{u \in U_t(\mathbf{s}_t)} (E[H_u^{t+1}(\mathbf{s}_t, \mathbf{s}_{t+1}, \psi_{t+1}^0(\mathbf{s}_{t+1}, \mathbf{y}_{t+1}^0), \mathbf{y}_t^0, u_t^0) | \mathbf{s}_t, \mathbf{y}_t^0])u$$

$$= (E[H_u^{t+1}(\mathbf{s}_t, \mathbf{s}_{t+1}, \psi_{t+1}^0(\mathbf{s}_{t+1}, \mathbf{y}_{t+1}^0), \mathbf{y}_t^0, \mathbf{u}_t^0) | \mathbf{s}_t, \mathbf{y}_t^0])\mathbf{u}_t^0 \qquad \text{a.s.} \quad \square \tag{32}$$

The proof of this statement follows exactly the proof of Theorem 3 (except that Theorem 2.2 plays the rôle of Theorem 2.1). We remind the reader (cf. the note at the end of §2.1.4) that the differential form of the maximum principle (32) is weaker than the statement (28).

3. THE METHOD OF DYNAMIC PROGRAMMING AND ITS CONNECTION WITH THE MAXIMUM PRINCIPLE

1. The Basic Idea of Dynamic Programming

In this section the method of dynamic programming will be illustrated by means of the optimal control problem (1)–(3), (5). For this problem a version of the Bellman functional equation will be given, and from it we shall derive the maximum principle (in differential form).

In dynamic programming, an *initial value* problem of optimal control is embedded in a family of problems which depends parametrically on the initial state. Hence, corresponding to the problem (1)–(3), (5), we shall consider the following family of optimal control problems:

$$\text{Maximize} \quad \sum_{k=t}^{N-1} E\phi^k(\mathbf{s}_k, \mathbf{y}_k, \mathbf{u}_k) \tag{33}$$

$$\text{subject to} \quad \mathbf{y}_{k+1} = f^{k+1}(\mathbf{s}_k, \mathbf{s}_{k+1}, \mathbf{y}_k, \mathbf{u}_k) \quad \text{a.s.,} \tag{34}$$

$$\mathbf{y}_t = \tilde{\mathbf{y}}_t \quad \text{a.s.,}$$

$$\mathbf{u}_k \in U_k(\mathbf{s}_k) \quad \text{a.s.,} \quad k = t+1, \ldots, N-1. \tag{35}$$

Here $\tilde{\mathbf{y}}_t := \tilde{\mathbf{y}}_t(\mathbf{s}^t)$ is an *initial state*, $t = 1, \ldots, N-1$, and the family of problems is parametrized by $(\tilde{\mathbf{y}}_t, t)$. The solution of each problem (33)–(35) is to be considered with respect to the class of Markov controls. It is assumed that the functional (33) takes finite values for any admissible pairs $\{(\mathbf{y}_k, \mathbf{u}_k)\}$.

Let $\{(\mathbf{y}_t^0, \mathbf{u}_t^0)\}_{t=0}^{N-1}$ be a solution of the problem (1)–(3), (5). An additional requirement which we impose on the problem (33)–(35) is the following:

There exists a sequence of measurable feedback control functions given by $v^0 := \{v_0^0(s, y), v_1^0(s, y), \ldots, v_{N-1}^0(s, y)\}$, *generating the control* $\{\mathbf{u}_t^0\}$ *such that for any* t, $1 \leq t \leq N-1$, *and for each* $\mathscr{F}_{\mathbf{s}_t}$-*measurable initial state* $\tilde{y}(\mathbf{s}_t)$, *the sequence* $v^{0t} := \{v_t^0(s, y), v_{t+1}^0(s, y),$

$\ldots, v^0_{N-1}(s, y)\}$ *generates the optimal Markov control for the problem* (33)–(35).

From Proposition 2 it follows that $P\{\forall y \in \mathbb{R}^n, v_t^0(\mathbf{s}_t, y) \in U_t(\mathbf{s}_t)\} = 1$, $t = 1, \ldots, N-1$, so the sequence of functions v^0 is a Markov strategy.

Let us agree to call the strategy v^0 satisfying the requirement of the previous paragraph *optimal in the wide sense.* If the strategy v^0 satisfies this requirement for all $\mathscr{F}_{\mathbf{s}^t}$-measurable initial states $\tilde{y}_t := \tilde{y}_t(\mathbf{s}^t)$, then it is called *optimal in the strict sense.*

2. The Bellman Value Function

We associate with the sequences v^{0t}, $t = 0, 1, \ldots, N-1$ $(v^{00} := v^0)$, and a corresponding *fixed* sequence of initial values $\tilde{\mathbf{y}}_t := \tilde{y}_t(\mathbf{s}^t)$ $[\tilde{\mathbf{y}}_0 := \tilde{y}_0(\mathbf{s}_0)]$, a sequence of $\mathscr{E} \times \mathscr{B}(\mathbb{R}^n)$-measurable functions W^t such that

$$W^t(\mathbf{s}_t, \tilde{\mathbf{y}}_t) = E\left[\sum_{k=t}^{N-1} \phi^k(\mathbf{s}_k, \hat{\mathbf{y}}_k, v_k^0(\mathbf{s}_k, \hat{\mathbf{y}}_k)) \middle| \mathbf{s}_t, \tilde{\mathbf{y}}_t\right] \quad \text{a.s.,} \tag{36}$$

where $\hat{\mathbf{y}}_k$, $k = t+1, \ldots, N-1$, satisfies equation (34) with $\mathbf{u}_k := v_k^0(\mathbf{s}_k, \hat{\mathbf{y}}_k)$ and initial condition $\hat{\mathbf{y}}_t := \tilde{\mathbf{y}}_t$. The function W^t as defined may depend on $\tilde{\mathbf{y}}_t$. However, we have the following:

Lemma 3. *The function W^t for $t = 1, 2, \ldots, N-1$ can be chosen in such a way that equation* (36) *holds for any $\mathscr{F}_{\mathbf{s}^t}$-measurable function $\tilde{\mathbf{y}}_t$.*

□ Let the sequence of measurable functions given by $\tilde{y}_t(s^t)$, $t = 0, \ldots, N-1$, be arbitrary. We introduce a sequence of random vectors $\mathbf{Y}_k(y)$, $k = t+1, \ldots, N-1$, defined by means of the recurrence relation

$$\mathbf{Y}_{k+1}(y) := f^{k+1}(\mathbf{s}_k, \mathbf{s}_{k+1}, \mathbf{Y}_k(y), v_k^0(\mathbf{s}_k, \mathbf{Y}_k(y))), \qquad \mathbf{Y}_t(y) := y.$$

Obviously, $\mathbf{Y}_k(\tilde{\mathbf{y}}_t) = \hat{\mathbf{y}}_k$. Let us also define

$$\Phi^t(\mathbf{s}_t, \mathbf{s}_{t+1}, \ldots, \mathbf{s}_{N-1}, y) := \sum_{k=t}^{N-1} \phi(\mathbf{s}_k, \mathbf{Y}_k(y), v_k^0(\mathbf{s}_k, \mathbf{Y}_k(y))).$$

The functions given by $\Phi^t(s_t, s_{t+1}, \ldots, s_{N-1}, y)$ are measurable in all variables and

$$\Phi^t(\mathbf{s}_t, \mathbf{s}_{t+1}, \ldots, \mathbf{s}_{N-1}, \tilde{\mathbf{y}}_t) = \sum_{k=t}^{N-1} \phi^k(\mathbf{s}_k, \hat{\mathbf{y}}_k, v_k^0(\mathbf{s}_k, \hat{\mathbf{y}}_k)) \qquad \text{a.s.}$$

Define

$$W^t(s, y) := \int_{S^{N-1-t}} \Phi^t(s, s_{t+1}, \ldots, s_{N-1}, y)\pi(s, ds_{t+1}, \ldots, ds_{N-1}),$$

where π denotes the $(N - t - 1)$-step joint transition probability measure of the Markov process from the state $\mathbf{s}_t = s$. The function W^t is measurable in both variables, and it follows that

$$\begin{aligned} E\left[\sum_{k=t}^{N-1} \phi^k(\mathbf{s}_k, \hat{\mathbf{y}}_k, v_k^0(\mathbf{s}_k, \hat{\mathbf{y}}_k)) \middle| \mathbf{s}_t, \hat{\mathbf{y}}_t\right] &= E[\Phi^t(\mathbf{s}_t, \ldots, \mathbf{s}_{N-1}, \tilde{\mathbf{y}}_t) | \mathbf{s}_t, \tilde{\mathbf{y}}_t] \\ &= \int_{S^{N-1-t}} \Phi^t(\mathbf{s}_t, s_{t+1}, \ldots, s_{N-1}, \tilde{\mathbf{y}}_t) \\ &\quad \times \pi(\mathbf{s}_t, ds_{t+1}, \ldots, ds_{N-1}) \\ &= W^t(\mathbf{s}_t, \tilde{\mathbf{y}}_t). \end{aligned}$$

Since this construction is clearly independent of the chosen sequence of initial values, the result follows. □

The function W^t satisfying (36) is called the *(Bellman) value function*, and W^N is conveniently defined to be identically 0.

3. The Bellman Functional Equation

Define for $t = 0, 1, \ldots, N - 1$ the $\mathscr{E} \times \mathscr{B}(\mathbb{R}^n) \times \mathscr{B}(U)$-measurable function given by

$$\begin{aligned} R^t(s, y, u) := \phi^t(s, y, u) + \int_S W^{t+1}(s_{t+1}, f^{t+1}(s, s_{t+1}, y, u)) \\ \times P_t(s, ds_{t+1}) - W^t(s, y), \end{aligned} \qquad (37)$$

where $W^N(s, y) :\equiv 0$.

Theorem 4. (Necessity and sufficiency of the Bellman functional equation for optimality). 1°. *If v^0 is optimal in the wide sense, then*

$$\max_{u \in U_0(\mathbf{s}_0)} R^0(\mathbf{s}_0, \tilde{\mathbf{y}}_0, u) = R^0(\mathbf{s}_0, \tilde{\mathbf{y}}_0, v_0^0(\mathbf{s}_0, \mathbf{y}_0)) = 0 \qquad \text{a.s.} \qquad (38)$$

and for any $\mathscr{F}^t$-measurable $\mathbf{y}_t$

$$\max_{u \in U_t(\mathbf{s}_t)} R^t(\mathbf{s}_t, \mathbf{y}_t, u) = R^t(\mathbf{s}_t, \mathbf{y}_t, v_t^0(\mathbf{s}_t, \mathbf{y}_t)) = 0 \qquad \text{a.s.} \tag{39}$$

for $t = 1, \ldots, N - 1$.

2°. *If the relations* (38) *and* (39) *hold for some Markov strategy* v^0, *then* v^0 *is optimal in the strict sense.* □

Corollary 2. *If a Markov strategy is optimal in the wide sense, then it is also optimal in the strict sense (and thus the two definitions are equivalent).* □

Using the definition of the function given by $R^t(s, y, u)$ and the relations (38) and (39) we may conclude that

$$W^t(\mathbf{s}_t, \mathbf{y}_t) = \max_{u \in U_t(\mathbf{s}_t)} \Big[\phi^t(\mathbf{s}_t, \mathbf{y}_t, u) + \int_S W^{t+1}(s_{t+1}, f^{t+1}(\mathbf{s}_t, s_{t+1}, \mathbf{y}_t, u)) \times P_t(\mathbf{s}_t, ds_{t+1})) \Big] \qquad \text{a.s.,}$$

$$W^N(s, y) :\equiv 0,$$

for $t = 1, \ldots, N - 1$, and any $\mathscr{F}^t$-measurable random vectors $\mathbf{y}_t$ with $\mathbf{y}_0 := \tilde{\mathbf{y}}_0$.

This relation for the function $W^t(s, y)$ is a version of the *Bellman functional equation* for the family of problems (1)–(3), (5), and (33)–(35).

4. Proof of Theorem 4

□ 1°. Necessity.

□ We obtain first (39). Let the Markov strategy v^0 be optimal in the wide sense. For arbitrary t $(1 \leqq t \leqq N - 1)$, we take an arbitrary $\mathscr{F}_{\mathbf{s}_t}$-measurable function given by $\tilde{\mathbf{y}}(s_t)$. Let $\mathbf{u}_t \in U_t(\mathbf{s}_t)$ a.s., and let $\mathbf{u}_t$ be measurable with respect to the σ-algebra $\mathscr{F}_{\mathbf{s}_t, \mathbf{y}(\mathbf{s}_t)}$. Consider the Markov control for the problem (33)–(35) with initial state $\tilde{y}(\mathbf{s}_t)$ given by

$$\{\mathbf{u}_t, v_{t+1}^0(\mathbf{s}_{t+1}, \mathbf{y}_{t+1}), \ldots, v_{N-1}^0(\mathbf{s}_{N-1}, \mathbf{y}_{N-1})\},$$

where the $\mathbf{y}_k$ satisfy equation (34) with initial state $\tilde{y}(\mathbf{s}_t)$ and $\mathbf{u}_k := v_k^0(\mathbf{s}_k, \mathbf{y}_k)$ for $k = t + 1, \ldots, N - 1$.

We evaluate the objective functional (33) at this control as follows:

$$E\left[\phi^t(\mathbf{s}_t, \tilde{y}(\mathbf{s}_t), \mathbf{u}_t) + \sum_{k=t+1}^{N-1} \phi^k(\mathbf{s}_k, \mathbf{y}_k, v_k^0(\mathbf{s}_k, \mathbf{y}_k))\right]$$

$$= E\left[\phi^t(\mathbf{s}_t, \tilde{y}(\mathbf{s}_t), \mathbf{u}_t) + E\left[\sum_{k=t+1}^{N-1} \phi^k(\mathbf{s}_k, \mathbf{y}_k, v_k^0(\mathbf{s}_k, \mathbf{y}_k)) \middle| \mathbf{s}_{t+1}, \mathbf{y}_{t+1}\right]\right]$$

$$= E[\phi^t(\mathbf{s}_t, \tilde{y}(\mathbf{s}_t), \mathbf{u}_t) + W^{t+1}(\mathbf{s}_{t+1}, \mathbf{y}_{t+1})]$$

$$= E\,[\phi^t(\mathbf{s}_t, \tilde{y}(\mathbf{s}_t), \mathbf{u}_t) + E[W^{t+1}(\mathbf{s}_{t+1}, f^{t+1}(\mathbf{s}_t, \mathbf{s}_{t+1}, \tilde{y}(\mathbf{s}_t), \mathbf{u}_t) | \mathbf{s}_t, \tilde{y}_t(\mathbf{s}_t)]]$$

$$= E\left[\phi^t(\mathbf{s}_t, \tilde{y}(\mathbf{s}_t), \mathbf{u}_t) + \int_S W^{t+1}(s_{t+1}, f^{t+1}(\mathbf{s}_t, s_{t+1}, \tilde{y}(\mathbf{s}_t), \mathbf{u}_t)))P_t(\mathbf{s}_t, ds_{t+1})\right]$$

$$= E[R^t(\mathbf{s}_t, \tilde{y}(\mathbf{s}_t), \mathbf{u}_t) + W^t(\mathbf{s}_t, \tilde{y}_t(\mathbf{s}_t))].$$

Consequently, the value of the functional (33) at the Markov control $\{v_t^0(\mathbf{s}_t, \tilde{y}(\mathbf{s}_t)), v_{t+1}^0(\mathbf{s}_{t+1}, \hat{\mathbf{y}}_{t+1}), \ldots, v_{N-1}^0(\mathbf{s}_{N-1}, \hat{\mathbf{y}}_{N-1})\}$ with the same initial state $\tilde{y}(\mathbf{s}_t)$, where $\hat{\mathbf{y}}_k$ denotes the corresponding trajectory, may be written

$$E[R^t(\mathbf{s}_t, \tilde{y}(\mathbf{s}_t), v_t^0(\mathbf{s}_t, \tilde{y}(\mathbf{s}_t)) + W^t(\mathbf{s}_t, \tilde{y}(\mathbf{s}_t))].$$

From the optimality of the strategy v^0 in the wide sense, we have that

$$ER^t(\mathbf{s}_t, \tilde{y}(\mathbf{s}_t), v_t^0(\mathbf{s}_t, \tilde{y}(\mathbf{s}_t)) \geqq ER^t(\mathbf{s}_t, \tilde{y}(\mathbf{s}_t), \mathbf{u}_t), \tag{40}$$

which is true for any $\mathscr{F}_{\mathbf{s}_t, \tilde{y}(\mathbf{s}_t)}$-measurable u_t such that $\mathbf{u}_t \in U_t(\mathbf{s}_t)$ a.s.

We shall show now that from (40) it follows that

$$R^t(\mathbf{s}_t, \tilde{y}(\mathbf{s}_t), v_t^0(\mathbf{s}_t, \tilde{y}(\mathbf{s}_t))) \geqq R^t(\mathbf{s}_t, \tilde{y}(\mathbf{s}_t), \mathbf{u}_t) \quad \text{a.s.} \tag{41}$$

for any $\mathscr{F}_{\mathbf{s}_t, \tilde{y}(\mathbf{s}_t)}$-measurable u_t such that $\mathbf{u}_t \in U_t(\mathbf{s}_t)$ a.s.

□ Suppose the contrary, i.e., that there exists a set $E \in \mathscr{F}_{\mathbf{s}_t, \tilde{y}(\mathbf{s}_t)}$ such that $P(E) > 0$ and an $\mathscr{F}_{\mathbf{s}_t, \tilde{y}(\mathbf{s}_t)}$-measurable function u_t such that $\mathbf{u}_t \in U_t(\mathbf{s}_t)$ and

$$R^t(s_t, \tilde{y}(s_t), u_t(s_t)) > R^t(s_t, \tilde{y}(s_t), v_t^0(s_t, \tilde{y}(s_t)))$$

on E. Define

$$\tilde{u}_t(s_t) := \begin{cases} u_t(s_t) & \text{on } E, \\ v^0(s_t, \tilde{y}(s_t)) & \text{on } \Omega \backslash E. \end{cases}$$

Obviously, $\tilde{\mathbf{u}}_t$ is $\mathscr{F}_{\mathbf{s}_t, \tilde{y}(s_t)}$-measurable, $\tilde{\mathbf{u}}_t \in U_t(\mathbf{s}_t)$ a.s. and

$$ER^t(\mathbf{s}_t, \tilde{y}(\mathbf{s}_t), \tilde{\mathbf{u}}_t) > ER^t(\mathbf{s}_t, \tilde{y}(\mathbf{s}_t), v_t^0(\mathbf{s}_t, \tilde{y}(\mathbf{s}_t)),$$

which contradicts (40). □

From (41) we can conclude that

$$R^t(\mathbf{s}_t, \tilde{y}(\mathbf{s}_t), v_t^0(\mathbf{s}_t, \tilde{y}(\mathbf{s}_t))) \geqq R^t(\mathbf{s}_t, \tilde{y}(\mathbf{s}_t), v_t(\mathbf{s}_t, \tilde{y}(\mathbf{s}_t))) \qquad \text{a.s.,} \tag{42}$$

which is true for any measurable functions given by $\tilde{y}(s_t)$ and $v_t(s, y)$ such that

$$P\{\forall y \in \mathbb{R}^n, v_t(\mathbf{s}_t, y) \in U_t(\mathbf{s}_t)\} = 1. \tag{43}$$

By Proposition 2 it follows from (42) that

$$P\{\forall y \in \mathbb{R}^n, R^t(\mathbf{s}_t, y, v_t^0(\mathbf{s}_t, y)) \geqq R^t(\mathbf{s}_t, y, v_t(\mathbf{s}_t, y))\} = 1 \tag{44}$$

for any measurable function v_t which satisfies (43). Further, from (44) it follows that

$$R^t(\mathbf{s}_t, \mathbf{y}_t, v_t^0(\mathbf{s}_t, \mathbf{y}_t) \geqq R^t(\mathbf{s}_t, \mathbf{y}_t, v_t(\mathbf{s}_t, \mathbf{y}_t)) \qquad \text{a.s.} \tag{45}$$

for each $\mathbf{y}_t := y_t(\mathbf{s}^t)$ and for any measurable function v_t satisfying (43).

From (45) it is immediate that, for each $\mathscr{F}^t$-measurable y_t and any $\mathscr{F}_{\mathbf{s}_t, \mathbf{y}_t}$-measurable u_t such that $\mathbf{u}_t \in U_t(\mathbf{s}_t)$ a.s.,

$$R^t(\mathbf{s}_t, \mathbf{y}_t, v_t^0(\mathbf{s}_t, \mathbf{y}_t)) \geqq R^t(\mathbf{s}_t, \mathbf{y}_t, \mathbf{u}_t) \qquad \text{a.s.} \tag{46}$$

By virtue of Lemma 1, any $\mathbf{u}_t$ with these properties can be represented in the form $\mathbf{u}_t = v_t(\mathbf{s}_t, \mathbf{y}_t)$ a.s., where v_t satisfies condition (43).

Now, by virtue of Proposition 2, the first equality in (39) follows immediately from (46).

We show next that the second equality, $R^t(s_t, \tilde{y}_t, v_t^0(s_t, \tilde{y}_t)) = 0$, is true for any $\tilde{\mathbf{y}}_t := \tilde{y}_t(\mathbf{s}^t)$, $t = 1, \ldots, N-1$, and for $t = 0$, $\tilde{\mathbf{y}}_0 := y_0(\mathbf{s}_0)$. Using the Markovian property of the process $\{\boldsymbol{\sigma}_k\} := \{(\mathbf{s}_k, \hat{\mathbf{y}}_k)\}$ and

Proposition 2, we have that

$$W^t(\mathbf{s}_t, \tilde{\mathbf{y}}_t) = E\left[\sum_{k=t+1}^{N-1} \phi^k(\mathbf{s}_k, \hat{\mathbf{y}}_k, v_k^0(\mathbf{s}_k, \hat{y}_k)) \middle| \mathbf{s}_t, \tilde{\mathbf{y}}_t\right] + \phi^t(\mathbf{s}_t, \tilde{\mathbf{y}}_t, v_t^0(\mathbf{s}_t, \tilde{\mathbf{y}}_t))$$

$$= E\left[E\left[\sum_{k=t+1}^{N-1} \phi^k(\mathbf{s}_k, \hat{\mathbf{y}}_k, v_k^0(\mathbf{s}_k, \tilde{\mathbf{y}}_k)) \middle| \mathbf{s}_t, \mathbf{s}_{t+1}, \tilde{\mathbf{y}}_t, \hat{\mathbf{y}}_{t+1}\right] \middle| \mathbf{s}_t, \tilde{\mathbf{y}}_t\right]$$

$$+ \phi^t(\mathbf{s}_t, \tilde{\mathbf{y}}_t, v_t^0(\mathbf{s}_t, \tilde{\mathbf{y}}_t))$$

$$= E[W^{t+1}(\mathbf{s}_{t+1}, \hat{\mathbf{y}}_{t+1}) | \mathbf{s}_t, \tilde{\mathbf{y}}_t] + \phi^t(\mathbf{s}_t, \tilde{\mathbf{y}}_t, v_t^0(\mathbf{s}_t, \tilde{\mathbf{y}}_t))$$

$$= \int_S W^{t+1}(s_{t+1}, f^{t+1}(\mathbf{s}_t, s_{t+1}, \tilde{\mathbf{y}}_t, v_t^0(\tilde{\mathbf{y}}_t, \mathbf{s}_t)))P_t(\mathbf{s}_t, ds_{t+1})$$

$$+ \phi^t(\mathbf{s}_t, \tilde{\mathbf{y}}_t, v_t^0(\mathbf{s}_t, \tilde{\mathbf{y}}_t)). \tag{47}$$

Finally, using Proposition 2, statement (38) follows from (47) on setting $t = 0$ and $\tilde{\mathbf{y}}_0 = y_0(\mathbf{s}_0)$. □

2°. Sufficiency.

□ By Lemma 1 it is sufficient to show that for each $t = 0, \ldots, N-1$ and any initial value $\tilde{\mathbf{y}}_t := \tilde{\mathbf{y}}_t(\mathbf{s}^t)$ ($\tilde{\mathbf{y}}_0 := \mathbf{y}_0$) we have

$$E\sum_{k=t}^{N-1} \phi^k(\mathbf{s}_k, \mathbf{y}_k^0, v_k^0(\mathbf{s}_k, \mathbf{y}_k^0)) \geqq E\sum_{k=t}^{N-1} \phi^k(\mathbf{s}_k, \mathbf{y}'_k, v'_k(\mathbf{s}_k, \mathbf{y}'_k)), \tag{48}$$

where $v'_k(s, y)$ is an arbitrary Markov strategy and $\mathbf{y}_t^0 = \mathbf{y}'_t = \tilde{\mathbf{y}}_t$. The random vectors $\mathbf{y}'_k$ satisfy the equations (34) with $\mathbf{u}_k := v'_k(\mathbf{s}_k, \mathbf{y}'_k)$ and the random vectors $\mathbf{y}_k^0$ satisfy these equations with $\mathbf{u}_k := v_k^0(\mathbf{s}_k, \mathbf{y}_k^0)$.

Note first of all that from (39) it follows that

$$R^t(\mathbf{s}_t, \tilde{\mathbf{y}}_t, v'_t(\mathbf{s}_t, \tilde{\mathbf{y}}_t) \leqq R^t(\mathbf{s}_t, \tilde{\mathbf{y}}_t, v_t^0(\mathbf{s}_t, \tilde{\mathbf{y}}_t)) \qquad \text{a.s.}$$

for any $\mathscr{F}^t$-measurable function $\tilde{\mathbf{y}}_t$. From this, by Proposition 2,

$$P\{\forall y \in \mathbb{R}^n, R^t(\mathbf{s}_t, y, v'_t(\mathbf{s}_t, y)) \leqq R^t(\mathbf{s}_t, y, v_t^0(\mathbf{s}_t, y))\} = 1.$$

Hence, for any t ($1 \leqq t \leqq N-1$) and any $\tilde{\mathbf{y}}_t := \tilde{y}_t(\mathbf{s}^t)$,

$$\phi^t(\mathbf{s}_t, \tilde{\mathbf{y}}_t, v'_t(\mathbf{s}_t, \tilde{\mathbf{y}}_t)) + \int_S W^{t+1}(s_{t+1}, f^{t+1}(v'_t(\mathbf{s}_t, \tilde{\mathbf{y}}_t)))P_t(\mathbf{s}_t, ds_{t+1})$$

$$\leqq \phi^t(\mathbf{s}_t, \tilde{\mathbf{y}}_t, v_t^0(\mathbf{s}_t, \tilde{\mathbf{y}}_t))$$

$$+ \int_S W^{t+1}(s_{t+1}, f^{t+1}(v_t^0(\mathbf{s}_t, \tilde{\mathbf{y}}_t)))P_t(\mathbf{s}_t, ds_{t+1}) \qquad \text{a.s.} \tag{49}$$

We prove the inequality (48) by induction. Suppose (48) holds for $t + 1$; we shall prove it for t. Altering v^0 to v' only at t and using (49) and induction, we have that

$$
\begin{aligned}
E \sum_{k=t}^{N-1} \phi^k(\mathbf{s}_k, \mathbf{y}_k^0, v_k^0(\mathbf{s}_k, \mathbf{y}_k^0)) \\
&= E\Bigg[\phi^t(\mathbf{s}_t, \mathbf{y}_t^0, v_t^0(\mathbf{s}_t, \mathbf{y}_t^0)) \\
&\quad + \int_S W^{t+1}(s_{t+1}, f^{t+1}(\mathbf{s}_t, s_{t+1}, \mathbf{y}_t^0, v_t^0(\mathbf{s}_t, \mathbf{y}_t^0)))P_t(\mathbf{s}_t, ds_{t+1})\Bigg] \\
&\geqq E\Bigg[\phi^t(\mathbf{s}_t, \mathbf{y}_t^0, v_t'(\mathbf{s}_t, \mathbf{y}_t^0)) \\
&\quad + \int_S W^{t+1}(s_{t+1}, f^{t+1}(\mathbf{s}_t, s_{t+1}, \mathbf{y}_t^0, v_t^0(\mathbf{s}_t, \mathbf{y}_t^0)))P_t(\mathbf{s}_t, ds_{t+1})\Bigg] \\
&\geqq E \sum_{k=t}^{N-1} \phi^k(\mathbf{s}_k, \mathbf{y}_k', v_k'(\mathbf{s}_k, \mathbf{y}_k')).
\end{aligned}
\tag{50}
$$

The general induction step is thus completed. The first step is effected similarly. □□

5. The Connection between the Bellman Equation and the Maximum Principle

In this section we use the Bellman functional equation as a necessary optimality condition and conclude from it the maximum principle for the problem (1)–(3), (5).

Theorem 5. *Let the following additional requirements hold for the problem defined by* (1)–(3), (5):

(1) *The multifunction given by* $U_t(s_t)$ *takes a.s. convex (set) values in* $\mathbb{R}^m$, $t = 1, \ldots, N - 1$.
(2) *The functions given by* $\phi^t(s_t, y, u)$, $f^{t+1}(s_t, s_{t+1}, y, u)$ *are a.s. differentiable with respect to* (y, u), $t = 0, \ldots, N - 1$.
(3) *The functions given by* $W^t(\mathbf{s}_t, y)$, $t = 1, \ldots, N - 1$, *are a.s.*

differentiable with respect to y, and there exists a random variable $\alpha := \alpha(\omega) > 0$, $E\alpha < \infty$, *such that*

$$|W_y^{t+1}(\mathbf{s}_{t+1}, \mathbf{Y}_{t+1}^0(u)) f_u^{t+1}(\mathbf{s}_t, \mathbf{s}_{t+1}, \mathbf{y}_t^0, u)| + |W_y^{t+1}(\mathbf{s}_{t+1}, \mathbf{Y}_{t+1}^0(y)) f_y^{t+1}(\mathbf{s}_t, \mathbf{s}_{t+1}, y, \mathbf{u}_t^0)| \leqq \alpha(\omega) \quad a.s.,^4 \tag{51}$$

where

$$\mathbf{Y}_{t+1}^0(u) := f^{t+1}(\mathbf{s}_t, \mathbf{s}_{t+1}, \mathbf{y}_t^0, u)$$

and

$$\mathbf{Y}_{t+1}^0(y) := f^{t+1}(\mathbf{s}_t, \mathbf{s}_{t+1}, y, \mathbf{u}_t^0).$$

Then all conclusions of Theorem 3′ are valid with $\psi_t^0(\mathbf{s}_t, \mathbf{y}_t^0) := W_y^t(\mathbf{s}_t, \mathbf{y}_t^0)$. □

Thus Theorem 5 (like Theorem 3′) represents the *differential form* of the maximum principle. Theorem 5 differs from Theorem 3′ mainly, first, in the assumption of the existence of the Markov strategy v^0 for the family of problems (33)–(35) needed to define the value functions W^t [cf. (36)] and, second, in the assumption of the smoothness of these functions. We note that this last requirement may not be satisfied even in the simplest examples.

□ In the proof of Theorem 5 we shall use the following result, which is easily checked.

Lemma 4. *Let a real-valued differentiable function on* $\mathbb{R}^m$ *be given by* $F(u)$, *and let* $U \subseteq \mathbb{R}^m$ *be a convex set. If* $F(u^*) = \max_{u \in U} F(u)$, $u^* \in U$, *then* $F_u(u^*)u^* = \max_{u \in U} F_u(u^*)u$. □

Let $\mathbf{y}_t^0, \mathbf{u}_t^0$ be a solution of the problem (1)–(3), (5). According to the conclusion of Theorem 4, for all $t = 0, \ldots, N-1$ the random function given by $R^t(\mathbf{s}_t, \mathbf{y}_t^0, u)$ a.s. reaches a maximum with respect to $u \in U_t(\mathbf{s}_t)$ at the point $\mathbf{u}_t^0$. From Lemma 4 it follows that

$$R_u^t(\mathbf{s}_t, \mathbf{y}_t^0, \mathbf{u}_t^0)\mathbf{u}_t^0 = \max_{u \in U_t(\mathbf{s}_t)} R_u^t(\mathbf{s}_t, \mathbf{y}_t^0, \mathbf{u}_t^0)u \quad \text{a.s.} \tag{52}$$

Condition (51) permits differentiation under the integral with respect to u of the function given by $W^{t+1}(s_{t+1}, f^{t+1}(s_t, s_{t+1}, y_t^0, u))$.

[4] The first term in (51) represents the norm of the matrix product of n-dimensional row vector W_y^{t+1} with the $n \times m$ matrix f_u^{t+1}. The second term has a similar interpretation.

Defining $\psi_t(s, y) := \partial W^t(s, y)/\partial y$ and recalling the definition (27) of the Hamiltonian $H^{t+1}(s_t, s_{t+1}, \psi, y, u)$, we have

$$R_u^t(\mathbf{s}_t, \mathbf{y}_t^0, \mathbf{u}_t^0) = E[H_u^{t+1}(\mathbf{s}_t, \mathbf{s}_{t+1}, \psi_{t+1}^0(\mathbf{s}_{t+1}, \mathbf{y}_{t+1}^0), \mathbf{y}_t^0, \mathbf{u}_t^0) | \mathbf{s}_t, \mathbf{y}_t^0] \quad \text{a.s.}$$

Taking account of (52), the statement (32) follows.

We turn next to establishing the conjugate system (29). From (39) it follows that

$$R^t(\mathbf{s}_t, \mathbf{y}_t, \mathbf{u}_t^0) \leqq R^t(\mathbf{s}_t, \mathbf{y}_t, v_t^0(\mathbf{s}_t, \mathbf{y}_t)) = 0 \quad \text{a.s.} \tag{53}$$

for any $\mathscr{F}_{\mathbf{s}_t, \mathbf{y}_t^0}$-measurable $\mathbf{y}_t$. On the other hand,

$$R^t(\mathbf{s}_t, \mathbf{y}_t^0, \mathbf{u}_t^0) = R^t(\mathbf{s}_t, \mathbf{y}_t^0, v_t^0(\mathbf{s}_t, \mathbf{y}_t^0)) = 0 \quad \text{a.s.} \tag{54}$$

From (53) and (54) it follows that

$$R^t(\mathbf{s}_t, \mathbf{y}_t, \mathbf{u}_t^0) \leqq R^t(\mathbf{s}_t, \mathbf{y}_t^0, \mathbf{u}_t^0) \quad \text{a.s.}$$

for any $\mathscr{F}_{\mathbf{s}_t, \mathbf{y}_t^0}$-measurable $\mathbf{y}_t$. By Proposition 2, we thus have

$$\max_{y \in \mathbb{R}^n} R^t(\mathbf{s}_t, y, \mathbf{u}_t^0) = R^t(\mathbf{s}_t, \mathbf{y}_t^0, \mathbf{u}_t^0) \quad \text{a.s.,} \tag{55}$$

from which it follows immediately that

$$R_y^t(\mathbf{s}_t, \mathbf{y}_t^0, \mathbf{u}_t^0) = 0 \quad \text{a.s.,} \quad t = 1, \ldots, N-1. \tag{56}$$

By condition (51) the function given by $W^{t+1}(s_{t+1}, f^{t+1}(s_t, s_{t+1}, y, u_t^0))$ may be differentiated with respect to y under the integral. Therefore from (56) we obtain

$$\begin{aligned} R_y^t(\mathbf{s}_t^0, \mathbf{y}_t^0, \mathbf{u}_t^0) &= \psi^0(\mathbf{s}_t, \mathbf{y}_t^0) \\ &\quad - E[H_y^{+1}(\mathbf{s}_t, \mathbf{s}_{t+1}, \psi_{t+1}^0(\mathbf{s}_{t+1}, \mathbf{y}_{t+1}^0), \mathbf{y}_t^0, \mathbf{u}_t^0) | \mathbf{s}_t, \mathbf{y}_t^0] \\ &= 0 \quad \text{a.s.,}\ t = 1, \ldots, N-1, \end{aligned} \tag{57}$$

$$\psi_N^0(\mathbf{s}_N, \mathbf{y}_N^0) = 0 \quad \text{a.s.,}$$

i.e., the conjugate system (29). □

Note. In the economics literature, supporting prices (shadow prices, objectively determined multipliers, etc.) are often defined as derivatives of the Bellman value function. In this context Theorem 5 states a connection between the prices of optimal planning and the conjugate variables (multipliers, dual variables, etc.) appearing in the formulation of the maximum principle for models of economic dynamics which reduce to the problem (1)–(3), (5).

4. CONSTRUCTION OF MARKOV CONTROLS

1. The Problem of Constructing Markov Controls

In §1 we established the sufficiency of the class of controls whose dependency on the past is Markovian. More specifically, it was proven that if there exists an optimal control of general type, then from it an optimal Markov control may be constructed. However, the question of an effective method for this construction was left open.

In this section effective methods for constructing Markov controls will be demonstrated for two problems which have some additional convexity properties (the linear convex problem and the Gale model). In all the constructions described below an averaging method plays the main rôle. This method allows the construction of Markov controls from given controls which are at least as good as the given control, not only with respect to some fixed functional, but (simultaneously) with respect to any objective functional which can be represented as the expectation of a sum of concave objective functions.

2. The Linear Convex Model

We consider the following particular case of the problem of optimal Markov control (cf. §1):

$$\text{Maximize} \quad E \sum_{t=0}^{N-1} \phi^t(\mathbf{s}_t, \mathbf{y}_t, \mathbf{u}_t) \tag{58}$$

$$\text{subject to} \qquad \mathbf{y}_{t+1} = A^{t+1}(\mathbf{s}_t, \mathbf{s}_{t+1})\mathbf{y}_t + B^{t+1}(\mathbf{s}_t, \mathbf{s}_{t+1})\mathbf{u}_t \quad \text{a.s.,} \tag{59}$$

$$g^t(\mathbf{s}_t, \mathbf{y}_t, \mathbf{u}_t) \leqq 0 \quad \text{a.s.,} \tag{60}$$

$$\mathbf{u}_t \in U_t(\mathbf{s}_t) \quad \text{a.s.,} \ t = 0, \ldots, N-1, \tag{61}$$

where the random vector $y_0(\mathbf{s}_0)$ is given, $U := \mathbb{R}^m$ and A^{t+1} and B^{t+1} are matrices of size $n \times n$ and $n \times m$, respectively, whose elements are bounded measurable functions. Suppose the following conditions hold:

The process $\{\mathbf{s}_t\}$ is Markovian. $U_t({}^s{}_t)$ is a convex subset in $\mathbb{R}^m$ which depends measurably on s_t. The functions ϕ^t, g^t are (jointly) measurable with respect to their arguments. For each s_t the functions $g^t(s, \cdot, \cdot): \mathbb{R}^n \times \mathbb{R}^m \to \mathbb{R}^k$ are convex, and the functions $\phi^t(s, \cdot, \cdot)$: $\mathbb{R}^n \times \mathbb{R}^m \to \mathbb{R}$ are concave.

Recall that a control $\{\mathbf{u}_t\}_{t=0}^{N-1}$ is termed *Markovian* if there exists a measurable function given by $v_t(s, y)$ such that $u_t(\mathbf{s}^t) = v_t(\mathbf{s}_t, y_t(\mathbf{s}^t))$ a.s.

Theorem 6. *Let $\{u_t(\mathbf{s}^t)\}$ be a control and $\{y_t(\mathbf{s}^t)\}$ the corresponding controlled process which satisfy the constraints* (59)–(61). *Suppose the following conditions hold for each t:*

$$E|\mathbf{y}_t| < \infty, \qquad E|\mathbf{u}_t| < \infty, \qquad E|\phi^t(\mathbf{s}_t, \mathbf{y}_t, \mathbf{u}_t)| < \infty. \tag{62}$$

Then the recurrence relation

$$\begin{aligned} \tilde{\mathbf{y}}_0 := \mathbf{y}_0, \qquad \tilde{\mathbf{y}}_t &:= E[\mathbf{y}_t | \mathbf{s}_{t-1}, \mathbf{s}_t, \tilde{\mathbf{y}}_{t-1}], \\ \tilde{\mathbf{u}}_t &:= E[\mathbf{u}_t | \mathbf{s}_t, \tilde{\mathbf{y}}_t] \end{aligned} \tag{63}$$

defines a control $\{\tilde{\mathbf{u}}_t\}$ and a corresponding process $\{\tilde{\mathbf{y}}_t\}$ which satisfy the constraints (59)–(61) *and are such that*

$$E\phi^t(\mathbf{s}_t, \tilde{\mathbf{y}}_t, \tilde{\mathbf{u}}_t) \geqq E\phi^t(\mathbf{s}_t, \mathbf{y}_t, \mathbf{u}_t), \qquad t = 0, \ldots, N-1. \quad \square \tag{64}$$

If the inequality (64) holds, we say that $\{(\tilde{\mathbf{u}}_t, \tilde{\mathbf{y}}_t)\}$ *majorizes* $\{(\mathbf{u}_t, \mathbf{y}_t)\}$ (or the control $\{\tilde{\mathbf{u}}_t\}$ *majorizes* $\{\mathbf{u}_t\}$). We emphasize that the function ϕ^t does not appear in the recurrence relation (63), and therefore a majorizing Markov control is simultaneously constructed in Theorem 6 for all ϕ^t which satisfy the assumptions made in this section.

3. A Lemma on Markov Dependency

We state a result needed for the proof of Theorem 6.

Lemma 5. *Suppose the process $\{\mathbf{s}_t\}$ is Markovian, and let an $\mathscr{F}_{\mathbf{s}^t}$-measurable function be given by $\alpha(s^t)$. Then for any $\mathscr{F}_{\mathbf{s}^t}$-measurable and integrable function given by $\beta(s^t)$ we have*

$$E[\boldsymbol{\beta} | \mathbf{s}_t, \mathbf{s}_{t+1}, \boldsymbol{\alpha}] = E[\boldsymbol{\beta} | \mathbf{s}_t, \boldsymbol{\alpha}] \qquad a.s. \tag{65}$$

$\square$ Relation (65), as a consequence of one of the definitions of the Markov property, is equivalent to the statement that the process $\{\boldsymbol{\sigma}_t : t = 1, 2, 3\}$ given by

$$\boldsymbol{\sigma}_1 := \mathbf{s}^t, \qquad \boldsymbol{\sigma}_2 := (\mathbf{s}_t, \boldsymbol{\alpha}), \qquad \boldsymbol{\sigma}_3 := \mathbf{s}_{t+1}$$

is Markovian. The necessity of (65) for the Markov property of $\{\boldsymbol{\sigma}_t\}$

follows from a consideration of indicator functions B of appropriately measurable sets.

To verify the Markov nature of $\{\boldsymbol{\sigma}_t\}$ it suffices to prove that $E[\gamma(\boldsymbol{\sigma}_3)|\boldsymbol{\sigma}_1, \boldsymbol{\sigma}_2] = E[\gamma(\boldsymbol{\sigma}_3)|\boldsymbol{\sigma}_2]$ for any integrable function γ. We have

$$\begin{aligned} E[\gamma(\mathbf{s}_{t+1})|\mathbf{s}^t, \mathbf{s}_t, \boldsymbol{\alpha}] &= E[\gamma(\mathbf{s}_{t+1})|\mathbf{s}^t] = E[\gamma(\mathbf{s}_{t+1})|\mathbf{s}_t] \\ &= E[\gamma(\mathbf{s}_{t+1})|\mathbf{s}_t, \alpha] \qquad \text{a.s.,} \end{aligned}$$

where the last two equalities are a simple consequence of the Markovian nature of the process $\{\mathbf{s}_t\}$. □

4. Proof of Theorem 6

□ We show first that $\{(\tilde{\mathbf{y}}_t, \tilde{\mathbf{u}}_t)\}_{t=0}^{N-1}$ satisfies the constraints (59).

□ We take the conditional expectation with respect to $(\mathbf{s}_{t-1}, \mathbf{s}_t, \mathbf{s}_{t+1}, \tilde{\mathbf{y}}_{t-1})$ of both sides of (59) to obtain

$$\begin{aligned} &E[\mathbf{y}_{t+1}|\mathbf{s}_{t-1}, \mathbf{s}_t, \mathbf{s}_{t+1}, \tilde{\mathbf{y}}_{t-1}] \\ &\quad = A^{t+1}(\mathbf{s}_t, \mathbf{s}_{t+1})E[\mathbf{y}_t|\mathbf{s}_{t-1}, \mathbf{s}_t, \mathbf{s}_{t+1}, \tilde{\mathbf{y}}_{t-1}] \\ &\qquad + B^{t+1}(\mathbf{s}_t, \mathbf{s}_{t+1})E[\mathbf{u}_t|\mathbf{s}_{t-1}, \mathbf{s}_t, \mathbf{s}_{t+1}, \tilde{\mathbf{y}}_{t-1}] \qquad \text{a.s.} \end{aligned}$$

Now we take the conditional expectation with respect to $(\mathbf{s}_t, \mathbf{s}_{t+1}, \tilde{\mathbf{y}}_t)$ of both sides of this equation. Using Lemma 5, since by (63) $\tilde{\mathbf{y}}_t$ is measurably dependent on $(\mathbf{s}_{t-1}, \mathbf{s}_t, \tilde{\mathbf{y}}_{t-1})$, and the Markov property of $\{\mathbf{s}_t\}$, we obtain

$$\begin{aligned} \tilde{\mathbf{y}}_{t+1} &= A^{t+1}(\mathbf{s}_t, \mathbf{s}_{t+1})\tilde{\mathbf{y}}_t + B^{t+1}(\mathbf{s}_t, \mathbf{s}_{t+1})E[\mathbf{u}_t|\mathbf{s}_t, \mathbf{s}_{t+1}, \tilde{\mathbf{y}}_t] \qquad \text{a.s.} \\ &= A^{t+1}(s_t, s_{t+1})\tilde{\mathbf{y}}_t + B^{t+1}(s_t, s_{t+1})\tilde{\mathbf{u}}_t \qquad \text{a.s.,} \end{aligned}$$

again using Lemma 5, since $\mathbf{u}_t$ is similarly measurably dependent. □

We show next that $\{(\tilde{\mathbf{y}}_t, \tilde{\mathbf{u}}_t)\}_{t=0}^{N-1}$ satisfies the constraints (60) and (61).

□ Consider for each s_t the convex set

$$C(s_t) := \{(y, u) : u \in U_t(s_t), g^t(s_t, y, u) \leqq 0\}.$$

It is obvious that the multifunction $s_t \mapsto C(s_t)$ is measurable and that

$$(\mathbf{y}_t, \mathbf{u}_t) \in C(\mathbf{s}_t) \qquad \text{a.s.}$$

By Lemma II.1

$$E[(\mathbf{y}_t, \mathbf{u}_t) | \mathbf{s}_{t-1}, \mathbf{s}_t, \tilde{\mathbf{y}}_{t-1}] \in C(\mathbf{s}_t) \qquad \text{a.s.};$$

i.e.,

$$(\tilde{\mathbf{y}}_t, E[\mathbf{u}_t | \mathbf{s}_{t-1}, \mathbf{s}_t, \tilde{\mathbf{y}}_{t-1}]) \in C(\mathbf{s}_t) \qquad \text{a.s.}$$

Again, using Lemma II.1, we find that

$$(\tilde{\mathbf{y}}_t, E[E[\mathbf{u}_t | \mathbf{s}_{t-1}, \mathbf{s}_t, \tilde{\mathbf{y}}_{t-1}] | \mathbf{s}_t, \tilde{\mathbf{y}}_t]) \in C(\mathbf{s}_t) \qquad \text{a.s.},$$

which may be rewritten, using the Markov property of $\{(\mathbf{s}_t, \tilde{y}_t)\}$, as $(\tilde{\mathbf{y}}_t, \tilde{\mathbf{u}}_t) \in C(\mathbf{s}_t)$ a.s.

It remains to note that, by virtue of Jensen's inequality (Lemma II.2) and Lemma 5,

$$\begin{aligned} E\phi^t(\mathbf{s}_t, \mathbf{y}_t, \mathbf{u}_t) &= EE[\phi^t(\mathbf{s}_t, \mathbf{y}_t, \mathbf{u}_t) | \mathbf{s}_{t-1}, \mathbf{s}_t, \tilde{\mathbf{y}}_{t-1}] \\ &\leqq EE[\phi^t(\mathbf{s}_t, \tilde{\mathbf{y}}_t, E[\mathbf{u}_t | \mathbf{s}_{t-1}, \mathbf{s}_t, \tilde{\mathbf{y}}_{t-1})] | \mathbf{s}_t, \tilde{\mathbf{y}}_t] \\ &\leqq E\phi^t(\mathbf{s}_t, \tilde{\mathbf{y}}_t, \tilde{\mathbf{u}}_t). \quad \square \end{aligned}$$

5. Markov Programmes in the Gale Model

We consider the probabilistic version of Gale's model in parametric form, described in §2.4.7. We say that this model is *Markovian* if its elements depend on the random parameters as

$$U_t(\mathbf{s}_t), \qquad a^t(\mathbf{s}_t, u), \qquad b^{t+1}(\mathbf{s}_t, \mathbf{s}_{t+1}, u), \qquad f_{t+1}(\mathbf{s}_t, \mathbf{s}_{t+1}, c)$$

and if the process $\mathbf{s}_0, \mathbf{s}_1, \ldots$ is Markovian. A *programme* $\{\mathbf{z}_t\} := \{x_{t-1}, \mathbf{y}_t)\}$ is called *Markovian* if it is generated by a sequence of Markov feedback control functions, i.e., functions given by $u_t(s^t)$ of the form $u_t(\mathbf{s}^t) = v_t(\mathbf{s}_t, \mathbf{y}_t)$ a.s., where the functions v_t are $\mathscr{E} \times \mathscr{B}(\mathbb{R}^n)$-measurable.

Let $\{\mathbf{z}_t\} = \{(\mathbf{x}_{t-1}, \mathbf{y}_t)\}$ be a programme with i.v. $\mathbf{y}_0$. Set $\tilde{\mathbf{y}}_0 := \mathbf{y}_0$ and construct recursively the sequence of random vectors $\{(\tilde{\mathbf{x}}_{t-1}, \tilde{\mathbf{y}}_t)\}$ by the following rule: If $\mathbf{y}_t$ has been constructed, define $(\tilde{\mathbf{x}}_t, \tilde{\mathbf{y}}_{t+1})$ as

$$\tilde{\mathbf{x}}_t := E[\mathbf{x}_t | \mathbf{s}_t, \tilde{\mathbf{y}}_t], \qquad \tilde{\mathbf{y}}_{t+1} := E[\mathbf{y}_{t+1} | \mathbf{s}_t, \mathbf{s}_{t+1}, \tilde{\mathbf{y}}_t]. \tag{66}$$

Theorem 7. *Under the conditions* (M_1)–(M_9) (§§2.4.7–2.4.8), *a sequence* $\{\tilde{\mathbf{z}}_t\} := \{(\tilde{\mathbf{x}}_{t+1}, \tilde{\mathbf{y}}_t)\}$ *defined by* (66) *is a Markov programme with i.v.* $\mathbf{y}_0$ *for which* $F_t(\tilde{\mathbf{z}}_t) \geqq F_t(\mathbf{z}_t)$. $\square$

If this last inequality holds, we say that the programme $\{\tilde{\mathbf{z}}_t\}$ *majorizes* the programme $\{\mathbf{z}_t\}$. The recursion relation (66) therefore gives a method for constructing majorizing Markov programmes, and (as in the proof of Theorem 6) this method does not depend on a specific given functional F_t.

6. Two Lemmas

The proof of Theorem 7 is based on two lemmas.

Lemma 6. *Let U be a Polish space, let u be an $\mathcal{F}_{\mathbf{s}^t}$-measurable function with values in U, let α be an $\mathcal{F}_{\mathbf{s}^t}$-measurable $\mathbb{R}^n$-valued function and let $\pi(du \mid s_t, \alpha)$ denote the conditional distribution of $u(\mathbf{s}^t)$ for given s_t and $\alpha(s^t)$, where $\{\mathbf{s}_t\}$ is a Markov process. Then for any measurable function given by $\beta(s_t, s_{t+1}, u)$ such that the function given by $\beta(s_t, s_{t+1}, u(s_t))$ is integrable,*

$$E[\beta(\mathbf{s}_t, \mathbf{s}_{t+1}, u(\mathbf{s}^t)) \mid \mathbf{s}_t, \mathbf{s}_{t+1}, \boldsymbol{\alpha}] = \int_U \beta(s_t, s_{t+1}, u)\, \pi(du \mid s_t, \alpha).$$

□ The proof of this lemma is a straightforward consequence of Lemma 5 and Proposition 1. □

Lemma 7. *Let U be a compact metric space, let $(S, \mathcal{E}, \nu)$ be a probability space and let the $\mathbb{R}^n$-valued function ϕ on $U \times S$ be continuous in u and measurable with respect to s. Suppose further that ϕ satisfies the following convexity condition:*

For any $u_1, u_2 \in U$ and $\alpha \in [0, 1]$ there exists a $u \in U$ such that

$$\alpha\phi(u_1, \mathbf{s}) + (1 - \alpha)\phi(u_2, \mathbf{s}) = \phi(u, \mathbf{s}) \qquad a.s.$$

Then for any probability measure μ on $(U, \mathcal{B}(U))$ there exists a $v \in U$ such that

$$\int_U \phi(u, \mathbf{s})\mu(du) = \phi(v, \mathbf{s}) \qquad a.s. \tag{67}$$

(The point v is termed a *centre of gravity* of the probability measure μ.)

□ It is well known that for any probability measure μ on a compact metric space U there exists a sequence of probability measures μ_n with finite support which converges weakly to μ.[5]

For such a sequence

$$\int_U \phi(u, s)\mu_n(du) \to \int_U \phi(u, s)\mu(du) \tag{68}$$

for each s. On the other hand, it follows from the convexity condition that for each measure μ_n there exists a u_n such that

$$\int_U \phi(u, \mathbf{s})\mu_n(du) = \phi(u_n, \mathbf{s}) \qquad \text{a.s.} \tag{69}$$

Choosing a convergent subsequence $u_n \to v$ (U is compact), we have, since $\phi(\cdot, s)$ is continuous for fixed s, $\phi(u_n, s) \to \phi(v, s)$. Using this, (68) and (69), we obtain (67). □

7. Proof of Theorem 7

□ We show first that $(\tilde{\mathbf{x}}_t, \tilde{\mathbf{y}}_{t+1})$ is a technological process generated by some Markov control function.

□ Let $u_t(\mathbf{s}_t)$ generate $(\mathbf{x}_t, \mathbf{y}_{t+1})$. We consider the conditional distribution $\pi(s_t, \tilde{y}_t, du)$ of $u_t(\mathbf{s}^t)$ for given s_t and $\tilde{y}_t$. Define

$$\mathrm{c}^{t+1}(\mathbf{s}_t, \mathbf{s}_{t+1}, u) := (a^t(\mathbf{s}_t, u), b^{t+1}(\mathbf{s}_t, \mathbf{s}_{t+1}, u)).$$

Using Lemma 6, we find

$$\begin{aligned}(\tilde{\mathbf{x}}_t, \tilde{\mathbf{y}}_{t+1}) &= (E[\mathbf{x}_t | \mathbf{s}_t, \tilde{\mathbf{y}}_t], E[\mathbf{y}_{t+1} | \mathbf{s}_t, \mathbf{s}_{t+1}, \tilde{\mathbf{y}}_t]) \\ &= \int_{U_t \mathbf{s}_t} c^{t+1}(\mathbf{s}_t, \mathbf{s}_{t+1}, u)\pi(\mathbf{s}_t, \tilde{\mathbf{y}}_t, du) \qquad \text{a.s.} \\ &:= I(\mathbf{s}_t, \tilde{\mathbf{y}}_t, \mathbf{s}_{t+1}).\end{aligned} \tag{70}$$

By Lemma 7 and the convexity condition (M_7) (see §2.4.7), for each

[5] The sequence μ_n can be constructed the following way. For each n we consider a partition of U into Borel sets with diameter less than $1/n$. We choose one point in each of these sets and place at this point a mass equal to the μ-measure of that set. The measure so obtained is designated μ_n. It is easy to verify that $\int_U f d\mu_n \to \int_U f d\mu$ for any continuous function on U; i.e., μ_n *converges weakly* to μ.

s_t and y there exists a $v \in U_t(s_t)$ such that

$$I(s_t, y, s_{t+1}) = c^{t+1}(s_t, s_{t+1}, v) \qquad \text{a.s. } [P_t(s_t, \cdot)].$$

From this and Filippov's lemma (Corollary I.4) we conclude that there exists a measurable function given by $v_t(s, y)$ such that $v_t(\mathbf{s}_t, \tilde{\mathbf{y}}_t) \in U_t(\mathbf{s}_t)$ a.s. and $I(\mathbf{s}_t, \tilde{\mathbf{y}}_t, \mathbf{s}_{t+1}) = c^{t+1}(\mathbf{s}_t, \mathbf{s}_{t+1}, v_t(\mathbf{s}_t, \tilde{\mathbf{y}}_t))$ a.s. Combining this with (70) gives the required result. □

We show next that $\tilde{\mathbf{y}}_t \geqq \tilde{\mathbf{x}}_t$ a.s.

□ Because $\mathbf{y}_t \geqq \mathbf{x}_t$ a.s.,

$$\tilde{\mathbf{y}}_t = E[\mathbf{y}_t | \mathbf{s}_{t-1}, \mathbf{s}_t, \tilde{\mathbf{y}}_{t-1}] \geqq E[\mathbf{x}_t | \mathbf{s}_{t-1}, \mathbf{s}_t, \tilde{\mathbf{y}}_{t-1}] \qquad \text{a.s.}$$

Taking the conditional expectation with respect to $\mathbf{s}_t, \tilde{\mathbf{y}}_t$ of both sides of this inequality, since $\tilde{\mathbf{y}}_t$ is measurably dependent on $\mathbf{s}_{t-1}, \mathbf{s}_t, \tilde{\mathbf{y}}_{t-1}$, we obtain $\tilde{\mathbf{y}}_t \geqq E[\mathbf{x}_t | \mathbf{s}_t, \tilde{\mathbf{y}}_t] = \mathbf{x}_t$. □

Thus we have shown that $\{\tilde{\mathbf{z}}_t\}$ is a Markov programme with i.v. $\mathbf{y}_0$. Finally, we show that $F_t(\tilde{\mathbf{z}}_t) \geqq F_t(\mathbf{z}_t)$.

□ By Lemma 5, $\tilde{\mathbf{z}}_t = E[\mathbf{z}_t | \mathbf{s}_{t-1}, \mathbf{s}_t, \tilde{\mathbf{y}}_{t-1}]$, and thus by Jensen's inequality (Lemma II.2)

$$\begin{aligned} F_t(\tilde{\mathbf{z}}_t) &= Ef_t(\mathbf{s}_{t-1}, \mathbf{s}_t, E[\mathbf{z}_t | \mathbf{s}_{t-1}, \mathbf{s}_t, \tilde{\mathbf{y}}_{t-1}]) \\ &\geqq EE[f_t(\mathbf{s}_{t-1}, \mathbf{s}_t, \mathbf{z}_t) | \mathbf{s}_{t-1}, \mathbf{s}_t, \tilde{\mathbf{y}}_{t-1}] = F_t(\mathbf{z}_t). \end{aligned}$$ □□

5. MARKOV PRICES IN MODELS OF ECONOMIC DYNAMICS

1. Markov Prices in the Gale Model

The existence result for Markov prices in the stochastic version of the Gale model is analogous to the Markov maximum principle established in §2.1 and follows from Theorem 2. However, we give here an independent derivation, since for models of economic dynamics the concept of average prices is particularly natural.

We consider the Markov version of the Gale model described in §4.5. Let $\{\mathbf{x}_{t-1}^0, \mathbf{y}_t^0\}_{t=1}^N$ be an optimal Markov programme of length N with i.v. $\mathbf{y}_0^0 := \mathbf{y}_0$ generated by the sequence of feedback control functions $\mathbf{u}_t^0 := v_t^0(\mathbf{s}_t, \mathbf{y}_t^0)$ a.s., and let $\{p_t^0(\mathbf{s}^t)\}_{t=0}^N$ be a price system supporting this programme.

We take an arbitrary technological process $(\mathbf{x}_t, \mathbf{y}_{t+1})$ generated by a control function of the form $\mathbf{u}_t = v_t(\mathbf{s}_t, \mathbf{y}_t^0)$ a.s. The reduced utility for this process may be written in the form

$$\begin{aligned} G_{t+1}(\mathbf{x}_t, \mathbf{y}_{t+1}) = & \ EE[f_{t+1}(\mathbf{s}_{t+1}, \mathbf{x}_t, \mathbf{y}_{t+1}) | \mathbf{s}_t, \mathbf{y}_t^0] \\ & + E(E[\mathbf{p}_{t+1}^0 | \mathbf{s}_t, \mathbf{s}_{t+1}, \mathbf{y}_t^0]\mathbf{y}_{t+1}) \\ & - E(E[\mathbf{p}_t^0 | \mathbf{s}_t, \mathbf{y}_t^0]\mathbf{x}_t), \end{aligned}$$

since $\mathbf{y}_{t+1} := b^{t+1}(\mathbf{s}_t, \mathbf{s}_{t+1}, v_t(\mathbf{s}_t, \mathbf{y}_t^0))$ depends only on $\mathbf{s}_t, \mathbf{s}_{t+1}, \mathbf{y}_t^0$, and $\mathbf{x}_t := a^t(\mathbf{s}_t, v_t(\mathbf{s}_t, \mathbf{y}_t^0))$ depends on $\mathbf{s}_t, \mathbf{y}_t^0$.

Define

$$\begin{aligned} \boldsymbol{\psi}_{t+1}^0 &:= E[\mathbf{p}_{t+1}^0 | \mathbf{s}_t, \mathbf{s}_{t+1}, \mathbf{y}_t^0], \\ \boldsymbol{\lambda}_t^0 &:= E[\mathbf{p}_t^0 | \mathbf{s}_t, \mathbf{y}_t^0], \\ \gamma^{t+1}(\mathbf{s}_t, \mathbf{s}_{t+1}, \mathbf{y}_t^0, u) &:= f_{t+1}(\mathbf{s}_{t+1}, a^t(\mathbf{s}_t, u), b^{t+1}(\mathbf{s}_t, \mathbf{s}_{t+1}, u)) \\ &\quad + \psi_{t+1}^0(\mathbf{s}_t, \mathbf{s}_{t+1}, \mathbf{y}_t^0) b^{t+1}(\mathbf{s}_t, \mathbf{s}_{t+1}, u) \\ &\quad - \lambda_t^0(\mathbf{s}_t, \mathbf{y}_t^0) a^t(\mathbf{s}_t, u), \\ \zeta^t(\mathbf{s}_t, \mathbf{y}_t^0, u) &:= \int_S \gamma^{t+1}(\mathbf{s}_t, s_{t+1}, \mathbf{y}_t^0, u) P_t(\mathbf{s}_t, ds_{t+1}). \end{aligned} \tag{71}$$

Then

$$\begin{aligned} G_{t+1}(\mathbf{x}_t, \mathbf{y}_{t+1}) &= EE[\gamma^{t+1}(\mathbf{s}_t, \mathbf{s}_{t+1}, \mathbf{y}_t^0, v_t(\mathbf{s}_t, \mathbf{y}_t)) | \mathbf{s}_t, \mathbf{y}_t^0] \\ &= E\zeta^t(\mathbf{s}_t, \mathbf{y}_t^0, v_t(\mathbf{s}_t, \mathbf{y}_t^0)). \end{aligned}$$

Therefore, by the definition of supporting prices

$$E\zeta^t(\mathbf{s}_t, \mathbf{y}_t^0, v_t(\mathbf{s}_t, \mathbf{y}_t^0)) \leqq E\zeta^t(\mathbf{s}_t, \mathbf{y}_t^0, v_t^0(\mathbf{s}_t, \mathbf{y}_t^0))$$

for any feedback control function $v_t(\mathbf{s}_t, \mathbf{y}_t^0) \in U_t(\mathbf{s}_t)$ a.s. From this and Proposition 2 it follows that

$$\max_{u \in U_t(\mathbf{s}_t)} \zeta^t(\mathbf{s}_t, \mathbf{y}_t^0, u) = \zeta^t(\mathbf{s}_t, \mathbf{y}_t^0, v_t^0(\mathbf{s}_t, \mathbf{y}_t^0)) \qquad \text{a.s.} \tag{72}$$

Further, from the relations

$$E\mathbf{p}_t^0(\mathbf{y}_t^0 - \mathbf{x}_t^0) = 0, \qquad \mathbf{x}_t^0 := a^t(\mathbf{s}_t, v_t^0(\mathbf{s}_t, \mathbf{y}_t^0))$$

and (71) it follows that

$$\boldsymbol{\lambda}_t^0(\mathbf{y}_t^0 - \mathbf{x}_t^0) = 0 \qquad \text{a.s.} \tag{73}$$

Finally, from (71) and the Markov property of the $\{(\mathbf{s}_t, \mathbf{y}_t^0)\}$ process it follows that

$$E[\boldsymbol{\psi}_t^0 | \mathbf{s}_t, \mathbf{y}_t^0] = \boldsymbol{\lambda}_t^0 \qquad \text{a.s.} \tag{74}$$

Using (71), we therefore substitute for supporting prices $\{\mathbf{p}_t^0\}$ two systems of prices $\{\boldsymbol{\psi}_t^0\}, \{\boldsymbol{\lambda}_t^0\}$ which have a simple Markov structure possessing the properties (72) and (73) and connected with each other by (74). The conditions (72) and (73) are analogous to the conditions for supporting almost surely described in §2.4.9 [cf. (2.80) and (2.81) with $\boldsymbol{\psi}_t^0$ replaced by $E[\boldsymbol{\psi}_t^0 | \mathbf{s}_t, \mathbf{y}_t]$.

We note that the value of the *prior price* ψ_t^0 is not defined, generally speaking, by the data (s_{t-1}, y_{t-1}^0) at time $t - 1$. Therefore the variables known at time t, its expectation conditional on $E[\boldsymbol{\psi}_t^0 | \mathbf{s}_t, \mathbf{y}_t^0]$ $(= \boldsymbol{\lambda}_t^0$ a.s.), should be understood as the *posterior price* of the output from the production interval $(t - 1, t]$. Thus relation (74) shows that, at an optimum, input prices λ_t^0 at the *beginning* of the period $(t, t + 1]$ must coincide a.s. with the posterior output prices at the *end* of the *previous* interval, $(t - 1, t]$.

2. The Stochastic Analogue of the Model of the Dynamic Distribution of Resources

We consider next a stochastic generalization of the model described in §1.7.4. Let $\mathbf{s}_0, \mathbf{s}_1, \ldots$ be a *Markov* process with values in a measurable space S. Suppose that the *utility* and *production functions* depend on the process $\{\mathbf{s}_t\}$ as

$$\phi^t(s_t, y_t), \qquad f^{t+1}(s_t, y_t).$$

The *dynamics* of the system are defined by the stochastic difference equation

$$y_{t+1}(\mathbf{s}^t) = y_t(\mathbf{s}^{t-1}) + u_t(\mathbf{s}_t, \mathbf{y}_t) f^{t+1}(\mathbf{s}_t, \mathbf{y}_t), \qquad t = 0, \ldots, \tau - 1, \tag{75}$$

where the sequence of measurable functions given by $u_t(s_t, y_t)$ (a *programme* of distribution of available resources) satisfies the conditions

$$\begin{gathered} \mathbf{u}_t := (\mathbf{u}_{t1}, \ldots, \mathbf{u}_{tn}) \geqq 0, \\ \sum_{i=1}^{n} u_i(\mathbf{s}_t, \mathbf{y}_t) = 1 \qquad \text{a.s.,} \quad t = 0, \ldots, \tau - 1. \end{gathered} \tag{76}$$

The initial vector $\mathbf{y}_0$ is considered to be given independently; i.e.,

$y_0(\mathbf{s}_0) := \mathbf{y}_0$ a.s. It is required to maximize the *utility functional*

$$E \sum_{t=1}^{\tau-1} \phi^t(\mathbf{s}_t, \mathbf{y}_t). \tag{77}$$

We note that the model described does not consider uncertainty in the technological process: The random parameter $\mathbf{s}_t$ on which the production function f^{t+1} depends is *known* at time t. By choosing at time t the control $u_t(s_t, y_t)$ we can define one period in advance the set of factors that will be available at the beginning of the next period. This follows from the fact that the random vectors $\mathbf{y}_t$ depend not on the complete set of parameters $\mathbf{s}^t$, but only on $\mathbf{s}^{t-1}$.

The problem of the dynamic distribution of resources (75)–(77) as formulated is a particular case of the general scheme of optimal control given by (1)–(3), (5). We suppose, for the precise formulation of the problem and the application of the maximum principle, that the functions f^{t+1} and ϕ^t satisfy the conditions imposed in §2.1.2. In addition, it is natural from the economic interpretation to consider that $f^{t+1} \geqq 0$, and $\phi^t(s, y)$ and $f^{t+1}(s, y)$ are nondecreasing with respect to y.

Let $\{\mathbf{u}_t^0\}_{t=0}^{\tau-1}$ be an optimal programme and let $\{\mathbf{y}_t^0\}_{t=0}^{\tau}$ be the corresponding trajectory. Applying the maximum principle (Theorem 3), we obtain the existence of Lagrange multipliers $\tilde{\boldsymbol{\psi}}_t^0 = \tilde{\psi}_t^0(\mathbf{s}_t, \mathbf{y}_t^0)$ corresponding to the constraint (75) for the problem (75)–(77). Defining $\boldsymbol{\psi}_t^0 := E[\tilde{\boldsymbol{\psi}}^0 | \mathbf{y}_{t-1}^0, \mathbf{s}_{t-1}]$, we obtain with the help of some simple reasoning (cf. §1.7.4) that the functions $\boldsymbol{\psi}_t^0$ (*Markov supporting prices*) possess the following properties:

(α) $u_{ti}^0(\mathbf{s}_t, \mathbf{y}_t^0) = 0$ for $f^{t+1}(\mathbf{s}_t, \mathbf{y}_t^0) > 0$ a.s., and

$$\boldsymbol{\psi}_{t+1,i}^0 < \bar{\boldsymbol{\psi}}_{t+1}^0 := \max_i \boldsymbol{\psi}_{t+1,i}^0 \qquad \text{a.s.}$$

(β)

$$\boldsymbol{\psi}_t^0 - E[\boldsymbol{\psi}_{t+1}^0 | \mathbf{y}_{t-1}^0, \mathbf{s}_{t-1}] = E[\bar{\boldsymbol{\psi}}_{t+1}^0 \mathbf{f}_y^{t+1}(\mathbf{s}_t, \mathbf{y}_t^0) - \boldsymbol{\phi}_y^t(\mathbf{s}_t, y_t^0) | \mathbf{y}_{t-1}^0, \mathbf{s}_{t-1}] \qquad \text{a.s.}$$

The interpretation of these relations is analogous to the interpretation given for the deterministic case in §1.7.4. The relations (α) show that the optimal output must be distributed a.s. amongst those factors whose value is greatest. Relation (β) equates the conditional expected value at the beginning of the tth period of the vector of optimal marginal resource value increments with the corresponding conditional expectation of the sum of the optimal vector of marginal returns and the optimal utility gradient.

COMMENTS ON CHAPTER 3

The results presented in Chapter 3 are due to Arkin.

Theorem 1 (stating the sufficiency of Markov controls) generalizes significantly the corresponding results of work by Arkin and Krechetov [3]. From Theorem 1′ it is not difficult to establish the theorem of Blackwell and Ryll-Nardzewski [1] and Strauch [1] on the sufficiency of simple strategies in Markov decision processes. For this, it is enough to notice that a decision process defined by a family of Markov transition probability functions can be represented (up to measure equivalence in the space of trajectories) as a solution of a stochastic difference equation of the form (2), where the process $\{\mathbf{s}_t\}$ is taken to be a sequence of independent random variables uniformly distributed in the interval $[0, 1]$.

The maximum principle for Markov controls (Theorem 2) was obtained earlier under more restrictive assumptions by Arkin and Krechetov [3].

A significant feature of the proof techniques used to establish the necessary and sufficient conditions for optimal Markov control by the method of dynamic programming (Theorem 4) is the absence of conditions of a topological character (continuity, compactness, etc.) such as are usually imposed on the problem.

Theorems 5 and 6 may be considered to be strengthened versions of the theorem on sufficiency of Markov controls for problems with convex structure. The description of these results follows mainly Arkin [2], who gives some generalizations of Theorems 5 and 6.

A problem of the dynamic distribution of resources similar to that described in §5 is investigated by Krechetov [1] by means of a stochastic maximum principle.

4 OPTIMAL ECONOMIC PLANNING OVER AN INFINITE HORIZON: WEAK TURNPIKE THEOREMS

1. THE STATIONARY INFINITE HORIZON MODEL

1. Preliminary Comments

In this chapter and the next (and last) we shall consider the probabilistic version of economic planning theory over an *infinite* horizon. The deterministic case was presented in Chapter 1. The basis of this study is the stochastic analogue of the Gale model described in §2.4.1.

We must modify the definition of that model in order to treat the infinite horizon case. To this end, we assume that the stochastic process $\{\mathbf{s}_t\}$ (representing the random factors influencing the economy) is given for all integers t, and at each time $t \geqq 0$ the *history*

$$s^t := (\ldots, s_{t-1}, s_t)$$

of the process up to time t is known.[1] In the space of pairs of $\mathbb{R}^n$-valued measurable functions $(x(\mathbf{s}^{t-1}), y(\mathbf{s}^t)) \geqq 0$ a.s., suppose given for each

[1] In Chapter 5 we consider the version of the model in which the history of process $\{\mathbf{s}_t\}$ starts from time 0 (or, more generally, from some time α). Such models can be reduced to the model described here in a great many instances.

$t \geqq 1$ a convex set Q_t (the *technology sets*) and a concave functional F_t defined on Q_t (the expected *utility functionals*).

Programmes, prices, supporting prices, etc. are defined analogously to those in §§2.4.1–2.4.3, the only difference being that t takes an infinite number of integer values. For example, *infinite programmes* are random infinite sequences of the form $\{(x_{t-1}(\mathbf{s}^{t-1}), y_t(\mathbf{s}^t))\}$ which satisfy the constraints $\mathbf{y}_t \geqq \mathbf{x}_t$ a.s., $(\mathbf{x}_{t-1}, \mathbf{y}_t) \in Q_t$ $(t \geqq 1)$. By analogy with the definition of §1.1.3, an infinite programme $\{\mathbf{z}_t\}$ with i.v. $\mathbf{y}_0$ is said to be *optimal* if the sequence of sums $F_1(\mathbf{z}_1) + \cdots + F_N(\mathbf{z}_N)$ overtakes the analogous sequence of sums for any other programme with i.v. $\mathbf{y}_0$.

Although the bulk of our presentation concerns the probabilistic model in functional form, we shall also need the *parametric* model which is defined for $s^t \in S^t$[2] by the entities

$$U_t(s^t), \qquad a^t(s^t, u), \qquad b^t(s^t, u), \qquad f_t(s^t, c), \tag{1}$$

which have the same meaning as in §2.4.7.

2. Definition of the Stationary Model

As for the deterministic case of Chapter 1, the theory of economic planning over an infinite horizon will be developed for the stationary stochastic model. We begin with its detailed description and some discussion.

In the stochastic case, the *stationary model* (in functional form) is defined as follows. First, the process $\{\mathbf{s}_t\}$ is assumed to be *stationary*.

This means, by definition, that for any k the distribution of the random vector

$$(\mathbf{s}_t, \mathbf{s}_{t+1}, \ldots, \mathbf{s}_{t+k})$$

does not depend on t.

Alternatively, consider the space Ω of sequences

$$(\ldots, s_{-1}, s_0, s_1, \ldots)$$

and the transformation T defined on it which transforms $\omega := \{s_t\}$ into $\omega' := \{s'_t\}$, where $s'_t := s_{t+1}$ (i.e., T is the *forward shift* operator which shifts sequences one place to the left). The stationarity of the process

[2] By S^t we designate the space of infinite sequences s^t.

$\{\mathbf{s}_t\}$ is equivalent to the requirement that the measure P induced on Ω by the process $\{\mathbf{s}_t\}$ is invariant with respect to T.[3]

The deterministic stationarity condition requiring Q_t and F_t to be independent of t becomes in the stochastic case the requirement that

$$Q_{t+1} = TQ_t, \tag{2}$$

$$F_{t+1}(Tz) = F_t(z). \tag{3}$$

We explain the meaning of these expressions. The transformation T on the space Ω induces an operator on the space of (measurable) functions on Ω which transforms $z(\omega)$ into $z(T\omega)$. We denote this operator (permitting ourselves some freedom of notation) by the same letter, T. Functions of the form $z(s_t)$, $z(s^t)$ involving the "coordinates" s_t of the process transform under the operator T to $z(s_{t+1})$, $z(s^{t+1})$. Condition (2) states that each function in Q_{t+1} with values $z(s^{t+1})$ has the form

$$(Tz')(s^t) \qquad \text{for some} \quad z' \in Q_t, \tag{4}$$

and all functions of the form (4) belong to Q_{t+1}. Condition (3) states that the functional F_{t+1} on Q_{t+1} is identical to F_t on Q_t.

It is easily seen that the operator T shifts the time scale forward one time period. With this interpretation, Conditions (2) and (3) imply that the structure of technology and utility does not change over time.

The *parametric model* is naturally termed *stationary* if the process $\{\mathbf{s}_t\}$ is stationary and the multifunction and functions in (1) given by

$$U(s^t), \qquad a(s^t, u), \qquad b(s^t, u), \qquad f(s^t, c), \tag{5}$$

do not depend explicitly on t. It is easy to see that this requirement guarantees the validity of (2) and (3).[4]

Although the assumption of stationarity is restrictive, the arguments justifying this assumption in the deterministic case (see §1.1.6) continue to hold in the stochastic case. It is also worth mentioning that many random factors which influence the economic environment (for example, meteorological factors) are usually modelled by stationary random processes.

[3] That is to say, $P(\Gamma) = P(T\Gamma) = P(T^{-1}\Gamma)$ for any measurable set $\Gamma \subseteq \Omega$.

[4] Property (3) holds since $F_t(\mathbf{z}) := Ef(\mathbf{s}^t, z(\mathbf{s}^t)) = Ef(\mathbf{s}^{t+1}, z(\mathbf{s}^{t+1})) = F_{t+1}(T\mathbf{z})$, where the second equality holds by virtue of the stationarity of the process $\{\mathbf{s}_t\}$.

Finally, analogous to the deterministic case (see §1.1.6) economic models of *stationary growth* can be reduced to stationary models. The former models are defined in terms of the latter by means of

$$\tilde{\mathbf{Q}}_t := \lambda(\mathbf{s}^0)\lambda(\mathbf{s}^1)\cdots\lambda(\mathbf{s}^{t-1})Q_t,$$

$$\tilde{F}_t(\mathbf{z}_t) := F_t(\mathbf{z}_t/\lambda(\mathbf{s}^0)\lambda(\mathbf{s}^1)\cdots\lambda(\mathbf{s}^{t-1})),$$

where Q_t, F_t define the stationary model, and $\lambda(\mathbf{s}^0), \lambda(\mathbf{s}^1), \lambda(\mathbf{s}^2), \ldots$ $[\lambda(\cdot) > 0]$ is the stationary stochastic process of expansion coefficients. (Recall that the random histories $\mathbf{s}^t$ are infinite sequences.)

3. Stationary Programmes and Prices

A programme $\{\mathbf{z}_t\}$ is said to be *stationary* if

$$\mathbf{z}_{t+1} = T\mathbf{z}_t. \tag{6}$$

This may be formulated alternatively as follows: The current state $z_t(\mathbf{s}^t)$ does not depend directly on t; i.e., $\mathbf{z}_t = z(\mathbf{s}^t)$. This means that the programme $\{\mathbf{z}_t\}$ directs the same action in the same circumstances, independent of the time period.

A programme $\{\mathbf{z}_t\} = \{(\mathbf{x}_{t-1}, \mathbf{y}_t)\}$ is stationary if and only if

$$\mathbf{z}_t = T^{t-1}\mathbf{z}_1, \tag{7}$$

where $\mathbf{z}_1 := (\mathbf{x}_0, \mathbf{y}_1)$ satisfies the following conditions:

$$\mathbf{z}_1 \in Q_1, \tag{8}$$

$$\mathbf{y}_1 \geqq T\mathbf{x}_0 \qquad \text{a.s.} \tag{9}$$

Indeed, these conditions are necessary, since (8) is the technological constraint for $\{\mathbf{z}_t\}$ at $t = 1$, and (9), in view of (6), may be written $\mathbf{y}_1 \geqq \mathbf{x}_1$ a.s. (the resource restriction in period 1). The implication in the other direction is easily seen to hold by applying T^{t-1} to both sides of (8) and (9).

Note that $\mathbf{y}_0 := T^{-1}\mathbf{y}_1$ is an initial vector for the programme (7). In the sequel, with each stationary programme of the form (7) an i.v. $T^{-1}\mathbf{y}_1$ will be associated. (This convention is convenient in treating supporting prices.)

We shall say that *generalized prices* $\{\pi_t\}$ are *stationary* if $\pi_{t+1}(T\mathbf{x}) = \pi_t(\mathbf{x})$ for any function $\mathbf{x} \in L_\infty(S^t)$. *Ordinary prices* (i.e., prices of integral type) $\{p_t(\mathbf{s}^t)\}$ are *stationary* if $p_t(\mathbf{s}^t)$ does not depend directly on t, i.e., if $p_t(\mathbf{s}^t) := p(\mathbf{s}^t)$ or, in other words, $\mathbf{p}_{t+1} = T\mathbf{p}_t$.

4. Assumptions for Stationary Models

As in §2.4.1, we shall assume that replacement of $(x(\mathbf{s}^{t-1}), y(\mathbf{s}^t)) \in Q_t$ by an equivalent (with respect to the given probability measure) pair of functions does not affect membership of Q_t or change the value of F_t. Furthermore, one or other of the conditions (I)–(VII) of §§2.2.2–2.2.5 will be introduced as necessary. Although these conditions were previously concerned only with a finite collection of Q_t and F_t, now t will run through the positive integers. Otherwise, with the exception of Condition (IV), their formulations remain unaltered.

For stationary models, we shall assume in addition that the programme $\tilde{\zeta}$ appearing in Condition (IV) is stationary.

Similarly, conditions (M_1)–(M_9), defined in §§2.4.7–2.4.8 for the parametric model, apply *mutatis mutandis* to the stationary parametric model over an infinite horizon.

2. THE TURNPIKE AND ITS SUPPORTING PRICES

1. The Existence of Turnpike Programmes

In the sequel we shall assume that

Conditions (I) *and* (II) *of* §2.4.2 *hold for all t.*

If the programme $\{\mathbf{z}_t\}$ is stationary, then the value $F_t(\mathbf{z}_t)$ does not depend on t. A (stationary) programme which maximizes this value is called a *turnpike programme* (or simply a *turnpike*). We emphasize that the maximum is taken here with respect to all possible stationary programmes (i.e., the initial vector is not considered to be fixed).

In general, several turnpike programmes may exist; however, conditions which guarantee the uniqueness of the turnpike (up to, of course, equivalence with respect to the probability measure P) will as a rule be applied below.

Theorem 1. (Existence of turnpikes.) *Under Conditions* (I) *and* (II), *a turnpike programme exists.*

□ We must show that $F_1(\mathbf{z}_1)$ achieves a maximum on the subset Q of the product space $L_1(S^0) \times L_1(S^1)$ defined by the constraints (8) and (9).

We use Komlós's theorem (Theorem III.5). To apply this result, it is sufficient to check that the constraint (9) holds a.s. in the almost sure limit; the remainder of its conditions are guaranteed by the hypotheses (I) and (II). To this end let $\mathbf{x}_0^k \to \mathbf{x}_0, \mathbf{y}_1^k \to \mathbf{y}_1$ a.s. and suppose $\mathbf{y}_1^k \geqq T\mathbf{x}_0^k$. Then $T\mathbf{x}_0^k \to T\mathbf{x}_0$ a.s. since T preserves the measure P. Hence $\mathbf{y}_1 \geqq T\mathbf{x}_0$ a.s., since the corresponding inequality holds a.s. for each k.[5] □

2. Stationary Generalized Prices Supporting the Turnpike

From now on we also assume that conditions (III) and (IV) hold.

Theorem 2. (Existence of stationary generalized supporting prices.) *Under conditions* (I)–(IV) *there exist stationary generalized prices supporting the family of turnpike programmes.*

□ We prove this result by means of two lemmas.

Lemma 1. *There exists a functional* $\bar{\pi}_1 \geqq 0$ *in the space* $L_\infty^*(S^1; \mathbb{R}^n)$ *such that*

$$F_1(\mathbf{z}_1) + \bar{\pi}_1(\mathbf{y}_1 - T\mathbf{x}_0) \leqq \bar{F}_1, \tag{10}$$

where $\bar{F}_1 := F_1(\bar{\mathbf{z}}_1)$ *denotes the maximum of* F_1 *subject to the constraints* (8) *and* (9), *and* $\mathbf{z}_1 = (\mathbf{x}_0, \mathbf{y}_1)$ *is an arbitrary function in* Q_1 *(treated here as a random vector).*

□ Consider the problem of maximizing the functional F_1 subject to

$$\mathbf{z}_1 = (\mathbf{x}_0, \mathbf{y}_1) \in Q_1,$$

satisfying the constraint (9). Functions in Q_1 will be treated as elements

[5] This argument is easily made precise by the consideration of appropriate P-null sets.

of the space

$$H := L_\infty(S^0; \mathbb{R}^n) \times L_\infty(S^1; \mathbb{R}^n).$$

[This is possible by Condition (III).] The constraint (9) may be rewritten

$$g(\mathbf{z}_1) \geqq 0,$$

where the linear map

$$g: H \to L_\infty(S^1; \mathbb{R}^n)$$

is defined by the formula

$$g(\mathbf{z}_1) := g(\mathbf{x}_0, \mathbf{y}_1) := \mathbf{y}_1 - T\mathbf{x}_0.^6 \tag{11}$$

By Condition (IV) there exists a function $\tilde{\mathbf{z}}_1 \in Q_1$ such that

$$g(\tilde{\mathbf{z}}_1) \geqq \delta 1 > 0;$$

i.e., $g(\tilde{\mathbf{z}}_1)$ belongs to the interior of the nonnegative cone in the space $L_\infty(S^1; \mathbb{R}^n)$. It follows that we may apply the Kuhn–Tucker theorem (see §III.2); consequently there exists a nonnegative functional $\bar{\pi}_1 \in L^*_\infty(S^t; \mathbb{R}^n)$ satisfying (10). ☐

Now define

$$\bar{\pi}_t(x) := \bar{\pi}_1(T^{-t+1}x) \tag{12}$$

for arbitrary $x \in L_\infty(S^t; \mathbb{R}^n)$, $t = 0, 1, 2, \ldots$. Theorem 2 follows immediately from the following lemma:

Lemma 2. *Condition* (10) *is necessary and sufficient for the prices given by* (12) *to support the family of turnpike programmes.*

☐ ⇐☐ To prove sufficiency, we take any turnpike programme

$$\{\bar{\mathbf{z}}_t\} := \{T^{t-1}\bar{\mathbf{z}}_1\}$$

and set $\mathbf{z}_1 := \bar{\mathbf{z}}_1$ in the left-hand side of (10). Then

$$\bar{\pi}_1(\bar{\mathbf{y}}_1 - T\bar{\mathbf{x}}_0) = 0, \tag{13}$$

and thus $\bar{\pi}_1(\bar{\mathbf{y}}_1 - \bar{\mathbf{x}}_1) = 0$ since $\bar{\mathbf{x}}_1 = T\bar{\mathbf{x}}_0$. Therefore Condition B of

[6] This formula does indeed specify a well defined mapping of H into $L_\infty(S^1; \mathbb{R}^n)$, since the equivalence class of functions (with respect to the measure P) defined by $(\mathbf{x}_0, \mathbf{y}_1)$ is mapped by g to the equivalence class of the image $\mathbf{y}_1 - T\mathbf{x}_0$. This follows from the fact that T preserves the measure P.

the definition of supporting prices holds. Moreover, from (10) and (13),

$$F_1(\mathbf{z}_1) + \bar{\pi}_1(\mathbf{y}_1) - \bar{\pi}_1(T\mathbf{x}_0) \leqq F_1(\bar{\mathbf{z}}_1) + \bar{\pi}_1(\bar{\mathbf{y}}_1) - \bar{\pi}_1(T\bar{\mathbf{x}}_0).$$

This is equivalent to the inequality

$$F_1(\mathbf{z}_1) + \bar{\pi}_1(\mathbf{y}_1) - \bar{\pi}_0(\mathbf{x}_0) \leqq F_1(\bar{\mathbf{z}}_1) + \bar{\pi}_1(\bar{\mathbf{y}}_1) - \bar{\pi}_0(\bar{\mathbf{x}}_0) \tag{14}$$

as a consequence of (12). Furthermore,

$$F_t(T^{t-1}\mathbf{z}_1) + \bar{\pi}_t(T^{t-1}\mathbf{y}_1) - \bar{\pi}_{t-1}(T^{t-1}\mathbf{x}_0)$$
$$\leqq F_t(T^{t-1}\bar{\mathbf{z}}_1) + \bar{\pi}_t(T^{t-1}\bar{\mathbf{y}}_1) - \bar{\pi}_{t-1}(T^{t-1}\bar{\mathbf{x}}_0).$$

Here $\mathbf{z}_1$ takes values in the set Q_1, and thus $T^{t-1}\mathbf{z}_1$ takes values in the set Q_t by the stationarity condition for the model. From this we may conclude that Condition A of the definition of supporting prices holds. □

⇒□ By the definition of support, both the inequality (14) and the equation $\bar{\pi}_1(\bar{\mathbf{y}}_1 - \bar{\mathbf{x}}_1) = 0$ hold. It follows, using $\bar{\pi}_0(\mathbf{x}_0) = \bar{\pi}_1(T\mathbf{x}_0)$, that

$$\bar{\pi}_1(\bar{\mathbf{y}}_1) = \bar{\pi}_1(\bar{\mathbf{x}}_1) = \bar{\pi}_1(T\bar{\mathbf{x}}_0) = \bar{\pi}_0(\bar{\mathbf{x}}_0),$$

and hence (14) implies that (10) holds, as required. □□□

3. Stationary Prices Supporting the Turnpike

Now suppose that, in addition to (I)–(IV), Conditions (V)–(VII) hold.

Theorem 3. (Existence of stationary supporting prices.) *Under Conditions* (I)–(VII) *there exist stationary prices of integral type supporting the family of turnpike programmes.*

□ Suppose that

$$\{\pi_t(\mathbf{x})\} = \{\pi_1(T^{t-1}\mathbf{x})\}$$

are stationary generalized prices supporting the turnpike. Then inequality (10) holds. We shall show that when the functional $\bar{\pi}_1$ satisfies (10) its absolutely continuous component $\bar{\pi}_1^a$, such that for $x \in L_\infty(S^1; \mathbb{R}^n)$

$$\bar{\pi}_1^a(\mathbf{x}) = E\mathbf{p}_1\mathbf{x},$$

also satisfies this inequality. Then, by Lemma 2, the prices

$$\{\bar{\mathbf{p}}_t\} = \{T^{t-1}\bar{\mathbf{p}}_1\}$$

support the family of turnpike programmes, as required.

Therefore, consider an arbitrary $\mathbf{z}_1 \in Q_1$. We expand $\bar{\pi}_1$ as the sum $\bar{\pi}_1^a + \bar{\pi}_1^s$ and consider the sets $\Gamma_k \subseteqq S^1$ on which the singular functional $\bar{\pi}_1^s$ is concentrated (see §III.6). Let

$$\mathbf{z}_1^k := (\mathbf{x}_0^k, \mathbf{y}_1^k) = \boldsymbol{\theta}_k \mathbf{z}_1,$$

where

$$\boldsymbol{\theta}_k := T^{-1}(1 - \mathbf{1}_{\Gamma_k}).$$

Since $\mathbf{1}_{\Gamma_k}$ is a measurable function of s^1, $\boldsymbol{\theta}_k$ is a measurable function of s^0 taking values 0 and 1, and it follows by Condition (VII) that $\mathbf{z}_1^k \in Q_1$ for any k. Therefore, we may put $\mathbf{z}_1^k$ in (10) to yield

$$F_1(\mathbf{z}_1^k) + \bar{\pi}_1^a(\mathbf{y}_1^k - T\mathbf{x}_0^k) + \bar{\pi}_1^s(\mathbf{y}_1^k - T\mathbf{x}_0^k) \leqq \bar{F}_1.$$

In this inequality $\bar{\pi}_1^s(\mathbf{y}_1^k) \geqq 0$ since $\bar{\pi}_1^s \geqq 0$ and $\mathbf{y}_1^k \geqq 0$. Furthermore,

$$\bar{\pi}_1^s(T\mathbf{x}_0^k) = \pi_1^s([(1 - \mathbf{1}_{\Gamma_k})\mathbf{x}_0]) = 0,$$

since the function in square brackets is zero on Γ_k. Therefore

$$F_1(\mathbf{z}_1^k) + \bar{\pi}_1^a(\mathbf{y}_1^k - T\mathbf{x}_0^k) \leqq \bar{F}_1.$$

Passing to the limit in this inequality as $k \to \infty$, we obtain (10) with $\bar{\pi}_1^a$ replacing $\bar{\pi}_1$. Indeed, $F_1(\mathbf{z}_1^k) \to F_1(\mathbf{z}_1)$ by (VI). Moreover,

$$\mathbf{x}_0^k \to \mathbf{x}_0, \quad \mathbf{y}_1^k \to \mathbf{y}_1, \qquad \text{a.s.},$$

and therefore $T\mathbf{x}_0^k \to T\mathbf{x}_0$ a.s. Finally, since $\bar{\pi}_1^a$ is a functional of integral type,

$$\bar{\pi}_1^a(\mathbf{y}_1^k - T\mathbf{x}_0^k) \to \bar{\pi}_1^a(\mathbf{y}_1 - T\mathbf{x}_0)$$

using (I) and the Lebesque dominated convergence theorem. □

3. UNIFORM STRICT CONCAVITY AND UNIFORM CONTINUITY CONDITIONS FOR UTILITY FUNCTIONALS[7]

1. Definition of Concavity Conditions

Conditions of uniform strict concavity for utility functionals play an important rôle in the proof of stochastic turnpike theorems. Here we study two such conditions and show that a sufficiently wide class of functionals satisfies them.

Let $(\Omega, \mathscr{F}, P)$ be a probability space, let Q be a convex set in the space

$$D := L_\infty(\Omega, \mathscr{F}, P; \mathbb{R}^m),$$

norm bounded by some constant C, and let F be a real-valued concave functional on Q. For $z, z' \in Q$ define

$$F(\mathbf{z}, \mathbf{z}') := F(\tfrac{1}{2}(\mathbf{z} + \mathbf{z}')) - \tfrac{1}{2}[F(\mathbf{z}) + F(\mathbf{z}')], \tag{15}$$

where $\mathbf{z}$ and $\mathbf{z}'$ are interpreted as random vectors. Consider the following two conditions:

(F.1) *For any* $\epsilon > 0$ *there exists a* $\delta_1 := \delta_1(\epsilon) > 0$ *such that, for* $\mathbf{z}, \mathbf{z}' \in Q$ *for which* $E|\mathbf{z} - \mathbf{z}'| \geqq \epsilon$, $F(\mathbf{z}, \mathbf{z}') \geqq \delta_1$.
(F.2) *For any* $\epsilon > 0$ *there exists a* $\delta_2 := \delta_2(\epsilon) > 0$ *such that for any* $\mathbf{z}, \mathbf{z}' \in Q$, $F(\mathbf{z}, \mathbf{z}') \geqq \delta_2 P\{|\mathbf{z} - \mathbf{z}'| \geqq \epsilon\}$.

In these conditions $|\cdot|$ denotes some fixed norm on $\mathbb{R}^m$.

We note in (F.1) that the function given by $\delta_1(\epsilon)$ may be taken as monotone nondecreasing (by replacing δ_1 by $\sup\{\delta_1(\epsilon') : 0 < \epsilon' \leqq \epsilon\}$). Therefore (F.1) may be restated as follows:

(F.1′) *There exists a nondecreasing function of* $\epsilon \geqq 0$ *given by* $\delta_1(\epsilon) \geqq 0$ *such that* $\delta_1(\epsilon) > 0$ *for* $\epsilon > 0$ *and*

$$F(\mathbf{z}, \mathbf{z}') \geqq \delta_1(E|\mathbf{z} - \mathbf{z}'|).$$

Lemma 3. (F.2) *implies* (F.1).

□ For $\epsilon > 0$ and any random variable ξ such that $|\xi| \leqq C$ a.s., we

[7] This section has a supplementary character. At first reading, it is only necessary to take note of the formulation of conditions and the statements of results.

have the inequality[8]

$$P\{|\xi| \geqq \epsilon\} \geqq (E|\xi| - \epsilon)/C. \tag{16}$$

Setting $\xi := |\mathbf{z} - \mathbf{z}'|$, we have that

$$F(\mathbf{z}, \mathbf{z}') \geqq \delta_2(\epsilon/2)P\{|\mathbf{z} - \mathbf{z}'| \geqq \epsilon/2\} \geqq \delta_2(\epsilon/2)[E|\mathbf{z} - \mathbf{z}'| - \epsilon/2]/C.$$

It follows that if $E|\mathbf{z} - \mathbf{z}'| \geqq \epsilon$,

$$F(\mathbf{z}, \mathbf{z}') \geqq \delta_2(\epsilon/2)(\epsilon/2C) := \delta_1(\epsilon). \quad \square$$

Lemma 4. *Let l be an arbitary (not necessarily continuous) linear functional on D. A functional F possesses the property* (F.1) [*resp.* (F.2)] *if and only if $\hat{F} := F + l$ possesses the property* (F.1) [*resp.* (F.2)].

□ The proof is obvious from the fact that $\hat{F}(\mathbf{z}, \mathbf{z}') = F(\mathbf{z}, \mathbf{z}')$. □

2. Integral Functionals Possessing Properties (F.1) and (F.2)

Let f be a real-valued function of $\omega \in \Omega$ and $a \in A(\omega)$, where $A(\omega)$ is a convex subset of $\mathbb{R}^m$ such that, for all $\mathbf{z} \in Q$, $\mathbf{z}(\boldsymbol{\omega}) \in A(\boldsymbol{\omega})$ a.s. Suppose that $f(\omega, a)$ is concave with respect to a on $A(\omega)$ and there exists a summable (i.e., finitely integrable) real-valued function $q(\omega)$ for which for $a \in A(\omega)$

$$|f(\omega, a)| \leqq q(\omega). \tag{17}$$

Suppose also that the function given by $\Phi(\omega, a)$, which is equal to ∞ outside $A(\omega)$ and to $f(\omega, a)$ on $A(\omega)$, is (jointly) measurable with respect to (ω, a). Then a concave functional can be defined on Q by the following formula:

$$F(\mathbf{z}) := Ef(\boldsymbol{\omega}, z(\boldsymbol{\omega})). \tag{18}$$

Now we give some examples of integral functionals of the form of (18) possessing the properties (F.1) and (F.2). For this purpose consider the following conditions:

(f.1) *There exists a real-valued function given by $\kappa_1(\omega, \epsilon) \geqq 0$ which is nondecreasing in ϵ and measurable in ω (with respect to the*

[8] Its proof is obtained by considering $E|\xi| = E|\xi|\mathbf{I}_\Delta + E|\xi|(1 - \mathbf{I}_\Delta) \leqq CP(\Delta) + \epsilon$, where $\Delta := \{\omega : |\xi(\omega)| \geqq \epsilon\}$.

σ-algebra $\mathscr{F}$ or its completion) such that for each ω, $\kappa_1(\omega, \epsilon) > 0$ if $\epsilon > 0$ and

$$f(\omega, a, a') \geqq \kappa_1(\omega, |a - a'|)$$

for all $a, a' \in A(\omega)$.

[Here $f(\omega, a, a')$ is defined from f analogously to (15).]

(f.2) *There exists a nondecreasing function given by $\kappa_2(\epsilon) \geqq 0$ (independent of ω) such that $\kappa_2(\epsilon) > 0$ for $\epsilon > 0$ and for each ω*

$$f(\omega, a, a') \geqq \kappa_2(|a - a'|)$$

for all $a, a' \in A(\omega)$.

Lemma 5. *If f possesses Property* (f.1) [*resp.* (f.2)], *then the functional F defined on Q by* (18) *satisfies Condition* (F.1) [*resp.* (F.2)].

□ We show first that (F.1) follows from (f.1).

□ For $\mathbf{z}, \mathbf{z}' \in Q$ we have that

$$F(\mathbf{z}, \mathbf{z}') = Ef(\boldsymbol{\omega}, z(\boldsymbol{\omega}), z'(\boldsymbol{\omega}))$$

and

$$f(\boldsymbol{\omega}, z(\boldsymbol{\omega}), z'(\boldsymbol{\omega})) \geqq \kappa_1(\boldsymbol{\omega}, \xi(\boldsymbol{\omega})) \qquad \text{a.s.,} \tag{19}$$

where $\xi(\omega) := |z(\omega) - z'(\omega)|$.

Choose $\mathbf{z}, \mathbf{z}' \in Q$ such that $E\boldsymbol{\xi} \geqq 2\epsilon > 0$. Then for $\Delta := \{\boldsymbol{\xi} \geqq \epsilon\}$ the inequality $P(\Delta) \geqq \epsilon/2C := \gamma$ holds. This follows from (16) using the fact that $|\mathbf{z}| \leqq C$ a.s. Hence, estimating the right-hand side of (19), it follows that

$$F(z, z') \geqq E1_\Delta(\boldsymbol{\omega})\kappa_1(\boldsymbol{\omega}, \epsilon). \tag{20}$$

Now the infimum of the right-hand side of (20) with respect to Δ, for which $P(\Delta) \geqq \gamma$, is bounded below by some positive value $\delta_1(\epsilon)$. Indeed, since the random variable $\kappa_1(\boldsymbol{\omega}, \epsilon)$ is a.s. positive, we may choose a $\sigma := \sigma(\epsilon) > 0$ to ensure for $\Gamma := \{\kappa_1 \geqq \sigma\}$ that $P(\Gamma) \geqq 1 - \gamma/2$. Then, for any event Δ such that $P(\Delta) \geqq \gamma$, we have

$$E1_\Delta(\boldsymbol{\omega})\kappa_1(\boldsymbol{\omega}, \epsilon) \geqq \sigma P(\Delta \cap \Gamma) \geqq \sigma[P(\Delta) + P(\Gamma) - 1]$$
$$\geqq \sigma[\gamma/2] = \sigma(\epsilon)\epsilon/4C := \delta_1(\epsilon).$$

Combining this inequality with (20) yields the required bound on F. □

Now we prove that (f.2) implies (F.2).

□ This follows from the chain of inequalities

$$F(z, z') \geqq E\kappa_2(|z(\boldsymbol{\omega}) - z'(\boldsymbol{\omega})|) \geqq E1_\Delta(\boldsymbol{\omega})\kappa_2(\epsilon) = \kappa_2(\epsilon)P(\Delta),$$

where $\Delta := \{|\mathbf{z} - \mathbf{z}'| \geqq \epsilon\}$. □□

Remark. *It is easy to see that* (f.1) *holds if the function given by* $f(\omega, a)$ *is continuous and strictly concave with respect to* a *on the compact set* $A(\omega)$.

□ In this case, the minimum of the positive function $f(\omega, a, a')$ over the compact

$$K_\epsilon(\omega) := \{(a, a'): a \in A(\omega),\ a' \in A(\omega),\ |a - a'| \geqq \epsilon\}$$

is achieved, and is therefore positive—in fact, equal to $\kappa_1(\omega, \epsilon)$. To see that the function given by $\kappa_1(\omega, \epsilon)$ is $\bar{\mathscr{F}}$-measurable with respect to ω, note that

$$\kappa_1(\omega, \epsilon) = \inf_i f(\omega, a_i(\omega), a_i'(\omega)),$$

where $\{(a_i(\omega), a_i'(\omega))\}$ is a countable family of selectors approximating the random set $\mathbf{K}_\epsilon$ (see Corollary I.2). □

3. Nonintegral Functionals Possessing Properties (F.1) and (F.2)

We mention one more construction yielding functionals possessing Properties (F.1) and (F.2). We begin with a particular case.

Let $F_1, \ldots, F_k$ be functionals satisfying (F.1) [resp. (F.2)], and let $d_1, \ldots, d_k$ be positive real numbers. Obviously, $d_1F_1 + \cdots + d_kF_k$ satisfies (F.1) [resp. (F.2)]. This comment may be generalized in the following way.

Let a real-valued concave function given by $g(r) := g(r_1, \ldots, r_k)$ be defined on a convex subset R of $\mathbb{R}^k$ containing all values in the range of the function Ψ given by

$$\Psi(\mathbf{z}) := (F_1(\mathbf{z}), \ldots, F_k(\mathbf{z})), \qquad \mathbf{z} \in Q.$$

Suppose that $g(r)$ is *strictly monotone* in the following sense. There exists a nonzero nonnegative vector ξ such that

$$g(r + r') - g(r) \geqq \xi r'$$

for $r, r + r' \in R$, $r' \geqq 0$.

Lemma 6. *If $F_1, F_2, \ldots, F_k$ are functionals possessing Property (F.1) [or (F.2)], then the functional given by $F(\mathbf{z}) := g(\Psi(\mathbf{z}))$, where g and Ψ are as defined above, possesses the same property.*

□ The lemma follows from the chain of relations

$$\begin{aligned} F(\mathbf{z}, \mathbf{z}') &= g(\Psi(\tfrac{1}{2}(\mathbf{z} + \mathbf{z}'))) - \tfrac{1}{2}[g(\Psi(\mathbf{z})) + g(\Psi(\mathbf{z}'))] \\ &= g(\tfrac{1}{2}[\Psi(\mathbf{z}) + \Psi(\mathbf{z}')] + \Psi(\mathbf{z}, \mathbf{z}')) - \tfrac{1}{2}[g(\Psi(\mathbf{z})) + g(\Psi(\mathbf{z}'))] \\ &\geqq g(\tfrac{1}{2}(\Psi(\mathbf{z}) + \Psi(\mathbf{z}')) + \xi\Psi(\mathbf{z}, \mathbf{z}') - \tfrac{1}{2}[g(\Psi(\mathbf{z})) + g(\Psi(\mathbf{z}'))] \\ &\geqq \xi\Psi(\mathbf{z}, \mathbf{z}'), \end{aligned}$$

where the first inequality is true by the monotonicity of g and the second by concavity. □

4. Uniform Continuity Conditions

Consider the integral functional F defined from the function given by $f(\omega, a)$ by means of (18). Suppose that $f(\omega, a)$ is continuous in a on $A(\omega)$, a compact set for each ω. Then we have the following result:

Lemma 7. *The functional F defined above is uniformly continuous (in the L_1 norm topology) and bounded on the set Q.*

□ Uniform continuity means here that

$$W(\beta) := \sup\{|F(\mathbf{z}) - F(\mathbf{z}')| : \mathbf{z}, \mathbf{z}' \in Q,\ E|\mathbf{z} - \mathbf{z}'| < \beta\} \to 0$$

as $\beta \to 0$.

Assume the contrary. Then there exist sequences $\{\mathbf{z}_k\}$ and $\{\mathbf{z}'_k\}$ in Q such that

$$E|\mathbf{z}_k - \mathbf{z}'_k| \to 0 \qquad \text{and} \qquad |F(\mathbf{z}_k) - F(\mathbf{z}'_k)| \geqq \kappa > 0.$$

Since $\mathbf{z}_k - \mathbf{z}'_k \to 0$ in L^1, we choose a subsequence $\{k_m\}$ such that $|\mathbf{z}_{k_m} - \mathbf{z}'_{k_m}| \to 0$ a.s. Then $f(\boldsymbol{\omega}, \mathbf{z}_{k_m}) - f(\boldsymbol{\omega}, \mathbf{z}'_{k_m}) \to 0$ a.s., since $f(\omega, \cdot)$

is uniformly continuous on $A(\omega)$. It follows, using (17) and the Lebesque dominated convergence theorem, that

$$F(\mathbf{z}_{k_m}) - F(\mathbf{z}'_{k_m}) = E[f(\boldsymbol{\omega}, \mathbf{z}_{k_m}) - f(\omega, \mathbf{z}'_{k_m})] \to 0,$$

which is a contradiction.

The boundedness of F is obvious from (17). □

In summary, if the function given by $f(\omega, a)$ is continuous, the set $A(\omega)$ is compact and Condition (f.1) or (f.2) holds, then the integral functional (18) is uniformly continuous and bounded and satisfies the corresponding condition (F.1) or (F.2). Taking a set $F_1, \ldots, F_k$ of such functionals satisfying one or other of these strict concavity conditions and setting

$$F(\mathbf{z}) = g(F_1(\mathbf{z}), \ldots, F_k(\mathbf{z})),$$

where g is a uniformly continuous, strictly monotone and concave function, we obtain a uniformly continuous bounded functional satisfying the corresponding strict concavity condition. Thus we have demonstrated a sufficiently wide class of functionals (not all of integral type) possessing the required properties.

4. WEAK TURNPIKE THEOREMS

1. Preliminary Comments

The content of this section follows the scheme of presentation of §§1.3 and 1.4. We assume in the remainder of this chapter that Conditions (I)–(V) (see §§2.4–2.5) hold. In addition, we shall assume the following condition.

(VIII) *The functionals F_t satisfy the uniform strict concavity condition* (F.1).

It is easy to see by the stationarity of the model that if one of the functionals F_t possesses the strict concavity property (F.1) [or (F.2)], then all the others possess the property and with the same function δ_1 (*or* δ_2).

We consider equivalent programmes $\{\mathbf{z}_t\}$ and $\{\mathbf{z}'_t\}$ such that $\mathbf{z}_t = \mathbf{z}'_t$ a.s. for all t (i.e., programmes which are equivalent with respect to the measure P). With this convention it is obvious that Condition

(VIII) guarantees the *uniqueness* of the turnpike, since there exists a single element $\bar{z} \in L_1$ which maximizes F_1 subject to the constraints (8) and (9). We fix any member of the class of equivalent turnpikes and designate it by $\bar{\zeta} := \{\bar{\mathbf{z}}_t\}$.

Let $\mathbf{y}_0 \in D_0$ be a nonnegative random vector.[9] We say that the vector $\mathbf{y}_0$ is *sufficient* if there exists a finite programme

$$\{(\mathbf{x}_0, \mathbf{y}_1), \ldots, (\mathbf{x}_{j-1}, \mathbf{y}_j)\}$$

with i.v. $\mathbf{y}_0$ and a nonrandom positive vector $\delta 1$ such that $\mathbf{y}_j \geqq \delta 1$ a.s.[10] In the following theorem $\mathbf{y}_0$ is assumed sufficient.

We let $\{\mathbf{z}_t^N\}$ denote an optimal programme of length N with i.v. $\mathbf{y}_0$.

2. Statement and Discussion of Results

Theorem 4. (Weak turnpike theorem.) *Under assumptions* (I)–(V) *and* (VIII) *we have the following:*

(a) *Let $t_N(\epsilon)$ be the number of time periods t, $1 \leqq t \leqq N$, for which*

$$E|\mathbf{z}_t^N - \bar{\mathbf{z}}_t| \geqq \epsilon.$$

Then, for any $\epsilon > 0$, the sequence $t_N(\epsilon)$ is bounded above.

(b) *Let $\boldsymbol{\theta}_N(\epsilon)$ denote the number of time periods t, $1 \leqq t \leqq N$, for which*

$$|\mathbf{z}_t^N - \bar{\mathbf{z}}_t| \geqq \epsilon \qquad a.s.$$

Then, if in addition the functionals F_t possess the property (F.2), *for each $\epsilon > 0$ the sequence $E\boldsymbol{\theta}_N(\epsilon)$ is bounded above.* □

This theorem contains two statements expressing the fact that optimal programmes stay near the turnpike most of the time. Indeed, from (a) it follows that $t_N/N \to 0$; i.e., the fraction of the time that the optimal programme $\{\mathbf{z}_t^N\}$ differs from the turnpike by more than ϵ in the metric $E|\mathbf{z}_t^N - \bar{\mathbf{z}}_t|$ tends to 0 as $N \to \infty$. Analogously, the boundedness of $E\boldsymbol{\theta}_N$ implies that $E(\boldsymbol{\theta}_N/N) \to 0$ as $N \to \infty$; i.e., the expected fraction of the time that the optimal programme $\{\mathbf{z}_t^N\}$ lies outside of the ϵ-neighbourhood of the turnpike tends to 0 as $N \to \infty$.

[9] Recall the notation $D_t := L_\infty^n(S^t)$ and the interpretation of elements of Lebesque function spaces over a probability space as random vectors.

[10] In this case we say the function given by $y_j(s^j)$ is *uniformly positive.*

We note that if $E\boldsymbol{\theta}_N(\epsilon)$ is bounded for each $\epsilon > 0$, then $t_N(\epsilon)$ is bounded for each $\epsilon > 0$.

□ This fact is immediate from the bound

$$E\boldsymbol{\theta}_N(\epsilon/2) \geqq \epsilon t_N(\epsilon)/4C,$$

where C is the constant from Condition (III).

To establish this estimate, note that

$$\boldsymbol{\theta}_N(\epsilon/2) = \sum_{t=1}^{N} 1_{\{\gamma_t^N \geqq \epsilon/2\}}, \tag{21}$$

where $\gamma_t^N := |\mathbf{z}_t^N - \bar{\mathbf{z}}_t|$. Thus

$$E\boldsymbol{\theta}_N(\epsilon/2) = \sum_{t=1}^{N} P\{\gamma_t^N \geqq \epsilon/2\}. \tag{22}$$

Consider in the right-hand-side summation only those items for which $E\gamma_t^N \geqq \epsilon$. For such t [they are $t_N(\epsilon)$ in number by definition] by the inequality (16), we have

$$P\{\gamma_t^N \geqq \epsilon/2\} \geqq \frac{(E\gamma_t^N - \epsilon/2)}{2C} \geqq \frac{\epsilon}{4C},$$

where C is the constant from (III). Combining this with (22) we obtain the necessary bound. □

In the stochastic case, therefore, at least two natural versions of the weak turnpike theorem appear. Note that in version (b) we use a stronger uniform strict concavity condition than in version (a) (cf. Lemma 3).

We make one more comment: In the formulation of Theorem 4, the L_1 norm

$$\|\mathbf{z}_t^N - \bar{\mathbf{z}}_t\|_1 := E|\mathbf{z}_t^N - \bar{\mathbf{z}}_t|$$

can be replaced by any L_p norm ($p \in [1, \infty)$)

$$\|\mathbf{z}_t^N - \bar{\mathbf{z}}_t\|_p := (E|\mathbf{z}_t^N - \bar{\mathbf{z}}_t|^p)^{1/p},$$

or by the value

$$P\{|\mathbf{z}_t^N - \bar{\mathbf{z}}_t| \geqq \beta\},$$

where β is a fixed positive number.

The statement regarding $\|\cdot\|_p$ follows easily from the fact that all random values $|\mathbf{z}_t^N - \bar{\mathbf{z}}_t|$ are bounded by the same constant $2C$. The second statement follows immediately from the Chebyshev inequality:

$$P\{|\mathbf{z}_t^N - \bar{\mathbf{z}}_t| \geqq \beta\} \leqq E|\mathbf{z}_t^N - \bar{\mathbf{z}}_t|/\beta.$$

Finally, we note that, analogous to the deterministic case, Theorem 4 is valid not only for optimal programmes but, more generally, for any *good family* of programmes.

Theorem 5. (The weak turnpike theorem for a good family.) *The statement of Theorem 4 is valid for any family of programmes* $\{\mathbf{z}_t^N\}_{t=1}^N$, $N = 1, 2, \ldots$, *such that the sums*

$$\sum_{t=1}^{N} [F_t(\bar{\mathbf{z}}_t) - F_t(\mathbf{z}_t^N)] \tag{23}$$

are bounded. □

3. Proof of Theorems 4 and 5

By the assumptions at the beginning of this section and Theorem 2, there exist stationary generalized prices $\{\bar{\pi}_t\}$ supporting $\bar{\zeta}$. Consider the *reduced utility*

$$G_t(\mathbf{x}, \mathbf{y}) := F_t(\mathbf{x}, \mathbf{y}) + \bar{\pi}_t(\mathbf{y}) - \bar{\pi}_{t-1}(\mathbf{x})$$

corresponding to these prices and define a pseudometric on Q_t by

$$\rho_t(\mathbf{z}, \mathbf{z}') := |G_t(\mathbf{z}) - G_t(\mathbf{z}')|$$

for $\mathbf{z}, \mathbf{z}' \in Q_t$ (cf. §1.3.4).

□ The proof of Theorem 5 is obtained from the following two lemmas.

Lemma 8. *There exists a constant K such that*

$$\sum_{t=1}^{N} \rho_t(\mathbf{z}_t^N, \bar{\mathbf{z}}_t) \leqq K.$$

□ By (1.17) (which in the present context relies only on the linearity possessed by generalized prices) we have for any programme $\{\mathbf{z}_t\}$

$$\sum_{t=1}^{N} \rho_t(\mathbf{z}_t, \bar{\mathbf{z}}_t) = \sum_{t=1}^{N} [F_t(\bar{\mathbf{z}}_t) - F_t(\mathbf{z}_t)] - \sum_{t=1}^{N-1} \bar{\pi}_t(\mathbf{y}_t - \mathbf{x}_t)$$
$$+ \bar{\pi}_0(\mathbf{x}_0) - \bar{\pi}_N(\mathbf{y}_N)$$
$$\leqq \sum_{t=1}^{N} [F_t(\bar{\mathbf{z}}_t) - F_t(\mathbf{z}_t)] + J, \tag{24}$$

where J is some constant. This follows since $\bar{\pi}_t(\mathbf{y}_t - \mathbf{x}_t) \geqq 0$ and the sequence $\{\bar{\pi}_N(\mathbf{y}_N)\}$ is bounded. Indeed,

$$|\bar{\pi}_N(\mathbf{y}_N)| = |\bar{\pi}_1(T^{-N+1}\mathbf{y}_N)| \leqq \|T^{-N+1}\mathbf{y}_N\|_\infty \|\bar{\pi}_1\|_{L^*_\infty} \leqq C\|\bar{\pi}_1\|_{L^*_\infty}. \tag{25}$$

The result now follows from the condition of Theorem 5 and the estimate (24). □

Lemma 9. *Let the function of the strict concavity condition* (F.1′) [*resp.* (F.2)] *for the functionals* F_t *be given by* $\delta_1(\epsilon)$ [*resp.* $\delta_2(\epsilon)$]. *Then, for any* t, $\mathbf{z} \in Q_t$ *and* $\epsilon > 0$, *if the condition* (F.1) *holds,*

$$\rho_t(\bar{\mathbf{z}}_t, \mathbf{z}) \geqq \delta_1(E|\bar{\mathbf{z}}_t - \mathbf{z}|), \tag{26}$$

and if (F.2) *holds,*

$$\rho_t(\mathbf{z}_t, \mathbf{z}) \geqq \delta_2(\epsilon)P\{|\bar{\mathbf{z}}_t - \mathbf{z}| \geqq \epsilon\}. \tag{27}$$

□ It is sufficient to check that

$$\rho_t(\bar{\mathbf{z}}_t, \mathbf{z}_t) \geqq F_t(\bar{\mathbf{z}}_t, \mathbf{z}_t),[11]$$

for then the result follows application of the appropriate condition. But

$$\rho_t(\bar{\mathbf{z}}_t, \mathbf{z}_t) \geqq \tfrac{1}{2}\rho_t(\bar{\mathbf{z}}_t, \mathbf{z}_t) = \tfrac{1}{2}[G_t(\bar{\mathbf{z}}_t) - G_t(\mathbf{z}_t)]$$
$$= G_t(\bar{\mathbf{z}}_t) - \tfrac{1}{2}[G_t(\bar{\mathbf{z}}_t) + G_t(\mathbf{z}_t)]$$
$$\geqq G_t(\tfrac{1}{2}[\bar{\mathbf{z}}_t + \mathbf{z}_t]) - \tfrac{1}{2}[G_t(\bar{\mathbf{z}}_t) + G(\mathbf{z}_t)]$$
$$= G_t(\bar{\mathbf{z}}_t, \mathbf{z}_t) = F_t(\bar{\mathbf{z}}_t, \mathbf{z}_t),$$

where the second inequality holds because $\bar{\mathbf{z}}_t$ is the maximum point of

[11] Recall from §3 that $F_t(\bar{\mathbf{z}}_t, \mathbf{z}_t)$ is defined by (15).

G_t, and the final equation holds because G_t is the sum of F_t and linear functionals (cf. the proof of Lemma 4). □

Theorem 5 can now be proven in a few lines. Statement (a) is obtained from the chain of inequalities

$$K \geqq \sum_{t=1}^{N} \rho_t(\mathbf{z}_t^N, \bar{\mathbf{z}}_t) \geqq t_N(\epsilon)\delta_1(\epsilon).$$

The first inequality holds by Lemma 8, and the second follows from (26).

To prove (b) we use (22) (with $\epsilon/2$ replaced by ϵ). From this formula, (27) and Lemma 8 we find that

$$E\boldsymbol{\theta}_N = \sum_{t=1}^{N} P\{|\mathbf{z}_t^N - \bar{\mathbf{z}}_t| \geqq \epsilon\} \leqq \frac{1}{\delta_2(\epsilon)} \sum_{t=1}^{N} \rho_t(\bar{\mathbf{z}}_t, \mathbf{z}_t^N) \leqq \frac{K}{\delta_2(\epsilon)},$$

as required. □

□ To prove Theorem 4, one needs to check the boundedness of the sum (23) for an optimal programme.

This will be proven if, among all infinite programmes with sufficient i.v. $\mathbf{y}_0$, we can find at least one good programme $\{\hat{\mathbf{z}}_t\}$ for which the sums $\sum_{t=1}^{N} [F_t(\bar{\mathbf{z}}_t) - F_t(\hat{\mathbf{z}}_t)]$ are uniformly bounded. The construction of such a programme is similar to that made for the deterministic case in §1.3.7. First we note that it may be assumed without loss of generality that the vector $\mathbf{y}_0$ is uniformly positive and greater than $\tilde{\mathbf{y}}_0$, the initial value of the programme of Condition (IV) of §2.4.4 (cf. Lemma 1.5). Then we choose $\theta \in (0, 1)$ and construct the sequence

$$\hat{\mathbf{z}}_t := \theta^t \tilde{\mathbf{z}}_t + (1 - \theta^t)\bar{\mathbf{z}}_t,$$

where $\{\tilde{\mathbf{z}}_t\}$ is the programme of Condition (IV) (cf. §§2.4.4 and 1.4). For a suitable choice of θ, $\{\hat{\mathbf{z}}_t\}$ is the required programme. This is checked exactly as in §1.3.7, and we leave the details to the reader.[12] □

4. The Turnpike Theorem for Good Programmes

Theorem 6. (Convergence of good infinite programmes to the turnpike.) *If* $\{\mathbf{z}_t\}$ *is a good programme, then*

$$\lim_{t \to \infty} E|\bar{\mathbf{z}}_t - \mathbf{z}_t| = 0.$$

Furthermore, if the functionals F_t satisfy the strict concavity condition (F.2), *then*

$$\lim_{t\to\infty} |\bar{\mathbf{z}}_t - \mathbf{z}_t| = 0 \qquad a.s.$$

□ By the definition of a good programme and the bound (24),

$$\sum_{t=1}^{\infty} \rho_t(\mathbf{z}_t, \bar{\mathbf{z}}_t) < \infty.$$

It follows that $\rho_t(\mathbf{z}_t, \bar{\mathbf{z}}_t) \to 0$, and this, in turn, gives by (26) the first statement of the theorem.

Further, under Condition (F.2) we have by (27) that

$$\delta_2(\epsilon) \sum_{t=1}^{\infty} P\{|\bar{\mathbf{z}}_t - \mathbf{z}_t| \geqq \epsilon\} < \infty.$$

By the Borel–Cantelli lemma the convergence of this series for arbitrary ϵ means that $\bar{\mathbf{z}}_t - \mathbf{z}_t \to 0$ a.s. □

5. THE EXISTENCE OF AN OPTIMAL PROGRAMME OVER AN INFINITE HORIZON

1. Statement of the Existence Theorem and Construction of the Brock *H* Functional

We continue to assume the conditions of §4, together with (VI) and (VII) of §2.4.5 (cf. §§1.4.1–1.4.3).

Theorem 7. (Existence and uniqueness of an optimal infinite programme.) *Under assumptions* (I)–(VIII) *there exists a unique optimal infinite programme with i.v.* $\mathbf{y}_0$ *for any sufficient vector* $\mathbf{y}_0$.

□ The scheme of proof is similar to that outlined in §1.4.1 for the deterministic case.

---

[12] One must use the fact that $F_t(\bar{\mathbf{z}}_t) - F_t(\tilde{\mathbf{z}}_t)$ does not depend on t, by the stationarity of the model and of the programmes $\{\bar{\mathbf{z}}_t\}, \{\tilde{\mathbf{z}}_t\}$.

First, consider stationary prices of integral type $\{\bar{\mathbf{p}}_t\}$ supporting the turnpike. On the set Π of all programmes $\zeta := \{\mathbf{z}_t\} = \{(\mathbf{x}_{t-1}, \mathbf{y}_t)\}$ with i.v. $\mathbf{y}_0$ define the functional

$$H(\zeta) := \sum_{t=1}^{\infty} [H_t(\bar{\zeta}) - H_t(\zeta)], \tag{28}$$

where

$$\begin{aligned} H_t(\zeta) &:= G_t(\mathbf{z}_t) - E[\bar{\mathbf{p}}_{t-1}(\mathbf{y}_{t-1} - \mathbf{x}_{t-1})] \\ &= F_t(\mathbf{z}_t) + E\bar{\mathbf{p}}_t\mathbf{y}_t - E\bar{\mathbf{p}}_{t-1}\mathbf{y}_{t-1}. \end{aligned} \tag{29}$$

Summing equation (29) with respect to t from 1 to N for the programmes $\bar{\zeta}$ and ζ, we obtain

$$\sum_{t=1}^{N} [H_t(\bar{\zeta}) - H_t(\zeta)] = \sum_{t=1}^{N} [F_t(\bar{\mathbf{z}}_t) - F_t(\mathbf{z}_t)] - E\bar{\mathbf{p}}_N\mathbf{y}_N + E\bar{\mathbf{p}}_0\mathbf{y}_0. \tag{30}$$

Since the sequence $\{E\mathbf{p}_N\mathbf{y}_N\}$ is uniformly bounded by (25), we conclude that a programme ζ is good if and only if $H(\zeta) < \infty$.

Next we shall interpret programmes ζ as elements of the product

$$L_1(S^0; \mathbb{R}^n) \times L_1(S^1; \mathbb{R}^n) \times L_1(S^1; \mathbb{R}^n) \times \cdots$$

and apply Theorem III.5 to conclude the existence of a solution to the problem of minimizing H over Π. To this end we check that the conditions of Komlós's theorem hold.

□ The set Π is closed with respect to a.s. convergence by (I) and the fact that the constraints $\mathbf{y}_t \geqq \mathbf{x}_t$ a.s. appearing in the definition of a programme hold in the a.s. limit.

Moreover, by (II) the functionals F_t are upper semicontinuous with respect to the topology of a.s. convergence, and therefore [see (29)], the functionals $H_t(\bar{\zeta}) - H_t(\cdot)$ are lower semicontinuous. It follows that the H functional is lower semicontinuous as the sum of a sequence of nonnegative lower semicontinuous functionals. Finally, the boundedness condition needed for Theorem III.5 follows from (I). □

Consequently, there exists a programme $\zeta^0 \in \Pi$ minimizing H.

Because there exists a programme $\hat{\zeta}$ with $H(\hat{\zeta}) < \infty$ (i.e., a good programme; see §§4.3 and 1.3.7), $H(\zeta^0) \leqq H(\hat{\zeta}) < \infty$.

Therefore, the problem of finding the optimal programme ζ^0 may be restricted to the set $\hat{\Pi}$ of good programmes with i.v. $\mathbf{y}_0$. But on this set the functional H is strictly concave by Condition (VIII) of §1, so the programme $\boldsymbol{\zeta}^0$ is unique.

2. Transition from the H Functional to the Sum $\sum F_t$

We prove now that for any programme $\boldsymbol{\zeta}$ with i.v. $\mathbf{y}_0$,

$$H(\boldsymbol{\zeta}) - H(\boldsymbol{\zeta}^0) = \sum_{t=1}^{\infty} [F_t(\mathbf{z}_t^0) - F_t(\mathbf{z}_t)]. \tag{31}$$

□ By (30),

$$\sum_{t=1}^{N} [H_t(\bar{\boldsymbol{\zeta}}) - H_t(\boldsymbol{\zeta})] - \sum_{t=1}^{N} [H_t(\bar{\boldsymbol{\zeta}}) - H_t(\boldsymbol{\zeta}^0)]$$

$$= \sum_{t=1}^{N} [F_t(\mathbf{z}_t^0) - F_t(\mathbf{z}_t)] + \beta_N, \tag{32}$$

where $\beta_N := E\bar{\mathbf{p}}_N(\mathbf{y}_N^0 - \mathbf{y}_N)$. The sequence $\{\beta_N\}$ is bounded by (25). It follows that if $H(\boldsymbol{\zeta}) = \infty$, the right- and left-hand sides of (31) are both infinite.

If $H(\boldsymbol{\zeta}) < \infty$, the programme $\boldsymbol{\zeta}$ is good, and hence by Theorem 6

$$E|\mathbf{y}_N^0 - \mathbf{y}_N| \leqq E|\mathbf{y}_N^0 - \bar{\mathbf{y}}_N| + E|\mathbf{y}_N - \bar{\mathbf{y}}_N| \to 0.$$

It follows that $E|\mathbf{w}_N| \to 0$, where $\mathbf{w}_N := T^{-N}(\mathbf{y}_N^0 - \mathbf{y}_N)$, and thus [13]

$$|\beta_N| = |E\bar{\mathbf{p}}_0\mathbf{w}_N| \leqq E|\bar{\mathbf{p}}_0\mathbf{w}_N| \leqq E|\bar{\mathbf{p}}_0||\mathbf{w}_N| \to 0,$$

using the summability of $\bar{\mathbf{p}}_0$. Therefore, taking limits in (32), we obtain (31). □

From (31) the optimality and uniqueness of $\boldsymbol{\zeta}^0$ follows immediately. Indeed, for any programme $\boldsymbol{\zeta} \neq \boldsymbol{\zeta}^0$,

$$0 < H(\boldsymbol{\zeta}) - H(\boldsymbol{\zeta}^0) = \sum_{t=1}^{\infty} [F_t(\mathbf{z}_t^0) - F_t(\mathbf{z}_t)],$$

so that from some N onwards all the sums $\sum_{t=1}^{N} [F_t(\mathbf{z}_t^0) - F_t(\mathbf{z}_t)]$ must be positive. □

[13] The following fact is used here. If $\boldsymbol{\alpha}$ is a random variable with a finite expectation and $\boldsymbol{\beta}_N$ is a sequence of uniformly bounded random variables, then $E|\boldsymbol{\beta}_N| \to 0$ implies that $E\boldsymbol{\alpha}\boldsymbol{\beta}_N \to 0$.

COMMENTS ON CHAPTER 4

Stationary economic planning models similar to those discussed in Chapter 4 and the stationary programmes and prices connected with them were considered independently—and at almost the same time—by Radner [3, 4] and Evstigneev [1–3]. Evstigneev proved the existence theorem for optimal programmes over an infinite horizon and the weak turnpike theorem. Problems of existence and convergence of optimal and good infinite programmes were also studied by Dana [1] and Jeanjean [1] (for models of Radner type) and Brock and Mirman [1, 2] (for the unisector model with independent identically distributed random parameters).

Results concerning infinite planning horizons are presented in this book for *stationary* models. Important results showing the possibility of a transition to *nonstationary* theory in the deterministic case have recently been obtained by Danilov [1] and Polterovich [1]. The study of nonstationary stochastic economic models is just beginning (see Kuznetsov [1], Evstigneev [3] (Theorems 1.2 and 1.4) and Föllmer and Majumdar [1]).

5 APPROXIMATION OF PROGRAMMES AND STRONG TURNPIKE THEOREMS

1. APPROXIMATION OF PROGRAMMES

1. The Canonical Approximation Scheme

In this section we present technical results which will be used in this chapter to prove various strong turnpike theorems for the stochastic version of the Gale model studied in previous chapters. The essence of the method developed lies in the approximation of an arbitrary programme by a progamme with specific required properties. These properties concern primarily the initial and terminal behaviour of the approximating programmes.

The point of departure for us is a construction used by Gale to prove the existence of good programmes (see §1.3.7). Gale's original construction is sufficient for the deterministic case and in proving weak turnpike theorems for the stochastic case (see §§4.4.2–4.4.4), but it needs to be considerably refined in order to be used in proving the deeper results of the present chapter.

In this chapter we assume that the economic model is *stationary* and satisfies Conditions (I)–(VIII) together with the following two requirements:

(IX) *For any* $\mathbf{z}, \mathbf{z}' \in Q_t$ *and any measurable function given by* $\theta(s^{t-1})$ *taking values* 0 *and* 1,

$$\boldsymbol{\theta}\mathbf{z} + (1 - \boldsymbol{\theta})\mathbf{z}' \in Q_t.$$

(X) *For each* $\beta > 0$ *there exists a real number* $W(\beta)$ *such that*

$$|F_t(\mathbf{z}) - F_t(\mathbf{z}')| \leqq W(\beta)$$

for any $\mathbf{z}, \mathbf{z}' \in Q_t$ *with* $E|\mathbf{z} - \mathbf{z}'| \leqq \beta$ *and*

$$\lim_{\beta \to 0} W(\beta) = 0.$$

The first requirement is stronger than Condition (VII) of §2.4.5; it postulates the possibility of random choice between *any* two technological processes in Q_t [whereas (VIII) assumes that one of these processes is (0, 0)]. Condition (X) implies the requirement of boundedness and uniform continuity in the L_1 norm of the functionals F_t. [Examples of functionals with the properties required by (X) were given in §4.3.2.]

In this chapter we consider programmes of the type $\{\mathbf{z}_a, \ldots, \mathbf{z}_b\}$ $(1 \leqq a < b)$ which begin at an arbitrary point a in time. They are defined by the usual relations (1.2) and (1.3).

Let $\gamma_t := \gamma_0 \gamma^t$ $(0 < \gamma < 1)$ be a geometric progression and let $\lambda \in (0, 1)$. We assign to each programme $\{\mathbf{z}_a, \ldots, \mathbf{z}_b\}$ $(1 \leqq a < b)$ the corresponding sequence

$$\mathbf{z}_t' := \gamma_t \lambda \tilde{\mathbf{z}}_t + (1 - \gamma_t)\mathbf{z}_t,$$

$t = a, \ldots, b$, where $\{\tilde{\mathbf{z}}_t\}$ is the programme of Condition (IV) of §2.4.4. This sequence we shall call the *canonical approximation* of programme $\{\mathbf{z}_a, \ldots, \mathbf{z}_b\}$ (corresponding to the parameters γ_0, γ and λ). In the sequel we shall find approximations possessing the properties we require by an appropriate choice of γ_0, γ and λ.

2. A Sufficient Condition for the Canonical Approximation to Be a Programme

Lemma 1. *A sufficient condition for the canonical approximation to be a programme is the following:*

$$\gamma_t \in [0, 1], \qquad t = a, \ldots, b, \tag{1}$$

$$\boldsymbol{\delta}_t(x) := \lambda \tilde{\mathbf{y}}_t - [\gamma \lambda \tilde{\mathbf{x}}_t + (1 - \gamma)x] \geqq 0 \quad \text{a.s.,} \quad \mathrm{t = a - 1, \ldots, b - 1}, \tag{2}$$

for any vector $x \in \mathbb{R}^n$ *such that* $|x| \leqq C$.

□ By the convexity of Q_t, (1), *(IV) and (V)*, $\mathbf{z}_t' \in Q_t$. Further, it can be directly checked that

$$\mathbf{y}_t' - \mathbf{x}_t' = \gamma_t \boldsymbol{\delta}_t(\mathbf{x}_t) + (1 - \gamma_t)(\mathbf{y}_t - \mathbf{x}_t),$$

from which we obtain immediately that $\mathbf{y}_t' - \mathbf{x}_t' \geqq 0$ a.s. □

3. Some Estimates

Lemma 2. *Let $\{\mathbf{z}_a, \ldots, \mathbf{z}_b\}$ be a programme, let $\{\mathbf{z}_a', \ldots, \mathbf{z}_b'\}$ be its canonical approximation, and let $\gamma_t \in [0, 1]$. Suppose further that β is a real number, Γ is an event*[1] *of $\mathscr{F}^{a-1}$ with $P(\Gamma) \leqq \beta$ and $\mathbf{z}_t''$ is a function equal to $\mathbf{z}_t'$ on Γ and to $\mathbf{z}_t$ outside Γ for $t = a, \ldots, b$. Then we have the inequality*

$$F_t(\mathbf{z}_t) - F_t(\mathbf{z}_t'') \leqq \gamma_t w(\beta), \tag{3}$$

where [cf. Condition (X)]

$$w(\beta) := W(2C\beta). \tag{4}$$

□ Consider the following chain of equalities [where $\mathbf{1}_\Gamma := 1_\Gamma(\boldsymbol{\omega})$]:

$$\begin{aligned}
\mathbf{z}_t'' &:= \mathbf{1}_\Gamma \mathbf{z}_t' + (1 - \mathbf{1}_\Gamma)\mathbf{z}_t \\
&= \mathbf{1}_\Gamma[\gamma_t \lambda \tilde{\mathbf{z}}_t + (1 - \gamma_t)\mathbf{z}_t] + (1 - \mathbf{1}_\Gamma)\mathbf{z}_t \\
&= \mathbf{1}_\Gamma[\mathbf{z}_t + \gamma_t(\lambda \tilde{\mathbf{z}}_t - \mathbf{z}_t)] + (1 - \mathbf{1}_\Gamma)\mathbf{z}_t \\
&= \mathbf{z}_t + \mathbf{1}_\Gamma \gamma_t(\lambda \tilde{\mathbf{z}}_t - \mathbf{z}_t) = \gamma_t \mathbf{z}_t + (1 - \gamma_t)\mathbf{z}_t + \mathbf{1}_\Gamma \gamma_t(\lambda \tilde{\mathbf{z}}_t - \mathbf{z}_t) \\
&= \gamma_t[\mathbf{z}_t + \mathbf{1}_\Gamma(\lambda \tilde{\mathbf{z}}_t - \mathbf{z}_t)] + (1 - \gamma_t)\mathbf{z}_t \\
&:= \gamma_t \mathbf{z}_t''' + (1 - \gamma_t)\mathbf{z}_t.
\end{aligned}$$

By (IX), $\tilde{\mathbf{z}}_t''' := \mathbf{1}_\Gamma \lambda \tilde{\mathbf{z}}_t + (1 - \mathbf{1}_\Gamma)\mathbf{z}_t \in Q_t$, so that the above expression for $\mathbf{z}_t''$ implies that

$$\begin{aligned}
F_t(\mathbf{z}_t) - F_t(\mathbf{z}_t'') &\leqq F_t(\mathbf{z}_t) - \gamma_t F_t(\mathbf{z}_t''') - (1 - \gamma_t)F_t(\mathbf{z}_t) \\
&= \gamma_t[F_t(\mathbf{z}_t) - F_t(\mathbf{z}_t''')] \leqq \gamma_t w(\beta).
\end{aligned}$$

The first inequality follows from the concavity of F_t and the second holds, using (X), because

$$E|\mathbf{z}_t''' - \mathbf{z}_t| \leqq 2CP(\Gamma) \leqq 2C\beta. \quad \square$$

[1] We let $\mathscr{F}^t$ denote the σ-algebra of events generated by $\mathbf{s}^t$.

Corollary 1. *There exists a constant H such that*

$$\sum_{t=a}^{b} [F_t(\mathbf{z}_t) - F_t(\mathbf{z}_t')] \leqq H \sum_{t=a}^{b} \gamma_t.$$

□ The proof is immediate from Lemma 2 on setting $H := w(1)$. □

4. Forward α-Approximation

Let α be a positive number. We choose $\lambda := \lambda(\alpha) \in (0, 1)$ such that

$$\lambda \tilde{\mathbf{y}}_t \leqq \alpha 1 \qquad \text{a.s.,} \quad t = 0, 1, 2, \ldots. \tag{5}$$

This is possible since $|\tilde{\mathbf{y}}_t| \leqq C$ a.s. With this $\lambda(\alpha)$ we choose $\gamma := \gamma(\alpha) \in (0, 1)$ sufficiently close to 1 so that the inequalities (2) hold for any x such that $|x| \leqq C$. Such a γ exists, since $\lambda\tilde{\mathbf{y}}_t - \lambda\tilde{\mathbf{x}}_t \geqq \lambda\delta 1$ a.s., where $\lambda\delta 1$ is a constant positive vector. Finally, we set $\gamma_0 := \gamma^{-a+1}$. The canonical approximation of the programme $\boldsymbol{\zeta} = \{\mathbf{z}_a, \ldots, \mathbf{z}_b\}$ with parameters $\lambda(\alpha)$, $\gamma(\alpha)$ and $\gamma_0(\alpha, a)$ is called its *forward α-approximation*[2] and will be denoted

$$\boldsymbol{\zeta}^{(\alpha)} := \{\mathbf{z}_a^{(\alpha)}, \ldots, \mathbf{z}_b^{(\alpha)}\}.$$

Lemma 3.

1. $\boldsymbol{\zeta}^{(\alpha)}$ *is a programme.*
2. $\mathbf{x}_{a-1}^{(\alpha)} \leqq \alpha 1$ *a.s.*
3. *If* $\Gamma \in \mathscr{F}^{a-1}$ *and* $P(\Gamma) \leqq \beta$, *then for any integers i, j such that* $a \leqq i \leqq j \leqq b$

$$\sum_{t=i}^{j} [F_t(\mathbf{z}_t) - F_t(\mathbf{1}_\Gamma \mathbf{z}_t^{(\alpha)} + (1 - \mathbf{1}_\Gamma)\mathbf{z}_t)] \leqq d(\alpha) w(\beta),$$

where $d(\alpha) := \gamma(\alpha)[1 - \gamma(\alpha)]^{-1}$.

4. *There exists an* $N := N(\alpha)$ (*not depending on a, b or* $\boldsymbol{\zeta}$) *such that if* $b - a > N(\alpha)$,

$$\mathbf{y}_b^{(\alpha)} \geqq \mathbf{y}_b - \alpha 1 \qquad \text{a.s.} \quad \square$$

[2] The term *forward* indicates that with increasing t the value of γ_t is decreasing [i.e., $\gamma \in (0, 1)$], and thus successive terms of the sequence $\{\mathbf{z}_t^{(\alpha)}\}$ move *closer* to those of the programme $\boldsymbol{\zeta}$. A *backward* α-approximation, defined below, is *initially close* to the original programme but *moves away* from it over time.

In this lemma all the properties of the programme $\zeta^{(\alpha)}$ required in the sequel have been formulated. Statement 2 says effectively that $\alpha 1$ is the initial vector for the programme $\zeta^{(\alpha)}$. Statement 3 may be interpreted as follows. Suppose that with some small probability (not exceeding β) we use the approximation $\zeta^{(\alpha)}$, and with the complementary probability we use the given programme ζ. Then the utility sum deriving from the mixed programme will differ little from the utility sum deriving from ζ, because $w(\beta) \to 0$ as $\beta \to 0$. It is essential here that the bound in Statement 3 does not depend either on the type of programme ζ or on its length. Statement 4 shows that by replacing ζ with its forward approximation $\zeta^{(\alpha)}$ we do not lose more than α of each good in the final production period.

□ Now we prove the lemma.

1. Since Condition (2) of Lemma 1 holds by construction, it suffices to check that (1) holds. This is so, since

$$\gamma_t = \gamma_0 \gamma^t = \gamma^{-a+1+t} \in (0, 1)$$

for $t \geqq a$.

2. *We have that*

$$\gamma_a = \gamma_0 \gamma^a = \gamma^{1-a} \gamma^a = \gamma,$$

$$\mathbf{x}_{a-1}^{(\alpha)} = \gamma\lambda\mathbf{x}_{a-1} + (1-\gamma)\mathbf{x}_{a-1} \leqq \lambda\tilde{\mathbf{y}}_{a-1} \leqq \alpha 1 \qquad \text{a.s.,}$$

where the first inequality holds by choice γ [cf. (2)] and the second inequality holds by (5).

3. This bound follows from Lemma 2, since

$$\sum_{t=i}^{j} \gamma^{t-a+1} \leqq \sum_{t=a}^{b} \gamma^{t-a+1} \leqq \frac{\gamma}{1-\gamma}.$$

4. We evaluate the final production vector for the programme $\zeta^{(\alpha)}$;

$$y_b^{(\alpha)} = \gamma_b \lambda \tilde{\mathbf{y}}_b + (1-\gamma_b)\mathbf{y}_b = \mathbf{y}_b + \gamma_b(\lambda\tilde{\mathbf{y}}_b - \mathbf{y}_b) = \mathbf{y}_b + \gamma^{b-a+1}(\lambda\tilde{\mathbf{y}}_b - \mathbf{y}_b).$$

This expression is bounded below a.s. by the vector $\mathbf{y}_b - \gamma^{b-a+1}C1$, since by Condition (1)

$$\lambda\tilde{\mathbf{y}}_b - \mathbf{y}_b \leqq \lambda\tilde{\mathbf{y}}_b \leqq C1 \qquad \text{a.s.}$$

It follows that $N(\alpha)$ must be chosen such that $\gamma^{N+1}C$ is not greater than α. □

5. Backward α-Approximation

The remaining results of this section are needed only for programmes of the type $\zeta = \{\mathbf{z}_1, \ldots, \mathbf{z}_b\}$ (i.e., with $a = 1$) having a strictly positive vector of initial resources $\mathbf{y}_0$. This initial random vector is considered to be given and fixed.

We fix permanently two numbers λ and γ with the following properties:

$$0 < \lambda < 1, \qquad \lambda\tilde{\mathbf{y}}_0 < \mathbf{y}_0 \quad \text{a.s.}, \qquad \gamma > 1 \tag{6}$$

and λ and γ are such that inequality (2) of Lemma 1 holds. Corresponding to each $\alpha > 0$ and natural number b, we set $\gamma_0 := \gamma_0(\alpha, b)$ to denote the smallest positive number satisfying the inequality

$$\gamma_0 \gamma^b \lambda \tilde{\mathbf{y}}_b \geqq \alpha 1 \qquad \text{a.s.} \tag{7}$$

The canonical approximation of the programme $\zeta = \{\mathbf{z}_1, \ldots, \mathbf{z}_b\}$ with parameters λ, γ and $\gamma_0(\alpha, b)$ defined above is called the *backward α-approximation* of ζ and will be denoted $\zeta^{[\alpha]} = \{\mathbf{z}_1^{[\alpha]}, \ldots, \mathbf{z}_b^{[\alpha]}\}$.

Lemma 4. *There exist constants $\alpha' > 0$ and c (not depending on b and ζ) such that the following statements are valid:*

1. *For $0 < \alpha < \alpha'$ the approximation $\zeta^{[\alpha]}$ is a programme with i.v. $\mathbf{y}_0$.*
2. $\sum_{t=1}^{b} [F_t(\mathbf{z}_t) - F_t(\mathbf{z}_t^{[\alpha]})] \leqq c\alpha$.
3. $\mathbf{y}_b^{[\alpha]} \geqq \alpha 1$.
4. $\mathbf{y}_b^{[\alpha]} \geqq \mathbf{y}_b - c\alpha 1$ *a.s.* □

Thus to each programme ζ there corresponds a programme $\zeta^{[\alpha]}$ close to ζ such that its final production vector $\mathbf{y}_b^{[\alpha]}$ is strictly positive and, moreover, for any good it is not less than α. The similarity of ζ and its backward approximation $\zeta^{[\alpha]}$ is expressed by Properties 2 and 4: In approximating ζ by $\zeta^{[\alpha]}$ we do not lose a substantial amount in either utility or final output.

□ Now we prove the lemma. We let μ denote the (essentially) smallest coordinate of $\tilde{\mathbf{y}}_b$. This vector is a.s. bounded below since $\tilde{\mathbf{y}}_b \geqq \delta + \tilde{\mathbf{x}}_b \geqq \delta 1$ a.s., where $\delta 1$ is a constant positive vector. Then by the definition of γ_0

$$\gamma_0 = \alpha/(\gamma^b \lambda \mu) \leqq \alpha/(\gamma^b \lambda \delta);$$

i.e.,

$$\gamma_0 \gamma^b \leqq \alpha/(\lambda\delta). \tag{8}$$

We may take α' to be any value of $\alpha > 0$ for which the right-hand side of (8) is less than 1.

We first check Statement 1. Since $\gamma > 1$, it follows from (8) that $\gamma_t < \gamma_0 \gamma^b < 1$, and so by Lemma 1 $\zeta^{[\alpha]}$ is a programme. Furthermore,

$$\begin{aligned}\mathbf{x}_0^{[\alpha]} &= \gamma_1 \lambda \tilde{\mathbf{x}}_0 + (1 - \gamma_1)\mathbf{x}_0 \leqq \gamma_1 \lambda \tilde{\mathbf{y}}_0 + (1 - \gamma_1)\mathbf{x}_0 \\ &\leqq \gamma_1 \mathbf{y}_0 + (1 - \gamma_1)\mathbf{y}_0 = \mathbf{y}_0 \quad \text{a.s.}\end{aligned}$$

by (6) and the fact that $\mathbf{y}_0$ is an i.v. for ζ. Therefore $\zeta^{[\alpha]}$ is a programme with i.v. $\mathbf{y}_0$.

Next we establish some bounds. As a consequence of Lemma 2,

$$\begin{aligned}\sum_{t=1}^{b} [F_t(\mathbf{z}_t) - F_t(\mathbf{z}_t^{[\alpha]})] &\leqq H \sum_{t=1}^{b} \gamma_t \leqq H\gamma_0(1 + \gamma + \cdots + \gamma^b) \\ &= H\gamma_0[(\gamma^{b+1} - 1)/(\gamma - 1)] \\ &= H\gamma_0[(\gamma^b - \gamma^{-1})/(1 - \gamma^{-1})] \\ &\leqq H[\gamma_0\gamma^b/(1 - \gamma^{-1})] \leqq \alpha H/[\lambda\delta(1 - \gamma^{-1})], \qquad (9)\end{aligned}$$

where the latter inequality holds by (8). From (8) it also follows that

$$\begin{aligned}\mathbf{y}_b^{[\alpha]} &:= \mathbf{y}_b + \gamma_b[\lambda\tilde{\mathbf{y}}_b - \mathbf{y}_b] \\ &\geqq \mathbf{y}_b - \gamma_b C\mathbf{1} \geqq \mathbf{y}_b - (C/\lambda\delta)\alpha\mathbf{1} \qquad \text{a.s.} \qquad (10)\end{aligned}$$

We conclude from (9) and (10) that we may take the constant c in Statements 2 and 4 to be equal to $\max\{H/[\lambda\delta(1 - \gamma^{-1})], C/\lambda\delta\}$.

Finally, by (7)

$$\mathbf{y}_b^{[\alpha]} = \gamma_b \lambda \tilde{\mathbf{y}}_b + (1 - \gamma_b)\mathbf{y}_b \geqq \gamma_b \lambda \tilde{\mathbf{y}}_b \geqq \alpha\mathbf{1};$$

i.e., Statement 3 holds. □

2. WINTER PROGRAMMES

1. Assumptions and Statement of the Existence Result

The goal of this section is to construct a family of *Winter programmes*, i.e., programmes which most of the time coincide with the turnpike and, in the stochastic case, yield a utility sum close to the optimal value.

In the remainder of this chapter, (I)–(X) are everywhere assumed to hold, together with the following condition:

(Int) *There exists a* $\gamma > 0$ *such that any function* $\mathbf{z}_t = (x(\mathbf{s}^{t-1}),$

$y(\mathbf{s}^t)$) differing from $\bar{\mathbf{z}}_t$ in the L_∞ norm $\|\cdot\|_\infty$ by less than γ belongs to Q_t.

This condition means that $\bar{\mathbf{z}}_t$ is an *interior point of the set Q_t* in the L_∞ norm topology.

We fix once and for all the positive initial vector $\mathbf{y}_0$.

Theorem 1. (Existence of a family of Winter programmes.) *Under the conditions* (I)–(X) *and* (Int), *for each $\epsilon > 0$ there exists a constant $D := D(\epsilon)$, independent of N, such that for any $N > 2D$ a programme $\zeta = \{\mathbf{z}_1, \ldots, \mathbf{z}_N\}$ with i.v. $\mathbf{y}_0$ exists with the following properties:*

$$\mathbf{z}_t = \bar{\mathbf{z}}_t \qquad \textit{for} \quad t = D, \ldots, N - D, \tag{11}$$

$$\sum_{t=1}^{N} F_t(\mathbf{z}_t^N) - \sum_{t=1}^{N} F_t(\mathbf{z}_t) < \epsilon, \tag{12}$$

where $\{\mathbf{z}_t^N\}$ denotes the optimal programme of length N with i.v. $\mathbf{y}_0$.

2. Sketch of the Proof

□ Recall that in the deterministic case described in §1.5.2 the main idea underlying the construction of the family of Winter programmes is as follows. Each programme of the family must at first agree with the optimal programme. As soon, however, as the optimal trajectory comes close to the turnpike, it must "jump" to the turnpike and move along it until a point in time close to the planning horizon, when it again shifts back to agree with the optimal programme until the horizon is reached.

In the stochastic case, an attempt to follow this simple scheme leads to a series of difficulties which must be overcome by suitable modification of the basic idea. Before proceeding to the technicalities, we shall first describe the modified scheme in an informal manner.

As in the deterministic case, we begin by choosing time periods close to the two ends of the planning interval when the optimal programme is close to the turnpike. More precisely, sufficiently small $\alpha > 0$ and $\beta > 0$ are fixed and, for each N, time periods $k := k(N)$ and $l := l(N)$ are chosen such that

$$\{k(N)\} \text{ and } \{N - l(N)\} \qquad \text{are bounded sequences} \tag{13}$$

and

$$P\{|\mathbf{z}_t^N - \bar{\mathbf{z}}_t| \geqq \alpha\} < \beta \qquad \text{for} \quad t = k \text{ and } l.^3 \tag{14}$$

The existence and boundedness of k and l for each sufficiently large N follows from the weak turnpike theorem (see Theorem 4.4 and the discussion following its statement).

The first difference from the deterministic case arises from the fact that the transition to the turnpike $\bar{\mathbf{z}}_{k+1}, \bar{\mathbf{z}}_{k+2}, \ldots$ at period $k+1$ is not possible a.s., but only with a probability close to 1. It follows from (Int) that the transition may be effected in the event

$$\Gamma_1 := \{|\mathbf{z}_k^N - \bar{\mathbf{z}}_k| < \alpha\} \tag{15}$$

(for α sufficiently small). But what should be done in the contrary case—when the complementary event $\bar{\Gamma}_1 := \{|\mathbf{z}_k^N - \bar{\mathbf{z}}_k| \geqq \alpha\}$ occurs? In this case we could try to use a forward approximation to construct a programme which extends the optimal programme $\{\mathbf{z}_1^N, \ldots, \mathbf{z}_k^N\}$ and approaches the turnpike with the speed of a geometric progression. However, it is possible to construct such a programme only if the vector $\mathbf{y}_k^N$ is uniformly positive. Generally speaking this is not so. To achieve the desired forward approximation in the contrary case we must first "correct" the *overture* $\{\mathbf{z}_1^N, \ldots, \mathbf{z}_k^N\}$ of the optimal programme by replacing it with its backward approximation $\{\mathbf{z}_1^N, \ldots, \mathbf{z}_k^N\}^{[\alpha]}$. After modification of the optimal overture, the resulting programme in the event $\bar{\Gamma}_1$ begins to move in the direction of the turnpike at time $k+1$. At some time $k+r$ (with r depending only on α) it arrives so close to the turnpike that by Condition (Int) it is possible to move onto it. Moreover, if we use the backward approximation of the optimal overture for all eventualities, it is still possible in the event Γ_1 to move to the turnpike at period $k+1$ in light of Statement 4 of Lemma 4.

Thus the programme constructed arrives at the turnpike in almost all random situations by time $k+r$. After this, it must move along the turnpike until time l. At this point, two possibilities again arise: Either the event $\Gamma_2 := \{|\mathbf{z}_l^N - \bar{\mathbf{z}}_l| < \alpha\}$ occurs with probability close to 1 or the complementary event $\bar{\Gamma}_2 := \{|\mathbf{z}_l^N - \bar{\mathbf{z}}_l| \geqq \alpha\}$ occurs. In the first event, it is possible to transfer immediately to the optimal *finale* $\{\mathbf{z}_{l+1}^N, \ldots, \mathbf{z}_N^N\}$. In the second event, the switch may be effected to its forward approximation $\{\mathbf{z}_{l+1}^N, \ldots, \mathbf{z}_N^N\}^{(\alpha)}$. The latter is possible since the vector $\bar{y}_l$ is a.s. uniformly positive by (Int), and it follows that $\bar{y}_l \geqq \alpha 1$ a.s. for sufficiently small α.

[3] It is assumed where necessary that N is sufficiently large.

If for each sufficiently large N a programme is constructed in the manner described above, then the resulting family is a family of Winter programmes. Each of them coincides with the turnpike over the bulk of the planning interval (i.e., on the interval $k + r$ to l) and yields a utility sum close to the optimum. The latter obtains because the programmes are constructed to be close (say, in the sense of L_1) to the optimal programme for $t \leqq k$ and $t \geqq l$ and close to the turnpike for $t = k + 1, \ldots, l$.

3. Formal Description of the Programme ζ

After this informal discussion, we now give a precise description. We take sufficiently small $\alpha > 0$ and $\beta > 0$, consider k and l as described in (13) and (14), and define the programme $\zeta = \{\mathbf{z}_1, \ldots, \mathbf{z}_N\}$ by composing it from the following four sequences:

$$\{\mathbf{z}_1, \ldots, \mathbf{z}_k\} := \{\mathbf{z}_1^N, \ldots, \mathbf{z}_k^N\}^{[\alpha]}, \tag{16}$$

$$\{\mathbf{z}_{k+1}, \ldots, \mathbf{z}_{k+r}\} := \begin{cases} \{(\bar{\mathbf{x}}_k - (c + 1)\alpha 1, \bar{\mathbf{y}}_{k+1}), \bar{\mathbf{z}}_{k+2}, \ldots, \bar{\mathbf{z}}_{k+r}\} & \text{for } \{|\mathbf{z}_k^N - \bar{\mathbf{z}}_k| < \alpha\}, \\ \{\bar{\mathbf{z}}_{k+1}, \ldots, \bar{\mathbf{z}}_{k+r}\}^{(\alpha)} & \text{for } \{|\mathbf{z}_k^N - \bar{\mathbf{z}}_k| \geqq \alpha\}, \end{cases} \tag{17}$$

$$\{\mathbf{z}_{k+r+1}, \ldots, \mathbf{z}_{l-1}, \mathbf{z}_l\} := \{(\bar{\mathbf{x}}_{k+r} - \alpha 1, \bar{\mathbf{y}}_{k+r+1}), \bar{\mathbf{z}}_{k+r+2}, \ldots, \bar{\mathbf{z}}_{l-1}, (\bar{\mathbf{x}}_{l-1}, \bar{\mathbf{y}}_l + \alpha 1)\}, \tag{18}$$

$$\{\mathbf{z}_{l+1}, \ldots, \mathbf{z}_N\} := \begin{cases} \{\mathbf{z}_{l+1}^N, \ldots, \mathbf{z}_N^N\} & \text{for } \{|\mathbf{z}_l^N - \bar{\mathbf{z}}_l| < \alpha\} \\ \{\mathbf{z}_{l+1}^N, \ldots, \mathbf{z}_N^N\}^{(\alpha)} & \text{for } \{|\mathbf{z}_l^N - \bar{\mathbf{z}}_l| \geqq \alpha\}, \end{cases} \tag{19}$$

where $r = N(\alpha)$, and c are the constants described in Lemmas 3 and 4.

4. ζ Is a Programme

□ To show that ζ is a programme, it is sufficient to prove that each of the sequences (16)–(19) is a programme and also that the linking constraints

$$\mathbf{y}_k \geqq \mathbf{x}_k, \qquad \mathbf{y}_{k+r} \geqq \mathbf{x}_{k+r}, \qquad \mathbf{y}_l \geqq \mathbf{x}_l \tag{20}$$

hold a.s.

That (16) is a programme, moreover with i.v. $\mathbf{y}_0$, is immediate from Statement 1 of Lemma 4.

To establish that (17) is a programme, it is sufficient, by (IX) and Statement 1 of Lemma 3, to check that

$$\{(\bar{\mathbf{x}}_k - (c+1)\alpha 1, \bar{\mathbf{y}}_{k+1}), \bar{\mathbf{z}}_{k+2}, \ldots, \bar{\mathbf{z}}_{k+r}\}$$

is a programme; Indeed, the resource constraints obviously hold, and it remains to note that

$$(\bar{\mathbf{x}}_k - (c+1)\alpha 1, \bar{\mathbf{y}}_{k+1}) \in Q_{k+1}$$

for sufficiently small α by (Int).

Similarly, use of (Int) shows that (18) is a programme.

Finally, (19) is obtained by a choice between two programmes (cf. Statement 1 of Lemma 3) depending on the event $\{|\bar{\mathbf{z}}_l - \mathbf{z}_l^N| < \alpha\}$ and thus by (IX) is also a programme.

Now we check the linking inequalities (20). The first holds, since in the event $\{|\mathbf{z}_k^N - \bar{\mathbf{z}}_k| < \alpha\}$,

$$\mathbf{y}_k \geqq \mathbf{y}_k^N - c\alpha 1 \geqq \bar{\mathbf{y}}_k - \alpha 1 - c\alpha 1 \geqq \bar{\mathbf{x}}_k - (c+1)\alpha 1 \qquad \text{a.s.,} \tag{21}$$

and for $\{|\mathbf{z}_k^N - \bar{\mathbf{z}}_k| \geqq \alpha\}$,

$$\mathbf{y}_k \geqq \alpha 1 \geqq \mathbf{x}_k \qquad \text{a.s.} \tag{22}$$

The first inequality in (21) follows from Statement 4 of Lemma 4, and (22) follows from Statement 3 of the same lemma and Statement 2 of Lemma 3. Further, $\mathbf{y}_{k+r} \geqq \mathbf{x}_{k+r}$ a.s. because

$$\mathbf{y}_{k+r} \geqq \bar{\mathbf{y}}_{k+r} - \alpha 1 \geqq \bar{\mathbf{x}}_{k+r} - \alpha 1 =: \mathbf{x}_{k+r},$$

where the first inequality holds by Statement 4 of Lemma 3.

It remains to check that $\mathbf{y}_l \geqq \mathbf{x}_l$. We have that

$$\mathbf{y}_l := \bar{\mathbf{y}}_l + \alpha 1 \geqq \begin{cases} \mathbf{y}_l^N \geqq \mathbf{x}_l^N =: \mathbf{x}_l \quad \text{a.s.} & \text{for } \{|\mathbf{z}_l^N - \bar{\mathbf{z}}_l| < \alpha\}, \\ \alpha 1 \geqq \mathbf{x}_l \quad \text{a.s.} & \text{for } \{|\mathbf{z}_l^N - \bar{\mathbf{z}}_l| \geqq \alpha\}, \end{cases}$$

where $\alpha 1 \geqq \mathbf{x}_l$ a.s. by Statement 2 of Lemma 3. □

5. Utility Estimates for ζ

Our aim is to estimate

$$\Delta := \sum_{t=1}^{N} F_t(\mathbf{z}_t^N) - \sum_{t=1}^{N} F_t(\mathbf{z}_t).$$

□ We decompose Δ as

$$\Delta := \Delta_1 + \Delta_2 + \Delta_3$$
$$:= \sum_{t=1}^{k} [F_t(\mathbf{z}_t^N) - F_t(\mathbf{z}_t)] + \sum_{t=k+1}^{l} [F_t(\mathbf{z}_t^N) - F_t(\mathbf{z}_t)]$$
$$+ \sum_{t=l+1}^{N} [F_t(\mathbf{z}_t^N) - F_t(\mathbf{z}_t)].$$

By Statement 2 of Lemma 4

$$\Delta_1 \leqq c\alpha. \tag{23}$$

Further,

$$\Delta_2 := \Delta_2' + \Delta_2'' = \sum_{t=k+1}^{l} [F_t(\mathbf{z}_t^N) - F_t(\bar{\mathbf{z}}_t)] + \sum_{t=k+1}^{l} [F_t(\bar{\mathbf{z}}_t) - F_t(\mathbf{z}_t)].$$

By an argument exactly analogous to that of Lemma 1.2 in which all valuations in terms of fixed prices must be replaced by expected valuations in terms of random prices, we have that

$$\Delta_2' \leqq \Delta_2''' := -E\bar{\mathbf{p}}_k(\bar{\mathbf{x}}_k - \mathbf{x}_k^N) + E\bar{\mathbf{p}}_l(\bar{\mathbf{y}}_l - \mathbf{y}_l^N).$$

The latter expression may be estimated, using the L_∞ norm boundedness of Q_t [Condition (III)] and the stationarity of the prices supporting the turnpike:

$$\begin{aligned}\Delta''' &\leqq \alpha E|\bar{\mathbf{p}}_k| + CE|\bar{\mathbf{p}}_k|\mathbf{1}_{\bar{\Gamma}_1} + \alpha E|\bar{\mathbf{p}}_l| + CE|\bar{\mathbf{p}}_l|\mathbf{1}_{\bar{\Gamma}_2}\\ &= 2\alpha E|\bar{\mathbf{p}}_0| + CE|\bar{\mathbf{p}}_0|(\mathbf{1}_{T^k\bar{\Gamma}_1} + \mathbf{1}_{T^l\bar{\Gamma}_2})\\ &\leqq 2\alpha E|\bar{\mathbf{p}}_0| + 2C \sup_{P(\Gamma)\leqq\beta} E|\bar{\mathbf{p}}_0|\mathbf{1}_\Gamma =: \gamma(\alpha,\beta).\end{aligned} \tag{24}$$

This bound $\gamma(\alpha, \beta)$ can be made arbitrarily small by choosing α and β sufficiently small.

Next we estimate Δ_2''. First, note that $\bar{\mathbf{z}}_t = \mathbf{z}_t$ for $t = k + r + 2, \ldots, l - 1$, so the corresponding terms in the sum Δ_2'' equal zero. The terms at times $t = k + 1$, $k + r + 1$ and l are each estimated using Condition (X) by the appropriate value of $W(\eta_t)$, where $\eta_t := E|\mathbf{z}_t - \bar{\mathbf{z}}_t|$. Thus, using (1) and the definition of $\bar{\Gamma}_1$,

$$\begin{aligned}\eta_{k+1} &= E|\mathbf{1}_{\Gamma_1}(\bar{\mathbf{x}}_k - (c+1)\alpha 1, \bar{\mathbf{y}}_{k+1}) + \mathbf{1}_{\bar{\Gamma}_1}(\bar{\mathbf{z}}_{k+1})^{(\alpha)} - \bar{\mathbf{z}}_{k+1}|\\ &\leqq E\mathbf{1}_{\Gamma_1}|(c+1)\alpha 1| + E\mathbf{1}_{\bar{\Gamma}_1}|(\bar{\mathbf{z}}_{k+1})^{(\alpha)} - \bar{\mathbf{z}}_{k-1}|\\ &\leqq (c+1)\alpha n + 2\beta C\end{aligned} \tag{25}$$

and

$$\eta_{k+r+1} = \eta_l = n\alpha, \tag{26}$$

where n is the dimension of the goods space. It remains only to estimate the terms in Δ_2'' corresponding to times $t = k + 2, \ldots, k + r$. But by the bound 3 of Lemma 3,

$$\sum_{t=k+2}^{k+r} [F_t(\bar{\mathbf{z}}_t) - F_t(\mathbf{z}_t)] \leqq d(\alpha)w(\beta). \tag{27}$$

Similarly,

$$\Delta_3 \leqq d(\alpha)w(\beta). \tag{28}$$

Summing the estimates (23)–(28), we find that

$$\begin{aligned} \Delta &\leqq c\alpha + \gamma(\alpha, \beta) + W[(c + 1)\alpha n + 2\beta C] \\ &\quad + 2W(n\alpha) + 2W(n\alpha) + 2d(\alpha)w(\beta) \\ &=: \Theta(\alpha, \beta). \end{aligned} \tag{29}$$

The bound denoted by Θ is independent of N and can be made as small as desired by choosing first a sufficiently small α, then a sufficiently small β. □

This proves Theorem 1. Indeed, we choose α and β such that $\Theta < \epsilon$ and use them to construct, for all sufficiently large N, $k := k(N, \alpha, \beta)$, $l := l(N, \alpha, \beta)$ and $\zeta := \zeta(N, \alpha, \beta)$. The utility of each such ζ differs from the corresponding optimal utility by not more than ϵ, and therefore $\{\zeta\} := \{\zeta(N)\}$ is a family of Winter programmes. □

3. THE STRONG TURNPIKE THEOREM

1. Statement of the Result

We assume that the conditions stated at the beginning of §2 hold.

Theorem 2. (Strong turnpike theorem.) *Under Conditions* (I)–(X) and (Int), *for each $\epsilon > 0$ there exists a constant $L_1 := L_1(\epsilon)$, independent of N, such that for any $N > 2L_1$ and $t = L_1, L_1 + 1, \ldots, N - L_1$, $E|\bar{\mathbf{z}}_t - \mathbf{z}_t^N| < \epsilon$.*

If, further, the functionals F_t satisfy the strict concavity condition (F.2), *then for any $\epsilon > 0$ and $\delta > 0$ there exists a constant $L_2 := L_2(\epsilon, \delta)$, independent of N, such that for any $N > 2L_2$*

$$P\{|\mathbf{z}_t^N - \bar{\mathbf{z}}_t| < \epsilon, t = L_2, \ldots, N - L_2\} \geqq 1 - \delta. \quad □ \tag{30}$$

It was stated in Theorem 4.4 that optimal programmes can deviate significantly from the turnpike (in the sense of expected norm) only in a small number of time periods. The first part of Theorem 2 states additionally that such periods must be situated close to the end points of the planning interval. The second part of the theorem states that, with probability close to 1, the optimal programme can leave an ϵ-neighbourhood of the turnpike only at time periods close to the end points of the planning interval.

The second statement is stronger than the first, since for $t = L_2, \dots, N - L_2$ we have the estimate

$$\begin{aligned} E|\mathbf{z}_t^N - \bar{\mathbf{z}}_t| &= E|\mathbf{z}_t^N - \bar{\mathbf{z}}_t|\mathbf{1}_{\{|\mathbf{z}_t^N - \bar{\mathbf{z}}_t| < \epsilon\}} + E|\mathbf{z}_t^N - \bar{\mathbf{z}}_t|\mathbf{1}_{\{|\mathbf{z}_t^N - \bar{\mathbf{z}}_t| \geqq \epsilon\}} \\ &\leqq \epsilon + 2C\delta. \end{aligned}$$

(C is a constant representing the L_∞ norm bound on Q_t.)

2. The Turnpike Theorem for the Pseudometric ρ_t

□ To prove Theorem 2 it is sufficient to establish the following statement.

Lemma 5. *For any $\tau > 0$ there exists a constant $L := L(\tau)$ such that for $N \geqq 2L$*

$$\sum_{t=L}^{N-L} \rho_t(\mathbf{z}_t^N, \bar{\mathbf{z}}_t) < \tau. \quad \square \tag{31}$$

Recall the definition of the pseudometric ρ_t on Q_t from §4.4.3:

$$\rho_t(\mathbf{z}, \mathbf{z}') := |G_t(\mathbf{z}) - G_t(\mathbf{z}')|,$$

where (under our current assumptions) the reduced utility is given by

$$G_t(\mathbf{z}) := F_t(\mathbf{z}) + E\bar{\mathbf{p}}_t\mathbf{y} - E\bar{\mathbf{p}}_{t-1}\mathbf{x}.$$

We show next how to derive the first statement of Theorem 2 from Lemma 5.

□ Fix $\epsilon > 0$ and set $\tau := \delta_1(\epsilon)$, where $\delta_1(\epsilon)$ is the function figuring in the strict concavity condition (F.1′) (see §4.3.1). Then if $E|\mathbf{z}_t^N - \bar{\mathbf{z}}_t| \geqq \epsilon$ for some t, by Lemma 4.9

$$\rho_t(\mathbf{z}_t^N, \bar{\mathbf{z}}_t) \geqq \delta_1(E|\mathbf{z}_t^N - \bar{\mathbf{z}}_t|) \geqq \delta_1(\epsilon) := \tau,$$

from which it follows, by (31), that $t \neq L, \dots, N - L$. □

The second statement of Theorem 2 is obtained from the lemma as follows:

□ Note first that by Lemma 4.9 it follows from (31) that

$$\sum_{t=L}^{N-L} P\{\Gamma_t^N\} \leqq \frac{\tau}{\delta_2(\epsilon)},$$

where $\Gamma_t^N := \{|\mathbf{z}_t^N - \bar{\mathbf{z}}_t| \geqq \epsilon\}$. But

$$\begin{aligned} P\{|\mathbf{z}_t^N - \bar{\mathbf{z}}_t| < \epsilon, t = L, \ldots, N - L\} & \\ = 1 - P\{\exists t, L \leqq t \leqq N - L, \text{ s.t.} |\mathbf{z}_t^N - \bar{\mathbf{z}}_t| \geqq \epsilon\} & \\ = 1 - P\left\{\bigcup_{t=L}^{N-L} \Gamma_t^N\right\} \geqq 1 - \sum_{t=L}^{N-L} P(\Gamma_t^N) \geqq 1 - \frac{\tau}{\delta_2(\epsilon)}. & \end{aligned}$$

From this it may be seen that if we take as $L_2(\epsilon, \delta)$ the value $L(\delta\, \delta_2(\epsilon))$ of Lemma 5, then the probability in (30) will not be less than $1 - \delta$. □

3. Estimation of $\sum \rho_t$

The proof of Lemma 5 is based on the following estimate of sums such as appear in (31).

Lemma 6. *For any programme $\{\mathbf{z}_t\}$ with i.v. $\mathbf{y}_0$ and for any N, k and l such that $1 \leqq k < l \leqq N$, the inequality*

$$\begin{aligned} \sum_{t=k+1}^{l} \rho_t(\mathbf{z}_t^N, \bar{\mathbf{z}}_t) \leqq \sum_{t=1}^{k} [F_t(\mathbf{z}_t^N) - F_t(\mathbf{z}_t)] & \\ + \sum_{t=l+1}^{N} [F_t(\mathbf{z}_t^N) - F_t(\mathbf{z}_t)] & \\ + \sum_{t=k+1}^{l} [F_t(\bar{\mathbf{z}}_t) - F_t(\mathbf{z}_t)] & \\ - E\bar{\mathbf{p}}_k(\bar{\mathbf{x}}_k - \mathbf{x}_k^N) + E\bar{\mathbf{p}}_l(\bar{\mathbf{y}}_l - \mathbf{y}_l^N) & \qquad (32) \end{aligned}$$

holds.

□ The statement of this lemma is similar to that of Lemma 1.11. The differences are that k is replaced by $k + 1$, the appropriate time indices are added and expectations of random terms are taken. Effecting the corresponding changes in the proof of Lemma 1.11 yields the proof of Lemma 6. □

4. Proof of Lemma 5

□ Consider the evaluation of the right-hand side of (32) for the programme $\zeta = \zeta(N, \alpha, \beta)$ constructed in this Chapter (§2.3) with $k := k(N, \alpha, \beta)$ and $l := l(N, \alpha, \beta)$. We have already estimated the sums appearing in the right-hand side of (32) in §2.5. The first sum is Δ_1, the second is Δ_3, the third is Δ_2'' and the sum of the last two expectations is Δ_2'''. It was proven in §2.5 that the sums of these values do not exceed $\Theta(\alpha, \beta)$ [see (29)]. We can make this value less than τ by choosing an appropriate α and β, and as L we take the constant bounding the previously constructed sequences $\{k(N) + 1\}$ and $\{N - l(N)\}$. For this L, by (32), the inequality (31) holds. □□

4. THE MODEL WITH HISTORY BEGINNING AT 0

1. Description of the Model

In the previous and present chapters it was assumed that the random values of the process $\{\mathbf{s}_t\}$ are defined for all integers t. This might be considered justifiable if $\mathbf{s}_t$ is interpreted as the state of the total environment which influences the economy at time t, but it is unnatural in some other interpretations. In the present section a model will be investigated for which the process $\{\mathbf{s}_t\}$ is given only at all *nonnegative* integers t (i.e., for which history begins at 0).

Let us agree that $\mathbf{s}_0^t$ will denote the *history* $(\mathbf{s}_0, \ldots, \mathbf{s}_t)$ of the given process (in order to distinguish it notationally from the infinite history $\mathbf{s}^t$ of a doubly infinite process $\ldots, \mathbf{s}_{-1}, \mathbf{s}_0, \mathbf{s}_1, \ldots$).

The model will be presented in terms of a *stationary Markov version* of the *parametric model* described in §2.4.7. Technology sets are defined as classes of functions $(x(\mathbf{s}_0^{t-1}), y(\mathbf{s}_0^t))$, represented (up to P-equivalence) as

$$x(\mathbf{s}_0^{t-1}) := a(\mathbf{s}_{t-1}, u(\mathbf{s}_0^{t-1})) \qquad \text{a.s.,} \tag{33}$$

$$y(\mathbf{s}_0^t) := b(\mathbf{s}_{t-1}, \mathbf{s}_t, u(\mathbf{s}_0^{t-1})) \qquad \text{a.s.,} \tag{34}$$

where $u(\mathbf{s}_0^{t-1}) \in U(\mathbf{s}_{t-1})$ a.s., and

$$F_t(\mathbf{z}) := Ef(\mathbf{s}_{t-1}, \mathbf{s}_t, z(\mathbf{s}_0^t)) \tag{35}$$

for $t = 1, 2, \ldots$. It will be assumed in the sequel that the mappings a, b, f and U satisfy the conditions (M_1)–(M_9) (see §2.4.7) and that the process $\{\mathbf{s}_t\}$ is stationary and Markovian.

We shall show that optimal planning theory over an infinite time horizon for such a model (denoted M) can be obtained as a corollary of the theory developed for stationary models with history beginning at $-\infty$.

2. The Model M' with History Beginning at $-\infty$ and Corresponding to the Model M

First, we construct a model M' with history beginning at $-\infty$ from the model M defined by (33)–(35). We extend indefinitely to the left the stationary process $\mathbf{s}_0, \mathbf{s}_1, \mathbf{s}_2, \ldots$, to obtain the stationary process

$$\ldots, \mathbf{s}_{-1}, \mathbf{s}_0, \mathbf{s}_1, \mathbf{s}_2, \ldots.$$ [4]

Supposing that at time t the (realization of the) history $s^t := (\ldots, s_{t-1}, s_t)$ is known, we consider the technological processes to be of type $(x(s^{t-1}), y(s^t))$ and define the technology sets Q_t' and utility functionals F_t' by (32)–(35) with $\mathbf{s}_0^t$ replaced by $\mathbf{s}^t$.

Note that any programme in the model M (an *M-programme*) may be interpreted as a programme in the model M' (an *M'-programme*). The class of M'-programmes of this type (i.e., corresponding to M-programmes) is denote by Π.

3. Existence of Majorizing M-Programmes

Let $0 \leqq y_0(\mathbf{s}_0) \in L_\infty^n(S_0)$.

Lemma 7. *For any M'-programme $\zeta = \{z_t(\mathbf{s}^t)\}$ with i.v. $y_0(\mathbf{s}_0)$ there exists an M-programme $\hat{\zeta} = \{\hat{\mathbf{z}}_t\} \in \Pi$ with i.v. $y_0(\mathbf{s}_0)$ majorizing ζ in the*

[4] Strictly speaking, this means that we extend the probability measure on the space of sequences $s_0, s_1, s_2, \ldots$ (corresponding to sample paths of the original process) to the space of doubly infinite sequences $\ldots, s_{-1}, s_0, s_1, \ldots$ (corresponding to the sample paths of the extended process) in such a way that the extended measure defines a stationary Markov process.

sense that

$$F_t(\hat{\mathbf{z}}_t) \geqq F_t(\mathbf{z}_t)$$

for each $t = 1, 2, \ldots$. *Furthermore, the programme* $\hat{\zeta}$ *may be taken to be Markovian, i.e., defined by a sequence of control functions of the type* $\mathbf{u}_t := v_t(\mathbf{s}_t, \hat{\mathbf{y}}_t)$.

□ Since the function $y_0(\mathbf{s}_0)$ depends only on $\mathbf{s}_0$, it is easy to see that any Markov programme belongs to the class Π. A Markov programme majorizing ζ can be constructed by the iterative procedure described by (66) of §3.4.5. The argument describing the properties of this construction corresponds word for word to the proof of Theorem 3.7. □

Corollary 2. *Any optimal* M*-programme* ζ^0 *(finite or infinite) with i.v.* $\mathbf{y}_0$ *is at the same time an optimal* M'*-programme with i.v.* $y_0(\mathbf{s}_0)$.

□ Any M'-programme ζ' with i.v. $\mathbf{y}_0$ is majorized by some M-programme $\hat{\zeta}'$ with i.v. $\mathbf{y}_0$. But this programme $\hat{\zeta}'$ cannot be strictly preferable to ζ^0 (in the sense of the appropriate definition of optimality). Hence ζ^0 considered as an M'-programme is optimal. □

Note also that Lemma 7 allows us to conclude immediately the existence of optimal M-programmes from the corresponding existence theorem for optimal M'-programmes (finite and infinite).

□ Indeed, suppose ζ^0 is an optimal programme of length N $(\leqq \infty)$ with i.v. $y_0(\mathbf{s}_0)$ in the model M'. Then it is majorized by some M-programme $\hat{\zeta}^0$ with the same i.v. The programme $\hat{\zeta}^0$ is not worse than any M'-programme with i.v. $\mathbf{y}_0$ and, in particular, is not worse than any M-programme with i.v. $\mathbf{y}_0$. Therefore, $\hat{\zeta}^0$ is an optimal M-programme. □

4. The Turnpike

In the model M the *rôle* of the turnpike is played by the turnpike $\bar{\zeta} := \{\bar{z}(\mathbf{s}^t)\}$ of the model M'. It follows from Corollary 2 and the turnpike theorems for the model M' that optimal M-programmes will be close to $\bar{\zeta}$.

Here, however, a noticeable difference between models with history beginning at 0 and models with history beginning at $-\infty$ arises. In the first type of model the turnpike is *not* a programme within the model, since at each time period it depends (potentially) on an infinite past; it is only a formal programme within the "extended" model.

However, it is possible to give another interpretation of the "programme" $\bar{\zeta}$ *within* the model M. If we fix the history s^{-1}, then the sequence

$$\bar{z}(s^{-1}, \mathbf{s}_0^1), \quad \bar{z}(s^{-1}, \mathbf{s}_0^2), \quad \ldots$$

defines an M-programme for each $s^{-1} \in \times_{t=-\infty}^{-1} S$.

Thus we have obtained a family of M-programmes depending on a random parameter $\mathbf{s}^{-1}$. Which of these programmes to use depends on the value of $\mathbf{s}^{-1}$ realized. In this sense, we may say that the *turnpike* $\bar{\zeta}$ is a *randomized M-programme.*

5. Results Concerning Prices

Results on the existence of supporting prices in the model M may be obtained from the analogous results for the model M' with the help of the following observation:

Lemma 8. *Suppose the prices* $\{p_t'(\mathbf{s}^t)\}$ *support the programmes of type* $\{z_t(\mathbf{s}_0^t)\}$ *in the model* M'. *Then the prices*

$$p_t(\mathbf{s}_0^t) := E[p_t'(\mathbf{s}^t) \mid \mathbf{s}_0^t]$$

support this programme in the model M.

□ By the definition of supporting prices, we have Property B:

$$\begin{aligned} 0 &= Ep_t'(\mathbf{s}^t)[y_t(\mathbf{s}_0^t) - x_t(\mathbf{s}_0^t)] = E(E[p_t'(\mathbf{s}^t)[y_t(\mathbf{s}_0^t) - x_t(\mathbf{s}_0^t)] \mid \mathbf{s}_0^t]) \\ &= E(E[p_t'(\mathbf{s}^t) \mid \mathbf{s}_0^t][y_t(\mathbf{s}_0^t) - x_t(\mathbf{s}_0^t)]) \\ &= E\mathbf{p}_t(\mathbf{y}_t - \mathbf{x}_t). \end{aligned}$$

Property A in the definition of supporting prices is obtained similarly from

$$\begin{aligned} &F_t(\mathbf{z}) + Ep_t'(\mathbf{s}^t)y(\mathbf{s}_0^t) - Ep_{t-1}'(\mathbf{s}^{t-1})x(\mathbf{s}_0^{t-1}) \\ &\quad = F_t(\mathbf{z}) + Ep_t(\mathbf{s}_0^t)y(\mathbf{s}_0^t) - Ep_{t-1}(\mathbf{s}_0^{t-1})x(\mathbf{s}_0^{t-1}) \end{aligned}$$

for $z(\mathbf{s}_0^t) := (x(\mathbf{s}_0^{t-1}), y(\mathbf{s}_0^t))$. □

Remark. *We can also consider a model in which the process* $\{\mathbf{s}_t\}$ *begins at some time* $-\alpha \leqq 0$ *(i.e., a model with history beginning at* $-\alpha$*).*

Then the $\{\mathbf{s}_t\}$ process is of the form $\mathbf{s}_{-\alpha}, \mathbf{s}_{-\alpha+1}, \ldots,$ and if the process given by

$$\boldsymbol{\sigma}_t := (\mathbf{s}_{-\alpha+t}, \ldots, \mathbf{s}_t), \qquad t = 0, 1, \ldots;$$

is Markov, then the model is trivially converted to the previous model by replacing $\{\mathbf{s}_t\}$ with $\{\boldsymbol{\sigma}_t\}$.

COMMENTS ON CHAPTER 5

The results of this chapter are due to Evstigneev and, in the context of the model described in §2.4.1, are published here for the first time.

Strong turnpike theorems were established earlier by Evstigneev [5] for a slightly simpler version of the present model. The techniques for the approximation of programmes were developed for the same paper.

Appendixes

I MEASURABLE SELECTION THEOREMS AND THEIR APPLICATIONS

1. Basic Definitions

Let $(\Omega, \mathscr{F})$ and $(X, \mathscr{B})$ be measurable spaces. We say that $\Gamma(\cdot)$ is a *multifunction* (*multivalued mapping, correspondence*) from Ω to X if to each $\omega \in \Omega$ there corresponds a set $\Gamma(\omega) \subseteq X$. We say that the multifunction $\omega \mapsto \Gamma(\omega)$ is *measurable* if the set

$$\Gamma := \operatorname{gr} \Gamma(\cdot) = \{(\omega, x) : x \in \Gamma(\omega)\}$$

[the *graph* of the mapping $\omega \mapsto \Gamma(\omega)$] belongs to $\mathscr{F} \times \mathscr{B}$.[1] In this case, it may also be said that $\Gamma(\cdot)$ is a *random subset* of X.

The function $\xi : \Omega \to X$ is called a *selector* of the multifunction $\omega \mapsto \Gamma(\omega)$ (or the set Γ) if

$$(\omega, \xi(\omega)) \in \Gamma \qquad \text{for} \quad \omega \in \operatorname{pr}_\Omega \Gamma.$$

Measurable spaces $(X, \mathscr{B})$ and $(X', \mathscr{B}')$ are said to be *isomorphic* if there exists a bijective function $i : X \to X'$ such that the functions i and i^{-1} are measurable.

A measurable space $(X, \mathscr{B})$ is called *standard* (*Borel*) if it is isomorphic to a Borel subset of a *Polish* (i.e., complete separable metric)

[1] $\mathscr{F} \times \mathscr{B}$ denotes the σ-algebra generated by all sets of the form $F \times B$, where $F \in \mathscr{F}$, $B \in \mathscr{B}$.

space with the Borel measurable structure generated by all open sets. It is known that any standard measurable space is isomorphic to one of the two following spaces: (1) a finite or countable set with all subsets measurable or (2) the unit interval $[0, 1]$ equipped with the Borel measurable structure (see, for example, Kuratovski [1], Ch. 3, §37, or Dynkin and Yushkevich [1], Appendix 2).

The intersection of all completions of the σ-algebra $\mathscr{F}$ with respect to all possible finite measures on it is called the *universal completion* of $\mathscr{F}$ and is denoted by $\bar{\mathscr{F}}$. $\mathscr{F}$ is said to be *universally complete* if $\bar{\mathscr{F}} = \mathscr{F}$.

The next result is due to Sainte-Beuve [1].

Theorem 1. (Measurable selection.) *Let $(X, \mathscr{B})$ be a standard measurable space and $(\Omega, \mathscr{F})$ an arbitrary measurable space. For any $\Gamma \in \mathscr{F} \times \mathscr{B}$ there exists an $\bar{\mathscr{F}}$-measurable selector.* □

To prove the theorem we reduce it to a particular case (described in Lemma 4). We begin with some needed preliminary results.

2. Lemmas Needed for the Reduction of the Measurable Selection Theorem to a Special Case

Lemma 1. *Let Δ be a Borel subset of a Polish space X. Then there exist a Polish space Y and a continuous mapping $\phi: Y \to X$ such that $\Delta = \phi(Y)$.*

□ The proof of this can be found in Naimark [1], Appendix III. □

We say that pairs of measurable spaces $(\Omega, \mathscr{F})$, $(X, \mathscr{B})$ possess the *measurable choice property* if the statement of Theorem 1 is true for them. The measurable space $(\Omega, \mathscr{F})$ is said to be a *measurable preimage* of the measurable space $(\Omega', \mathscr{F}')$ if there exists a mapping $i: \Omega \to \Omega'$ such that $i^{-1}(\mathscr{F}') = \mathscr{F}$.

Lemma 2. *If the pair of measurable spaces $(\Omega', \mathscr{F}')$, $(X, \mathscr{B})$ possesses the measurable choice property and $(\Omega, \mathscr{F})$ is a measurable preimage of $(\Omega', \mathscr{F}')$, then the pair of spaces $(\Omega, \mathscr{F})$, $(X, \mathscr{B})$ also possesses the measurable choice property.*

□ Let $i: \Omega \to \Omega'$ be the mapping which generates $\mathscr{F}$. Then each set $\Gamma \in \mathscr{F} \times \mathscr{B}$ may be represented as $j^{-1}(\Delta)$, where $\Delta \in \mathscr{F}' \times \mathscr{B}$ and

$j(\omega, x) := (i(\omega), x)$. Indeed, by the definition of measurable preimage, this representation is valid for the "rectangle" $F \times B$ ($F \in \mathscr{F}$, $B \in \mathscr{B}$). Furthermore, since the class of sets permitting the required representation is a σ-algebra, this class coincides with $\mathscr{F} \times \mathscr{B}$.

Note that if $\xi(\omega')$ is a selector of Δ, then $\eta(\omega) := \xi(i(\omega))$ is a selector of Γ. Indeed, if $\omega \in \mathrm{pr}_\Omega \Gamma$, then $(\omega, x) \in \Gamma$ for some x and thus $(i(\omega), x) \in \Delta$; i.e., $i(\omega) \in \mathrm{pr}_{\Omega'} \Delta$. But then $(i(\omega), \xi(i(\omega))) \in \Delta$ implies $(\omega, \xi(i(\omega))) \in \Gamma$.

We show now that the mapping $\eta: (\Omega, \bar{\mathscr{F}}) \to (X, \mathscr{B})$ is measurable if $\xi: (\Omega, \bar{\mathscr{F}}') \to (X, \mathscr{B})$ is measurable. It is sufficient to show that $i^{-1}(\bar{\mathscr{F}}') \subseteq \bar{\mathscr{F}}$.

To this end, fix a finite measure μ on $\mathscr{F}$. For any $A' \in \bar{\mathscr{F}}'$ we must find sets $A_1, A_2 \in \mathscr{F}$, such that $A_1 \subseteq A := i^{-1}(A') \subseteq A_2$ and $\mu(A_1) = \mu(A_2)$. Consider a measure $\nu(\cdot) := \mu(i^{-1}(\cdot))$ on $\mathscr{F}'$ and sets $A_1' \in \mathscr{F}'$ and $A_2' \in \mathscr{F}'$ such that $A_1' \subseteq A' \subseteq A_2'$ and $\nu(A_1') = \nu(A_2')$. It remains only to set $A_1 := i^{-1}(A_1')$, $A_2 := i^{-1}(A_2')$. □

A σ-algebra $\mathscr{F}$ is said to be *separable* if there exists a countable family of sets which generate $\mathscr{F}$. It is known that the σ-algebra $\mathscr{F}$ is separable if and only if the measurable space $(\Omega, \mathscr{F})$ is a measurable preimage of $(\mathbb{R}, \mathscr{B}(\mathbb{R}))$, where $\mathbb{R}$ is the real line and $\mathscr{B}(\cdot)$ denotes the Borel σ-algebra (see, for example, Meyer [1], Ch. III, §1, for the construction of a suitable generating mapping).

Lemma 3. *For any $\Gamma \in \mathscr{F} \times \mathscr{B}$, a separable σ-algebra $\mathscr{F}_0 \subseteq \mathscr{F}$ can be found such that $\Gamma \in \mathscr{F}_0 \times \mathscr{B}$.*

□ Consider the class $\mathscr{G}$ of sets $\Gamma \in \mathscr{F} \times \mathscr{B}$ for which $\mathscr{F}_0$ exists with the required properties. It is obviously closed with respect to complements. Further, if $\Gamma^k \in \mathscr{G}$ ($k = 1, 2, \ldots$), i.e., $\Gamma^k \in \mathscr{F}_0^k \times \mathscr{B}$, where the σ-algebras $\mathscr{F}_0^k$ are separable, then

$$\bigcup_{k=1}^{\infty} \Gamma^k \in \bigvee_{k=1}^{\infty} (\mathscr{F}_0^k \times \mathscr{B}) \subseteq \Big(\bigvee_{k=1}^{\infty} \mathscr{F}_0^k\Big) \times \mathscr{B},$$

where $\vee_{k=1}^{\infty} \mathscr{F}_0^k$ is a separable σ-algebra.[2] Since $\mathscr{G}$ is thus a σ-algebra which contains the cylinders, it follows that $\mathscr{G} = \mathscr{F} \times \mathscr{B}$. □

[2] The symbol $\vee_{k=1}^{\infty} \mathscr{F}_0^k$ is used to designate the smallest σ-algebra containing all the $\mathscr{F}_0^k$.

3. The Special Case of the Measurable Selection Theorem

Lemma 4. *Let X, Y be Polish spaces, $\Gamma \in \mathscr{B}(X) \times \mathscr{B}(Y)$, and suppose that for each x the set $\Gamma(x)$ is closed. Then there exists a $\overline{\mathscr{B}(X)}$-measurable selector of Γ.*

□ The proof of this lemma is based on a fundamental fact—the universal measurability of *analytic* sets—given by the following proposition (see, for example, Meyer [1], III.1.13 and III.2.24).

Lemma 5. *If X, Y are Polish spaces and $B \in \mathscr{B}(X) \times \mathscr{B}(Y)$, then* $\mathrm{pr}_X B \in \overline{\mathscr{B}(X)}$. □

Let ρ be a metric on Y. From Lemma 5 it follows that for any $y_0 \in Y$ the function $x \mapsto \rho(y_0, \Gamma(x))$ is $\overline{\mathscr{B}(X)}$ measurable. Indeed,

$$\{x : \rho(y_0, \Gamma(x)) < h\} = \mathrm{pr}_X[\Gamma \cap \{(x, y) : \rho(y_0, y) < h\}],$$

where Γ is closed and therefore belongs to $\mathscr{B}(X) \times \mathscr{B}(Y)$.

Now, let $y_1, y_2, y_3, \ldots$ be a denumeration of a countable everywhere dense subset of the complete separable space Y. For $x \in X' = \mathrm{pr}_X \Gamma$, define by induction the sequence of functions given by $n_1(x), n_2(x), \ldots$ and $\eta_i(x) := y_{n_i}(x)$ as follows. Set $n_1(x) := j$, where j is the smallest natural number for which $\rho(y_j, \Gamma(x)) < 2^{-1}$ and take as $n_{k+1}(x)$ the smallest natural number j such that $\rho(y_j, \Gamma(x)) < 2^{-k-1}$ and $\rho(y_j, \eta_k(x)) < 2^{-k}$.[3] For $x \notin X'$, let $\eta_i(x) := 1$, $\eta_i(x) := y_1$.

The functions n_i and η_i are easily seen by induction to be measurable with respect to $\overline{\mathscr{B}(X)}$. Indeed, the induction step from k to $k + 1$ is established by noticing that the set $\{n_{k+1}(x) = j\}$ is expressed in terms of a countable number of operations with the sets $\{x : \rho(y_i, \Gamma(x)) < 2^{-k-1}\}$, $\{x : \rho(y_i, \eta_k(x)) < 2^{-k}\}$ and X. The measurability of n_{k+1}, η_{k+1} follows. The case $k = 1$ is established similarly.

Because $\rho(\eta_k(x), \eta_{k+1}(x)) < 2^{-k}$ for each x, the Cauchy sequence $\{\eta_k(x)\}$ has a limit $\eta(x)$. By construction, the limit function $\eta : X \to Y$ is $\overline{\mathscr{B}(X)}$ measurable, and $\eta(x) \in \Gamma(x)$ for $x \in X$, because $\Gamma(x)$ is closed for $x \in X'$. □

[3] We check to see that at least one such j exists. It suffices to prove that the open set $\{y \in Y : \rho(y, \Gamma(x)) < 2^{-k-1}, \rho(y, \eta_k(x)) < 2^{-k}\}$ is nonempty. But, since the distance from $\eta_k(x)$ to $\Gamma(x)$ is less than 2^{-k}, a $y \in \Gamma(x)$ with $\rho(y, \eta_k(x)) < 2^{-k}$ can always be found. This point clearly satisfies the first inequality.

4. Proof of the Measurable Selection Theorem

□ By Lemma 3 we may suppose that the σ-algebra $\mathscr{F}$ is separable. Moreover, by Lemma 2 and the remark following it, it may be supposed without loss of generality that $(\Omega, \mathscr{F}) = (\mathbb{R}, \mathscr{B}(\mathbb{R}))$.

Suppose further without loss of generality that $(X, \mathscr{B})$ is a Polish space with Borel σ-algebra. Then by Lemma 1 Γ may be represented as $\phi(Y)$, where Y is some Polish space, and ϕ is a continuous mapping:

$$\phi: Y \to R \times X, \qquad y \mapsto \phi(y) := (\lambda(y), \xi(y)).$$

Consider the $\overline{\mathscr{B}(\mathbb{R})}$-measurable selector $\zeta(r)$ of the multifunction $r \mapsto \lambda^{-1}(r) \subseteqq Y$; it exists by Lemma 4. For $r \in \{r: \lambda^{-1}(r) \neq \emptyset\} = \mathrm{pr}_{\mathbb{R}} \Gamma$, we have $\lambda(\zeta(r)) = r$ and $(\lambda(\zeta(r)), \xi(\zeta(r))) \in \Gamma$. Thus for $(r, \xi(\zeta(r))) \in \Gamma$, i.e., the function given by $\eta(r) := \xi(\zeta(r))$ is a selector of Γ. It remains only to observe that this function $\eta: (\mathbb{R}, \overline{\mathscr{B}(\mathbb{R})}) \to (X, \mathscr{B})$ is measurable as the composition of the measurable mapping $\zeta: (\mathbb{R}, \overline{\mathscr{B}(\mathbb{R})}) \to (Y, \mathscr{B}(Y))$ and the continuous mapping $\xi: Y \to X$. □

Note. Theorem 1 is one of the most usable forms of the wealth of results about measurable choice. Various generalizations of, and details relating to, Theorem 1 can be found in Wagner's review [1]. Applications of measurable choice in the theory of extremum problems and in mathematical economics can be seen in the work of Hildenbrand [1], Arkin and Levin [1], Evstigneev [6] and Arkin [1].

5. Some Corollaries of the Measurable Selection Theorem

Corollary 1. *Under the hypotheses of Theorem* 1, $\mathrm{pr}_{\Omega} \Gamma \in \overline{\mathscr{F}}$.

□ Let ξ be a selector of Γ. Then $\mathrm{pr}_{\Omega} \Gamma$ can be represented as $\phi^{-1}(\Gamma)$, where $\phi(\omega) := (\omega, \xi(\omega))$ is a measurable mapping from $(\Omega, \overline{\mathscr{F}})$ into $(\Omega \times X, \mathscr{F} \times \mathscr{B}(X))$. □

Corollary 2. (Castaing [1].) *Let X be a Polish space, $(\Omega, \mathscr{F})$ an arbitrary measurable space and $\Gamma \in \mathscr{F} \times \mathscr{B}(X)$. Then there exists a countable family of $\overline{\mathscr{F}}$-measurable selectors given by $x_k(\omega)$ $(k = 1, 2, \ldots)$*

such that for each $\omega \in \mathrm{pr}_\Omega \Gamma$ *the sequence* $\{x_k(\omega)\}$ *is dense in* $\Gamma(\omega) := \{x : (\omega, x) \in \Gamma\}$.

[The selectors $\{x_k\}$ are said to *approximate* $\Gamma(\omega)$.]

□ Let $y_1, y_2, \ldots$ be a denumeration of a countable everywhere dense subset of the complete separable space X. Define

$$V_{m,i} := \{y : \rho\{y, y_i) \leqq 1/m\}, \qquad \Gamma_{m,i}(\omega) := \Gamma(\omega) \cap V_{m,i}$$

($i, m = 1, 2, \ldots$). Obviously, $\omega \mapsto \Gamma_{m,i}(\omega)$ are measurable multifunctions. By Theorem 1 they possess $\bar{\mathscr{F}}$-measurable selectors $y_{m,i}(\omega)$. Let $x(\omega)$ be an arbitrary $\bar{\mathscr{F}}$-measurable selector of Γ. Then the selectors

$$x_{m,i}(\omega) := \begin{cases} x(\omega) & \text{if } \Gamma_{m,i}(\omega) = \varnothing, \\ y_{m,i}(\omega) & \text{if } \Gamma_{m,i}(\omega) \neq \varnothing \end{cases}$$

are $\bar{\mathscr{F}}$ measurable and possess the required property. □

The next result is an immediate corollary of Theorem 1; it was first obtained by Aumann [1].

Corollary 3. *Let* $(\Omega, \mathscr{F})$, $(X, \mathscr{B})$ *and* Γ *be as in Theorem* 1, *and let* P *be a finite measure on* $\mathscr{F}$. *Then there exists an* $\mathscr{F}$*-measurable function* $x(\omega)$ *such that* $(\omega, x(\omega)) \in \Gamma$ *for all* $\omega \in \mathrm{pr}_\Omega \Gamma$ *except possibly for some set with measure* 0. □

In optimal control problems measurable choice theorems are often used in the form of *Filippov's lemma*, a version of which is set out next.

Corollary 4. *Let* U *be a Polish space;* $(\Omega_1, \mathscr{F}_1)$, $(\Omega_2, \mathscr{F}_2)$ *two measurable spaces;* $P_1(d\omega_1)$ *a probability measure on* $\mathscr{F}_1$ *and* $\pi(\omega_1, d\omega_2)$ *a probability measure on* $\mathscr{F}_2$ *such that* $\pi(\omega_1, \Gamma)$ *is an* $\mathscr{F}_1$*-measurable function with respect to* ω_1 *for any* $\Gamma \in \mathscr{F}_2$. *Let measurable functions with values in* $\mathbb{R}^{n_i}$ *be given by* $h_i(\omega_1, \omega_2)$, $f_i(u, \omega_1, \omega_2)$ $(i = 1, 2)$, *and let* $\omega_1 \mapsto U(\omega_1) \subseteq U$ *be a* $\mathscr{B}(U)$*-measurable multifunction. Suppose that for each* ω_1 *we can find a* $u \in U(\omega_1)$ *for which* $h_1(\omega_1, \omega_2) = f_1(u, \omega_1, \omega_2)$ *and* $h_2(\omega_1, \omega_2) \leqq f_2(u, \omega_1, \omega_2)$ *a.s.* $[\pi(\omega_1, \cdot)]$.

Then there exists a measurable function given by $u(\omega_1)$ *such that* $u(\omega_1) \in U(\omega_1)$, $h_1(\omega_1, \omega_2) = f_1(u(\omega_1), \omega_1, \omega_2)$ and $h_2(\omega_1, \omega_2) \leqq f_2(u(\omega_1), \omega_1, \omega_2)$ a.s. *with respect to the measure given by* $P(d\omega_1, d\omega_2) := P_1(d\omega_1)\pi(\omega_1, d\omega_2)$.

□ *Define*

$$V(\omega_1) := \{u \in U(\omega_1): h_1(\omega_1, \omega_2) = f_1(u, \omega_1, \omega_2),$$
$$h_2(\omega_1, \omega_2) \leq f_2(u, \omega_1, \omega_2) \text{ a.s. } [\pi(\omega_1, \cdot)]\}.$$

In light of Corollary 3, it is sufficient to check that $V(\omega_1)$ is measurably dependent on ω_1, but this is so, since

$$V(\omega_1) = \left\{u: \int_{\Omega_2} |h_1(\omega_1, \omega_2) - f_1(u, \omega_1, \omega_2)| \pi(\omega_1, d\omega_2) = 0, \right.$$
$$\left. \int_{\Omega_2} (h_2(\omega_1, \omega_2) - f_2(u, \omega_1, \omega_2))_+ \pi(\omega_1, d\omega_2) = 0, u \in U(\omega_1)\right\},$$

by virtue of Corollary 1 of Theorem III.8.[4] □

This version of Filippov's lemma was used by Arkin and Krechetov [2].

[4] For a vector $a = (a_1, \ldots, a_k)$, a_+ denotes the vector with coordinates $\max(0, a_i)$, $i = 1, \ldots, k$.

II CONDITIONAL DISTRIBUTIONS

1. Existence Theorem for Conditional Distributions

Theorem 1. *Let $(\Omega, \mathcal{F}, P)$ be a probability space, $(X, \mathcal{A})$ and $(Y, \mathcal{B})$ measurable spaces, and $\xi: \Omega \to X$ and $\eta: \Omega \to Y$ measurable functions. Suppose that the space $(Y, \mathcal{B})$ is standard (see Appendix* I). *Then there exists a real-valued function given by $\pi(x, \Gamma)$ for $x \in X$ and $\Gamma \in \mathcal{B}$ which possesses the following properties:*

(a) *$\pi(\cdot, \Gamma)$ is $\mathcal{A}$ measurable for fixed $\Gamma \in \mathcal{B}$;*
(b) *$\pi(x, \cdot)$ is a probability measure on $\mathcal{B}$ for each $x \in X$;*
(c) *if f is a measurable real-valued function on $X \times Y$, then*

$$E[f(\xi, \eta) \mid \xi] = \int_Y f(\xi, y)\pi(\xi, dy) \qquad a.s. \tag{1}$$

whenever the mean $Ef(\xi, \eta)$ exists.

□ We prove Theorem 1 by reduction to a special case.

2. Reduction of the Existence Theorem to a Special Case

□ First note by the definition of the integral that formula (1) is true for all f if it is true for nonnegative f. A nonnegative function f may be considered as the pointwise limit of bounded functions (in terms of a monotone sequence of functions of the type $f_n := \min(n, f)$, $n = 1, 2, \ldots$). Finally, by virtue of Theorem III.8, it is sufficient to state the truth of formula (1) for an f which has the form $f(x, y) = \phi(x)\psi(y)$, where ϕ and ψ are nonnegative and bounded. In this case (1) may be rewritten as

$$\phi(\xi)E[\psi(\eta)|\xi] = \phi(\xi)\int_Y \psi(y)\pi(\xi, dy) \qquad \text{a.s.,}$$

and therefore (c) holds if

$$E[\psi(\eta)|\xi] = \int_Y \psi(y)\pi(\xi, dy) \qquad \text{a.s.} \tag{2}$$

for any nonnegative bounded ψ. □

We make a further observation.

Let Q be the probability measure induced on $\mathscr{A}$ by the random variable ξ through the equation $Q(A) = P(\xi^{-1}(A))$ $(A \in \mathscr{A})$ and let $\mathscr{A}(Q)$ denote the completion of $\mathscr{A}$ with respect to Q. Suppose there exists a function given by $\pi(x, \Gamma)$ which possesses properties (b), (c) *and*

(a′) $\pi(\cdot, \Gamma)$ *is $\mathscr{A}(Q)$-measurable for any $\Gamma \in \mathscr{B}$.*

Then $\pi(x, \Gamma)$ may be modified so that properties (a)–(c) *hold.*

□ For this purpose we consider a countable algebra $\mathscr{C}$ generating $\mathscr{B}$ [$\mathscr{C}$ exists because the space $(Y, \mathscr{B})$ is standard]. As the function $\pi(\cdot, C)$ is $\mathscr{A}(Q)$ measurable, then for each $C \in \mathscr{C}$ may be found a set $\Delta := \Delta(C) \in \mathscr{A}$ such that $Q(\Delta) = 1$ and the function given by $1_\Delta(x)\pi(x, C)$ is $\mathscr{A}$ measurable. Taking the intersection of all such $\Delta(C)$ over $C \in \mathscr{C}$, we obtain a set A such that $Q(A) = 1$ and $1_A(x)\pi(x, C)$ is $\mathscr{A}$ measurable for every $C \in \mathscr{C}$. The $\mathscr{A}$-measurability of $1_A(x)\pi(x, \Gamma)$ in x for any $\Gamma \in \mathscr{B}$ follows.[1]

Now we fix some probability measure m on $\mathscr{B}$ and set

$$\pi'(x, \Gamma) = 1_A(x)\pi(x, \Gamma) + [1 - 1_A(x)]m(\Gamma).$$

Obviously, π' possesses Properties (a) and (b). Property (2) is also

[1] Indeed, all the sets $\Gamma \in \mathscr{B}$ for which the function $1_A(\cdot)\pi(\cdot, \Gamma)$ is measurable with respect to $\mathscr{A}$ form a monotone class. This monotone class contains the algebra $\mathscr{C}$ generating $\mathscr{B}$, which implies that it must coincide with $\mathscr{B}$ (see Theorem III.7).

valid since

$$\int_Y \psi(y)\pi'(\xi(\omega), dy) = \int_Y \psi(y)\pi(\xi(\omega), dy)$$

for all ω such that $\xi(\omega) \in A$, i.e., with probability 1.[2] □

3. Liftings

It remains to construct a function π with the properties (a′), (b) and (c). We use a theorem about liftings. It is known (see, for example, Meyer [1], Dinculeanu [1]) that in each equivalence class of measurable functions $\tilde{\gamma} \in L_\infty(X, \mathscr{A}(Q), Q)$ a member γ may be chosen such that the mapping

$$\rho : \tilde{\gamma} \mapsto \gamma$$

satisfies the following conditions:

(1) ρ is a linear operator;
(2) $\sup_x |\gamma(x)| = \|\tilde{\gamma}\|_{L_\infty}$;
(3) if $\tilde{\gamma} \geqq 0$ (i.e., this property holds a.s. for each random variable in $\tilde{\gamma}$), then $\gamma(x) \geqq 0$ for all x;
(4) $\rho(\tilde{1}) = 1$ ($\tilde{1}$ is the equivalence class of functions containing the constant function 1).

Such a mapping ρ from L_∞ into the space of bounded $\mathscr{A}(Q)$ measurable functions is called a *(linear) lifting*.

4. Proof of the Special Case of the Existence Theorem

□ Represent $(Y, \mathscr{B})$ as the interval $[0, 1]$ with Borel measurable structure (see Appendix I), and for continuous functions $\psi \in C(Y)$ set

$$\pi(x, \psi) := \rho(\tilde{E}[\psi(\boldsymbol{\eta})|\boldsymbol{\xi} = x]).^3$$

By virtue of the properties of the lifting, $\pi(x, \cdot)$ defines for each x a bounded nonnegative functional on $C(Y)$ satisfying the condition

[2] Indeed, $P\{\omega : \xi(\omega) \in A\} = Q(A) = 1$.
[3] Here $\tilde{E}[\psi(\boldsymbol{\eta})|\boldsymbol{\xi} = (\cdot)]$ denotes the class of $\mathscr{A}(Q)$ measurable functions g, equivalent with respect to Q, such that $g(\boldsymbol{\xi}) = E[\psi(\boldsymbol{\eta})|\boldsymbol{\xi}]$ a.s.

$\pi(x, 1) = 1$. Such a functional is defined by a probability measure $\pi(x, dy)$ on $\mathscr{B}$, so

$$\int_Y \psi(y)\pi(x, dy) = \rho\tilde{E}[\psi(\boldsymbol{\eta})|\boldsymbol{\xi} = x]$$

$$= E[\psi(\boldsymbol{\eta})|\boldsymbol{\xi} = x] \qquad \text{a.s. } [Q],$$

from which it follows by construction that $\pi(\cdot, \psi) = \int_Y \psi(y)\pi(\cdot, dy)$ is $\mathscr{A}(Q)$ measurable and

$$\int_Y \psi(y)\pi(\boldsymbol{\xi}, dy) = E[\psi(\boldsymbol{\eta})|\boldsymbol{\xi}] \qquad \text{a.s.}$$

The previous relation, together with $\mathscr{A}(Q)$ measurability of $\pi(\cdot, \psi)$, is true for all $\psi \in C(Y)$ and so (see Theorem III.8) for all bounded measurable ψ. Therefore, $\pi(x, dy)$ is a probability measure on $\mathscr{B}$ and satisfies conditions (a′) and (c).[4] □□

5. Random Convex Sets and the Generalized Jensen's Inequality

Now we present a few applications of Theorem 1.

Lemma 1. *Let $(\Omega, \mathscr{F}, P)$ be a probability space, $(X, \mathscr{A})$ a measurable space and $\xi: \Omega \to X$ a measurable mapping. Suppose that a set $A(x) \subseteq \mathbb{R}^n$ is put in correspondence with each $x \in X$ and that the following condition holds:*

> (C) *The multifunction $x \mapsto A(x)$ is measurable, and for each x the set $A(x)$ is nonempty and convex.*[5]

Let $\boldsymbol{\eta}$ be a random vector such that $\boldsymbol{\eta} \in A(\boldsymbol{\xi})$ a.s. and $E|\boldsymbol{\eta}| < \infty$. Then $E[\boldsymbol{\eta}|\boldsymbol{\xi}] \in A(\boldsymbol{\xi})$ a.s.

□ By Theorem 1 the conditional distribution $\pi(x, dy)$ of the random vector $\boldsymbol{\eta}$ exists at fixed values x of $\boldsymbol{\xi}$. By the definition of π and the stated

[4] Various theorems about the existence of conditional distributions may be found in textbooks on probability theory (see, for example, Hennequin and Tortrat [1], V.21.2). We have given the result here in a form most useful for the applications in this book.

[5] Some useful facts concerning measurable multifunctions taking convex values are presented by Rockafellar [1].

properties of ξ and η,

$$1 = 1_{A(\xi)}(\eta) = E[1_{A(\xi)}(\eta)|\xi]$$
$$= \int_Y 1_{A(\xi)}(y)\pi(\xi, dy) = \pi(\xi, A(\xi)) \qquad \text{a.s.}$$

and

$$E[\eta|\xi] = \int_Y y\pi(\xi, dy) \qquad \text{a.s.}$$

Thus for each ω, a.s. $[P]$, $\pi(\xi(\omega), A(\xi(\omega)) = 1$ and $E(\eta|\xi)(\omega) = \int_Y y\pi(\xi(\omega), dy)$, where the latter has finite $\mathbb{R}^n$ norm since $E|\eta| < \infty$. Hence it suffices to prove the following statement: If $\pi(dy)$ is a probability measure on $\mathbb{R}^n$ such that $\pi(A) = 1$ for some convex Borel set A and $\int_Y |y|\pi(dy) < \infty$, then $\bar{y}(A) := \int_A y\pi(dy) \in A$.

To this end, note first of all that the given statement is obviously true in the following cases: (a) $A \subseteq \mathbb{R}^1$; (b) A is an open halfspace. The general case we establish by induction on the dimension.

Assume the statement is proven for dimension $n - 1$. Let $A \subseteq \mathbb{R}^n$ and suppose that $\bar{y}(A) \notin A$. Then we can find a hyperplane M containing $\bar{y}$ such that $A \subseteq M \cup N$, where N is one of the two open halfspaces with boundary M. Let $A_1 := A \cap M$, $A_2 := A \cap N$. If $\pi(A_2) = 0$, then $\bar{y}(A) = \bar{y}(A_1)$ and $\bar{y}(A_1) \in A_1$ by the induction hypothesis. If $\pi(A_1) = 0$, then $\bar{y}(A) = \bar{y}(A_2) = \bar{y}(N) \in N$ using (b). Finally, if $\pi(A_1) > 0$ and $\pi(A_2) = 1 - \pi(A_1) > 0$, then since

$$\bar{y}(A) = \pi(A_1)\int_{A_1} y\pi(dy)/\pi(A_1) + \pi(A_2)\int_{A_2} y\pi(dy)/\pi(A_2),$$

it follows from the previous two cases that $\bar{y}(A)$ is an *interior* point of an interval with one of its end points in M and the other in N.

In all three cases, we have a contradiction. □

Lemma 2. (Generalized Jensen's inequality.) *Suppose the random variable ξ and the multifunction A satisfy the assumptions of Lemma* 1, *and for each $x \in X$ let a real-valued function given by $f(x, a)$ be defined on $A(x)$, concave with respect to a, such that the function given by*

$$\Phi(x, a) := \begin{cases} f(x, a) & \text{if } a \in A(x), \\ \infty & \text{if } a \notin A(x) \end{cases}$$

is jointly measurable in (x, a). Let ζ be a random vector such that $\zeta \in A(\xi)$

a.s., $E|\zeta| < \infty$ and $E|f_-(\xi, \zeta)| < \infty$, where $f_- := \min(f, 0)$. Then

$$E[f(\xi, \zeta)|\xi] \leqq f(\xi, E[\zeta|\xi]) \qquad a.s.$$

□ It is easy to show that the multifunction

$$x \mapsto B(x) := \{(z, r)\colon -\infty < r \leqq f(x, z)\}$$

satisfies Condition C of Lemma 1. If $E|f(\xi, \zeta)| < \infty$, then it is sufficient to apply Lemma 1 to $B(x)$ and the vector function given by $\eta(\omega) := (\zeta(\omega), f(\xi(\omega), \zeta(\omega))$ to obtain

$$-\infty < E[f(\xi, \zeta)|\xi] \leqq f(\xi, E[\zeta|\xi]) \qquad \text{a.s.}$$

The general case follows by replacing f with $f_N := \min(f, N)$ for $N = 1, 2, \ldots$ and then taking monotone increasing limits in the a.s. inequality

$$E[f_N(\xi, \zeta)|\xi] \leqq f_N(\xi, E[\zeta|\xi]). \quad \square$$

III SOME GENERAL RESULTS FROM MEASURE THEORY AND FUNCTIONAL ANALYSIS

Appendix III contains statements of some general facts from measure theory and functional analysis used in the book. Proofs of most results are omitted; however, references to the literature are given.

1. The Separation Theorem

Theorem 1. (Schaefer [1], II.9.1.) *Let A and B be convex subsets of a (locally convex) topological vector space such that* $\operatorname{int} A \neq \varnothing$ *and* $(\operatorname{int} A) \cap B = \varnothing$. *Then there exists a continuous linear functional $l \neq 0$, which* separates *A and B*; i.e.,

$$l(a) \leqq l(b) \qquad (a \in A, b \in B). \quad \square$$

2. The Kuhn–Tucker Theorem

Let D and H be (locally convex) topological vector spaces. Suppose that D is endowed with a partial ordering by fixing a convex cone K and defining $x \geqq y$ if and only if $x - y \in K$. A mapping g from some subset $Q \subseteq H$ to D is *concave* if

$$g(\alpha_1 z_1 + \alpha_2 z_2) \geqq \alpha_1 g(z_1) + \alpha_2 g(z_2) \qquad (\alpha_1 + \alpha_2 = 1, \alpha_1 \geqq 0, \alpha_2 \geqq 0).$$

We say that a linear functional π in the space D^* dual to D (i.e., the space of all continuous linear functionals on D) is *nonnegative* if $\pi(x) \geqq 0$ for $x \in K$.

Theorem 2. *Let Q be a convex subset of H, let K be a convex cone with interior in D defining the partial order $\geqq$ and let $F: Q \to \mathbb{R}$ and $g: Q \to D$ be concave mappings. Suppose that the maximum of F on $Q \cap \{z : g(z) \geqq 0\}$ is achieved at some point z^0 and the following condition holds:*

(Slater's condition.) *$g(z)$ belongs to the interior of K for some $z \in Q$. Then a nonnegative functional $\pi^0 \in D^*$ can be found such that*

$$F(z) + \pi^0(g(z)) \leqq F(z^0) \tag{1}$$

for all $z \in Q$. □

We explain the meaning of this result. By the conditions of the theorem z^0 is a solution of the following *mathematical programming problem:*

(∗) *Find the maximum of $F(z)$ over Q subject to*

$$g(z) \geqq 0. \tag{2}$$

The expression $L(z, \pi) := F(z) + \pi(g(z))$ appearing in the left-hand side of (1) defines the *Lagrangian function* of problem (∗) [corresponding to the *constraint* (2)]. It follows from the nonnegativity of π^0 and inequality (1) [put z^0 in the left-hand side of (1)] that $\pi^0(g(z^0)) = 0$, and so

$$L(z, \pi^0) \leqq L(z^0, \pi^0)$$

for all $z \in Q$. Therefore, if π^0 is the functional whose existence is asserted by Theorem 2, then a *constrained maximum* z^0 of the functional F is an *unconstrained maximum* of the Lagrangean function $L(z, \pi)$ evaluated at π^0. In this sense π^0 is said to *remove* the constraint (2).

Theorem 2 is known as the (*abstract*) *Kuhn–Tucker theorem*. Various versions of this result exist. Here the statement is taken from Hurwicz [1] (Theorem 5.3.1).

3. Liusternik's Theorem

Let M be a subset of a Banach space X. A vector $x \in X$ is called a *tangent* to the set M at the point $x_0 \in M$ if there exists an $\epsilon > 0$ and a mapping $t \mapsto r(t)$ of the interval $[0, \epsilon]$ into X such that

$$x_0 + tx + r(t) \in M \qquad \text{for all} \quad t \in [0, \epsilon]$$

and $\|r(t)\|/t \to 0$.

Theorem 3. *Let X and Y be Banach spaces, let U be a neighbourhood of point $x_0 \in X$ and let F be a Fréchet differentiable mapping of the set U into Y. Suppose that the mapping F is* regular *at the point x_0 [i.e., $\operatorname{im} F'(x_0) = Y$] and its derivative is continuous at that point (in the uniform operator topology). Then the set of vectors tangent to the set $\{x \in U : F(x) = F(x_0)\}$ at the point x_0 coincides with the null space (i.e., the set of roots) of the (continuous) linear mapping $F'(x^0)$.* □

The formulation of this result is taken from Ioffe and Tichomirov [1].

4. L_p Spaces

Let $(\Omega, \mathscr{F}, P)$ be a probability space, let D be a finite-dimensional linear space with some fixed norm $|\cdot|$ and let $p \in [1, +\infty]$. The space

$$L_p(\Omega, \mathscr{F}, P; D)$$

is defined as the space of equivalence classes of measurable functions $x(\omega)$ with values in D such that the *norm*

$$\|\mathbf{x}\|_p := \begin{cases} (\int |x(\omega)|^p \, dP)^{1/p} & \text{if} \quad 1 \leqq p < \infty, \\ \operatorname{ess\,sup} |x(\omega)| & \text{if} \quad p = \infty \end{cases}$$

is finite. Here $\operatorname{ess\,sup}|x|$ denotes the *essential supremum* with respect to the measure P, i.e.,

$$\inf\{c : c > |x(\omega)| \text{ a.s.}\}.$$

In this book we may omit some symbols in writing $L_p(\Omega, \mathscr{F}, P; D)$ (if this causes no confusion) and write, for example, $L_p(\Omega)$, $L_p(\Omega; D)$ and so on. If D is n-dimensional space, then we replace $L_p(D)$ by L_p^n. It is convenient in this case to equip $D := \mathbb{R}^n$ with the compatible norm

$$|(a_1, \ldots, a_n)| := \begin{cases} (a_1^p + \cdots + a_n^p)^{1/p} & \text{if } p < \infty, \\ \max_i |a_i| & \text{if } p = \infty. \end{cases}$$

Everywhere in the text we suppose that L_p^n spaces are ordered in a natural way: For $\mathbf{x}, \mathbf{y} \in L_p^n$, $\mathbf{x} \geqq \mathbf{y}$ ($\mathbf{x} > \mathbf{y}$) means that

$$x_i(\boldsymbol{\omega}) \geqq y_i(\boldsymbol{\omega}) \quad (x_i(\boldsymbol{\omega}) > y_i(\boldsymbol{\omega})) \qquad \text{a.s.}$$

for each i. [Here we consider (representatives of) the (equivalence class) elements of L_p^n as random n-vectors, and $x_i(\omega)$, $y_i(\omega)$ are the components of the corresponding vector-valued functions given by $x(\omega)$ and $y(\omega)$, respectively.]

5. Komlós's Theorem and Its Application to Optimization Problems

Theorem 4. (Komlós.) *Let $\{\mathbf{z}_m\}$ be a sequence of elements of the space $L_1^n(\Omega, \mathscr{F}, P)$ such that $\sup_m \|\mathbf{z}_m\|_1 < \infty$. Then there exists a sequence of natural numbers $m_1 < m_2 < \cdots$ and an element $\mathbf{z} \in L_1^n$ for which*

$$(\mathbf{z}_{m_1} + \cdots + \mathbf{z}_{m_k})/k \to \mathbf{z} \qquad \text{a.s.} \tag{3}$$

(we consider the elements of L_1^n as random n-vectors with finite expectation) as $k \to \infty$, and (3) remains true if the sequence $\{m_k\}$ is replaced by any of its (infinite) subsequences. □

We shall not give the proof of this important result here because of its length, but we refer the reader to Komlós [1].

Consider a countable number of spaces

$$G_i := L_1(\Omega_i, \mathscr{F}_i, P_i; \mathbb{R}^{n_i}), \qquad i = 1, 2, \ldots.$$

If $\mathbf{g}^m := (\mathbf{g}_1^m, \mathbf{g}_2^m, \ldots)$ is a sequence of elements of $G := G_1 \times G_2 \times \cdots$ and $\mathbf{g} := (\mathbf{g}_1, \mathbf{g}_2, \ldots) \in G$, we say that $\mathbf{g}^m$ *converges to* $\mathbf{g}$ *almost surely* if $\mathbf{g}_i^m \to \mathbf{g}_i$ almost surely with respect to the probability measure P_i for each i.

Theorem 5. *Let Q be a convex subset of G and F a concave functional on Q with values in $[-\infty, +\infty)$. Suppose further that F is upper semicontinuous with respect to a.s. convergence and Q is closed with respect to a.s. convergence and bounded in the sense that for each i a* *constant C_i can be found such that $\|\mathbf{q}_i\|_1 \leqq C_i$ for $(\mathbf{q}_1, \mathbf{q}_2, \ldots) \in Q$. Then F achieves a maximum on Q.*

□ Let $\mathbf{q}^m$ be a maximizing sequence for the functional F; i.e.,

$$F(\mathbf{g}^m) \to F^0 := \sup_{\mathbf{q} \in Q} F(\mathbf{q})$$

(possibly equal to $\pm\infty$.) Using Komlos's theorem and applying Kantor's diagonal process, we construct a subsequence $m_1 < m_2 < \cdots$ and $\mathbf{q}^0 \in G$ for which

$$\bar{\mathbf{q}}^k := (\mathbf{q}^{m_1} + \cdots + \mathbf{q}^{m_k})/k \to \mathbf{q}^0 \qquad \text{a.s.}$$

Since Q is convex, $\bar{\mathbf{q}}^k \in Q$, and thus $\mathbf{q}^0 \in Q$ since Q is closed. Moreover,

$$+\infty > F(\mathbf{q}^0) \geqq \overline{\lim_{k\to\infty}} F(\bar{\mathbf{q}}^k) \geqq \overline{\lim_{k\to\infty}} [F(\mathbf{q}^{m_1}) + \cdots + F(\mathbf{q}^{m_k})/k] = F^0,$$

since F does not take $+\infty$ values on Q and is upper semicontinuous and concave. Since $F(\mathbf{q}_0) \leqq F^0$, we may conclude that $F(\mathbf{q}^0) = F^0 < +\infty$; i.e., $\mathbf{q}^0$ is a maximum of F over Q. □

6. The Yosida–Hewitt Theorem

A continuous linear functional π on the space $L_\infty^n(\Omega, \mathscr{F}, P)$ is called *absolutely continuous* if its action on $\mathbf{x} \in L_\infty^n$ can be represented in the form

$$\pi(\mathbf{x}) = \int x(\omega)p(\omega)P(d\omega)$$

for some $\mathbf{p} \in L_1^n$. The functional λ is called *singular* if a sequence $\Gamma_1 \supseteqq \Gamma_2 \supseteqq \cdots$ of measurable subsets of Ω can be found such that

(a) $\lambda(\mathbf{x}) = 0$ for any function $\mathbf{x}$ which is identically equal to zero on one of the Γ_k;
(b) $P(\Gamma_k) \to 0$ as $k \to \infty$.

Theorem 6. *Each functional $\pi \in (L_\infty^n)^*$ can be uniquely represented in the form*

$$\pi = \pi^a + \pi^s,$$

where π^a *is absolutely continuous and* π^s *is singular. If* $\pi \geqq 0$, *then* $\pi^a \geqq 0$ *and* $\pi^s \geqq 0$. □

The proof of this theorem can be found in the Yosida and Hewitt article [1] or the book by Castaing and Valadier [1].

7. Monotone Class Theorems

In measure theory we often wish to make statements valid for some system of measurable functions or measurable sets as a consequence of their validity for some narrow class of "simple" functions or sets. For this purpose, various theorems about monotone classes are frequently used.

Let Ω be a set. A system $\mathscr{C}$ of subsets of Ω is called a monotone class if for any monotone sequence of sets $A_1 \subseteqq A_2 \subseteqq \cdots$ or $B_1 \supseteqq B_2 \supseteqq \cdots$ in $\mathscr{C}$

$$\bigcup_{i=1}^{\infty} A_i \in \mathscr{C} \qquad \text{and} \qquad \bigcap_{i=1}^{\infty} B_i \in \mathscr{C}.$$

Theorem 7. (See, for example, Neveu [1], Remark I.4.2.) *If* $\mathscr{A}$ *is an algebra of subsets of* Ω, *then the smallest monotone class containing* $\mathscr{A}$ *coincides with the smallest* σ*-algebra containing* $\mathscr{A}$. □

Theorem 8. (See Meyer [1], Theorem I.20.) *Let* $\mathscr{H}$ *be a system of bounded real-valued functions on* Ω *possessing the following properties:*

(1) $\mathscr{H}$ *is a vector space containing the constant* 1;
(2) $\mathscr{H}$ *is closed with respect to the topology of uniform convergence;*
(3) *if* $\{f_n\}$ *is a uniformly bounded (pointwise) monotone increasing sequence of nonnegative functions in* $\mathscr{H}$ *which converges to a function* f, *then* $f \in \mathscr{H}$.

Further, let D be a subset of $\mathscr{H}$ *which is closed with respect to multiplication. Then* $\mathscr{H}$ *contains all bounded functions which are measurable with respect to the* σ*-algebra generated by the elements of D.* □

It is easy to derive the following fact from Theorem 8 (see, for example, Dynkin and Yushkevich [1], Appendix 5, Lemma 2).

Corollary 1 *Let* $\Omega_1, \Omega_2, \Omega_3$ *be measurable spaces,* f *a measurable bounded (or nonnegative) real-valued function on* $\Omega_1 \times \Omega_3$ *and* $\pi(\omega_2, d\omega_3)$

a probability measure on Ω_3 *which depends measurably on* ω_2 [*i.e.,* $\pi(\omega_2, \Gamma)$ *is measurable in* ω_2 *for fixed* Γ]. *Then*

$$g(\omega_1, \omega_2) = \int f(\omega_1, \omega_3)\pi(\omega_2, d\omega_3)$$

is a (jointly) measurable function on $\Omega_1 \times \Omega_2$. □

REFERENCES

Arkin, V. I.

1. On the infinite-dimensional analogue of problems of nonconvex programming, *Cybernetics* (*Kibernetika*) **2** (1967) (in Russian). *Cybernetics* **2** (1967).
2. The construction of Markov programmes of models of economic dynamics, in *Probabilistic Models and Control of Economic Processes*. CEMI, USSR Academy of Sciences, Moscow, 1978 (in Russian).

Arkin, V. I. and L. M. Krechetov

1. A stochastic maximum principle for control problems in discrete time, in *Proceedings of the Third Japan–USSR Symposium on Probability Theory*. (Lect. Notes in Math. No. 550). Springer-Verlag, Berlin, 1976.
2. Stochastic Lagrange multipliers in control problems and economic dynamics, in *Probabilistic Control Problems in Economics*. Nauka, Moscow, 1977 (in Russian).
3. Markov controls for problems in discrete time: The stochastic maximum principle, in *Stochastic Processes and Control*. Nauka, Moscow, 1978 (in Russian).

Arkin, V. I. and V. L. Levin

1. The convexity of values of vector integrals: Measurable choice theorems and variational problems, *Progress of Math. Sci.* (*Uspehi Mat. Nauk*) **27**(3) (1972), 165 (in Russian). *Progress of Math. Sci.* **27**(3) (1972).

Arkin, V. I. and M. T. Saksonov

1. The stochastic maximum principle for problems of control of differential equations with random coefficients, in *Probabilistic Models and Control of Economic Processes*. CEMI, USSR Academy of Sciences, Moscow, 1978 (in Russian).
2. Necessary conditions for optimality in problems of control of stochastic differential equations, *Proc. USSR Acad. of Sci.* (*Dokl. Akad. Nauk SSSR*) **244**(1) (1979) (in Russian). *Soviet Math. Dokl.* **20** (1979).

Arrow, K. J.

1. Application of control theory to economic growth, in *Mathematical Economics*. Mir, Moscow, 1974 (in Russian).

Aumann, R. J.

1. Measurable utility and the measurable choice theorems, in *La Decision*, Vol. 2 (Actes Coll. du CNRS 1967). Paris, 1969.

Bewley, T.

1. Existence of equilibria in economics with infinitely many commodities, *J. Econom. Theory* **4** (1972), 514–540.

Blackwell, D. and C. Ryll-Nardzewski

1. Non-existence of everywhere proper conditional distributions, *Ann. Math. Stat.* **34** (1963), 223–225.

Boltyanski, V. G.

1. *Optimal Control of Discrete Systems*. Nauka, Moscow, 1973 (in Russian). Wiley, New York, 1978.

Brock, W. A.

1. On existence of weakly maximal programmes in a multisector economy, *Rev. Econom. Stud.* **37** (1970), 275–280.
2. Sensitivity of optimal growth paths with respect to a change in target stocks, *Z. Nationalökonom.* **Suppl. 1** (1971), 73–89.

Brock, W. A. and L. J. Mirman

1. Optimal economic growth and uncertainty: The discounted case, *J. Econom. Theory* **4**(3) (1972).
2. Optimal economic growth and uncertainty: The no discounting case, *Internat. Econom. Rev.* **14** (1973), 560–573.

Castaing, C.

1. Sur les multi-applications measurables, *Rev. Franc. Informatique et Rech. Opér.* **1** (1967), 91–126.

Castaing, C. and M. Valadier

1. *Convex Analysis and Measurable Multifunctions* (Lect. Notes in Math. No. 580). Springer-Verlag, Berlin, 1977.

Dana, R. A.

1. Evaluation of development programs in a stationary stochastic economy with bounded primary resources, in *Mathematical Models in Economics*. North-Holland, Amsterdam, 1974.

Danilov, V. I.

1. Optimal economic growth with changing technology, in *Methods of Functional Analysis in Mathematical Economics*. Nauka, Moscow, 1978 (in Russian).

Dinculeanu, N.

1. *Vector Measures*. Pergamon Press, Berlin, 1967.

Dorfman, R., P. A. Samuelson, and R. M. Solow

1. *Linear Programming and Economic Analysis*. McGraw-Hill, New York, 1958.

Dubovitski, A. and A. A. Milyutin

1. Necessary conditions for a weak extremum in optimal control problems with mixed inequality constraints, *U.S.S.R. Comput. Math. and Math. Phys.* (*Ž. Vyčisl. Mat. i*

Mat. Fiz.) **8** (1968), 725–779 (in Russian). *U.S.S.R. Comput. Math. and Math. Phys.* **8** (1968).

Dynkin, E. B.

1. Some probabilistic models of economic growth. *Proc. USSR Acad. of Sci.* **200**(3) (1971) (in Russian). *Soviet Math. Dokl.* **12** (1971).

Dynkin, E. B. and A. A. Yushkevich

1. *Controlled Markov Processes and Their Applications.* Nauka, Moscow (1975) (in Russian). Springer-Verlag, New York, 1979.

Evstigneev, I. V.

1. Optimal economic planning with respect to stationary random factors, *Proc. USSR Acad. of Sci.* **206**(5) (1972) (in Russian). *Soviet Math.* **13** (1972).
2. Asymptotic behaviour of optimal programs in stochastic models of economic development, in *International Conference on Probability Theory and Mathematical Statistics: Proceedings.* Chapter 1. Vilnus, 1973.
3. Optimal stochastic programs and their stimulating prices, in *Mathematical Models in Economics.* North-Holland, Amsterdam, 1974.
4. Models of economic dynamics taking into account uncertainty in the production process, *Proc. USSR Acad. of Sci.* **233**(3) (1975) (in Russian). *Soviet Math.* **16** (1975).
5. Turnpike theorems in probabilistic models of economic dynamics, *Math. Notes* (*Mat. Zametki*) **19**(2) (1976) (in Russian). *Math. Notes.* **19**(2) (1976).
6. Measurable selection and dynamic programming, *Math. Oper. Res.* **1**(3) (1976).
7. Optimal economic planning under production uncertainty, *Publ. Économétriques.* **9**(1) (1976).
8. Lagrange multipliers for the problems of stochastic programming, in Lect. Notes Econ. and Math. Syst. No. 133. Springer-Verlag, Berlin, 1976.

Evstigneev, I. V. and S. E. Kuznetsov

1. Stationary programmes in probabilistic models of economic growth, in *Selected Questions in Probability Theory and Mathematical Economics.* CEMI, USSR Academy of Sciences, Moscow, 1977 (in Russian).

Follmer, H. and M. Majumdar

1. On the asymptotic behavior of stochastic economic processes, *J. Math. Econom.* **5**(3) (1978).

Gale, D.

1. On optimal development in a multi-sector economy, *Rev. Econom. Stud.* **34** (1967), 1–18.
2. Mathematical theory of optimal growth, *Mathematica* **14**(6) (1970) (in Russian).

Hurwicz, L.

1. Programming in linear spaces, in *Studies in Linear and Nonlinear Programming.* II, Moscow, 1962 (in Russian). (K. J. Arrow, J. Hurwicz and H. Uzawa, eds.) 38–102. Stanford University Press, Stanford, California, 1958.

Hennequin, P. and A. Tortrat

1. *Probability Theory and Some Applications.* Nauka, Moscow, 1974 (in Russian).

Hildenbrand, W.

1. *Core and Equilibria of a Large Economy.* Princeton University Press, Princeton, New Jersey, 1974.

Ioffe, A. D. and V. M. Tichomirov

1. *Theory of Extremal Problems*. Nauka, Moscow 1974 (in Russian). North-Holland, New York, 1979.

Jeanjean, P.

1. Optimal development programs under production uncertainty: The undiscounted case, *J. Econom. Theory* **7**(1) (1974).

Kantorovich, L. V.

1. On an effective method of solution of a class of extremum problems, *Proc. USSR Acad. Sci.* **28** (1940), 212–215 (in Russian).
2. *Economic Assessment of Optimal Resource Use*. Nauka, Moscow, 1959 (in Russian).

Komlós, J.

1. A generalization of a problem of Steinhaus, *Acta Math. Acad. Sci. Hungar.* **18** (1967), 217–229.

Krechetov, L. I.

1. Application of the stochastic maximum principle to the analysis of relations amongst economic "norms", in *Probabilistic Models and Control of Economic Processes*. CEMI, USSR Academy of Sciences, Moscow, 1978 (in Russian).

Kuznetsov, S. E.

1. Weakly optimal programs in models with changing technology, in *Mathematical Models in Economics*. North-Holland, Amsterdam, 1979.

Kuratovski, K.

1. *Topology*, Vol. I. Mir, Moscow, 1966 (in Russian).
2. *Topology*, Vol. II. Mir, Moscow, 1969 (in Russian).

Makarov, V. L. and A. M. Rubinov

1. *Mathematical Theory of Economic Dynamics and Equilibria*. Nauka, Moscow, 1973 (in Russian). Springer-Verlag, New York, 1977.

McKenzie, L. W.

1. Turnpike theorems for a generalized Leontief model, *Econometrica* **31**(1–2) (1963).

Meyer, P. A.

1. *Probability and Potentials*. Mir, Moscow, 1973 (in Russian). Ginn (Blaisdell), Boston, Massachusetts, 1966; 2nd Ed., North-Holland, New York, 1978.

Naimark, M. A.

1. *Normed Rings*. Nauka, Moscow, 1968 (in Russian). Wolters-Nordhoff, Groningen, 1970.

Neveu, J.

1. *Mathematical Foundations of the Calculus of Probability Theory*. Mir, Moscow, 1969 (in Russian). Holden Day, San Francisco, 1965.

Nikaido, H.

1. Persistence of continual growth near the von Neumann ray: A strong version of the Radner turnpike theorem, *Econometrica* **32**(1–2) (1964).
2. *Convex Structures and Economic Theory*. Mir, Moscow, 1972 (in Russian). Academic Press, New York, 1968.

Phelps, E. S.

1. The accumulation of risky capital: A sequential utility analysis, *Econometrica* **30**(3) (1962).

Polterovich, V. M.

1. Equilibrium trajectories of economic growth, in *Methods of Functional Analysis in Mathematical Economics*. Nauka, Moscow, 1978 (in Russian).

Pontryagin, L. S., V. G. Boltyanski, R. V. Gamkrelidze and E. F. Mishchenko

1. *Mathematical Theory of Optimal Processes*. Fizmatgiz, Moscow, 1961. 2nd Ed., Nauka, Moscow, 1973 (in Russian). Pergamon Press, Oxford, 1964.

Propoi, A. I.

1. *Elements of the Theory of Optimal Discrete Processes*. Nauka, Moscow, 1973 (in Russian).

Pshenichni, B. N.

1. *Necessary Conditions for an Extremum*. Nauka, Moscow, 1969 (in Russian). Dekker, New York, 1971.

Pshenichni, B. N. and E. I. Nenahov

1. Necessary conditions for extrema in problems with operator constraints, *Cybernetics* **3** (1971) (in Russian). *Cybernetics* **3** (1971).

Radner, R.

1. Paths of economic growth that are optimal with regard only to final states: A turnpike theorem, *Rev. Econom. Stud.* **28**(2) (1961).
2. Balanced stochastic growth at the maximum rate, *Z. Nationalökonom.* **Suppl. 1** (1971), 39–52.
3. Optimal steady-state behavior of an economy with stochastic production and resources, in *Mathematical Topics in Economic Theory and Computation*. SIAM, Philadelphia, 1972.
4. Optimal stationary consumption with stochastic production and resources, *J. Econom. Theory* **6**(1) (1973).

Rockafellar, R. T.

1. Measurable dependence of convex sets and functions on parameters, *J. Math. Anal. Appl.* **28**(1) (1969).

Rockafellar, R. T. and R. J-B. Wets

1. Stochastic convex programming: Kuhn–Tucker conditions, *J. Math. Econom.* **2** (1975), 349–370.
2. Non-anticipativity and L^1-martingales in stochastic optimization problems, *Math. Programming Stud.* **6** (1976).
3. Stochastic convex programming: Relatively complete recourse and induced feasibility, *SIAM J. Control Optim.* **14** (1976), 574–589.

Romanovski, I. V.

1. Asymptotic behavior of discrete deterministic processes with continuous state spaces. in *Optimal Planning* Vol. 8. Nauka, Novosibirsk, 1967.

Ramsey, F.

1. A mathematical theory of savings, *Econom. J.* **38** (1928), 543–559.

Sainte-Beuve, M. F.

1. On the extension of von Neumann–Aumann's theorem, *J. Funct. Anal.* **17** (1974), 112–129.

Schaefer, H. H.

1. *Topological Vector Spaces*. Mir, Moscow, 1971 (in Russian). Springer, Berlin, 1966.

Strauch, R. E.
1. Negative dynamic programming, *Mathematica* **13**(5) (1969) (in Russian). *Ann. Math. Stat.* **37** (1966), 871–890.

Ter-Krikorov, A. M.
1. *Optimal Control and Mathematical Economics*. Nauka, Moscow, 1977 (in Russian).

Tsukui, J.
1. Turnpike theorem in a generalized dynamic input–output system, *Econometrica* **34**(2) (1966).

von Neuman, J.
1. On an economic equation system and an application of Brouwer's fixed point theorem, in *Proceedings of Mathematical Colloquia*, Vol. 8. Leipzig, Vienna, 1936 (in German).

Wagner, D. H.
1. Survey of measurable selection theorems, *SIAM J. Control Optim.* **15** (1977), 859–903.

Winter, S. G.
1. The norm of a closed technology and the straight-down-the-turnpike theorem, *Rev. Econom. Stud.* **34** (1967), 67–84.

Yosida, K. and E. Hewitt
1. Finitely additive measures, *Trans. Amer. Math. Soc.* **72** (1952), 45–66.

FURTHER REFERENCES

0. GENERAL

Specifically Relevant Journals

As well as a large number of related contributions appearing in the general mathematics, operations research and economics literature, work specifically related to the topics of this monograph appear in the following journals:

Econometrica
International Economic Review
J. of Economic Dynamics and Control
J. of Economic Theory
J. of Mathematical Economics
J. of Optimization Theory and Its Applications
Mathematics of Operations Research
Review of Economic Studies
SIAM J. on Control and Optimization.

Related Monographs, Texts and Special Journal Issues

The following provide background, alternative approaches and recent research results.

Arkin, V.I. *et al.*, eds. (1981). *Stochastic Models and Control.* Central Economic Mathematics Institute, USSR Academy of Sciences, Moscow. (In Russian.)

Arkin, V.I., V.I. Danilov, A. Ya. Kiruta & L.I. Kretchetov, eds. (1982). *Studies in Mathematical Economics and Control Theory.* Central Economic Mathematics Institute, USSR Academy of Sciences, Moscow. (In Russian.)

Arkin, V.I. & P.K. Katyshev, eds. (1983). *Models and Methods of Stochastic Optimization.* Central Economic Mathematics Institute, USSR Academy of Sciences, Moscow. (In Russian.)

Arkin, V.I. & A.D. Slastnikov, eds. (1985). *Probabilistic Problems of Control and Mathematical Economics.* Central Economic Mathematics Institute, USSR Academy of Sciences, Moscow. (In Russian.)

Bertsekas, D.P. & S.E. Shreve (1978). *Stochastic Optimal Control: The Discrete Time Case.* Academic, New York.

Clarke, F.H. (1983). *Optimization and Nonsmooth Analysis.* Wiley Interscience, New York.

Fleming, W.H. & R.W. Rishel (1975). *Deterministic and Stochastic Optimal Control.* Springer, Berlin.

Kamien, M.I. & N.L. Schwartz (1981). *Dynamic Optimization: The Calculus of Variations and Optimal Control in Economics and Management.* North Holland, New York.

Rader, T. (1972). *Theory of General Economic Equilibrium.* Academic, New York.

Special Symposium Issue on Economic Dynamics. *J. Econ. Th.* **12.1** (1976).

Special Conference Issue. *J. Econ. Dynamics Control* **10.1–2** (1986).

Special Issue on Nonlinear Economic Dynamics. *J. Econ. Th.* **40.1** (1986).

1. CHAPTER 1

Existence and Stability Results for Deterministic Optimal Control Models

These papers concern existence, characterization and stability results for optimal control models—including those of optimal growth and dynamic capital theory—(usually) under more general assumptions than those of the present monograph.

Araujo, A. & J.A. Scheinkman (1983). Maximum principle and transversality condition for concave infinite horizon economic models. *J. Econ. Th.* **30**, 1–16.

d'Aspremont, C. & J.H. Drèze (1979). On the stability of dynamic processes in economic theory. *Econometrica* **47**, 733–737.

Benhabib, J. & K. Nishimura (1979). The Hopf bifurcation and the existence and stability of closed orbits in multisector models of economic growth. *J. Econ. Th.* **21**, 421–444.

Benhabib, J. & K. Nishimura (1981). Stability of equilibrium in dynamic models of capital theory. *Intl. Econ. Rev.* **22**, 275–293.

Dechart, W.D. (1982). Lagrange multipliers in infinite horizon discrete time optimal control models. *J. Math. Econ.* **9**, 285–302.

Dechart, W.D. & K. Nishimura (1983). A complete characterization of optimal growth paths in an aggregated model with a non-concave production function. *J. Econ. Th.* **31**, 332–354.

Epstein, L.G. (1986). Implicitly additive utility and the nature of optimal economic growth. *J. Math. Econ.* **15**, 111–128.

Hartl, R.F. (1987). A simple proof of the monotonicity of state trajectories in autonomous control problems. *J. Econ. Th.* **41**, 211–215.

Pereira, F. & R.B. Vinter (1986). Necessary conditions for optimal control problems with discontinuous trajectories. *J. Econ. Dynamics Control* **10**, 115–118.

Romer, P. (1986). Cake eating, chattering and jumps: Existence results for variational problems. *Econometrica* **54**, 897–908.

Rosser, J.B., Jnr. (1983). Reswitching as a cusp catastrophe. *J. Econ. Th.* **31**, 182–193.

Sutherland, W.R.S. & L.C. MacLean (1987). Sensitivity analysis of optimal growth plans with exogenous capital stocks. Research Report DAL TR-87-3, Dept. of Maths., Stats. & Comp. Sci., Dalhousie U.

Turnpike Results for Dynamic Economic Models

Under this heading are collected papers developing the classical deterministic results surveyed in this monograph.

Ali Khan, M. & T. Mitra (1986). On the existence of a stationary optimal stock for a multi-sector economy: A primal approach. *J. Econ. Th.* **40**, 319–328.

Araujo, A. & J.A. Scheinkman (1977). Smoothness, comparative dynamics, and the turnpike property. *Econometrica* **45**, 601–620.

Benevista, L.M. & J.A. Scheinkman (1979). On the differentiability of the value function in dynamic models of economics. *Econometrica* **47**, 727–732.

Dasgupta, S. & L.W. McKenzie (1983). The comparative statics and dynamics of stationary states. Working Paper, Dept. of Economics, Dalhousie U.

Feinstein, C.D. & S.S. Oren (1985). A 'funnel' turnpike theorem for optimal growth problems with discounting. *J. Econ. Dynamics Control* **9**, 25–40.

Fershtman, C. & E. Mullar (1986). Turnpike properties of capital accumulation games. *J. Econ. Th.* **38**, 167–177.

Fujimoto, T. (1986). Non-linear Leontief models in abstract spaces. *J. Math. Econ.* **15**, 151–156.

Giavazzi, F. & C. Wyplosz (1985). The zero root problem: A note on the dynamic determination of the stationary equilibrium in linear models. *Rev. Econ. Studies* **52**, 353–357.

Krause, U. (1986). Perron's stability theorem for non-linear mappings. *J. Math. Econ.* **15**, 275–282.

McKenzie, L.W. (1980). Optimal growth and turnpike theorems. In: *Handbook of Mathematical Economics, Vol. III.* K.A. Arrow & M.D. Intriligator, eds. North Holland, New York, to appear.

McKenzie, L.W. (1982). A primal route to the turnpike and Liapounov stability. *J. Econ. Th.* **27**, 194–209.

McKenzie, L.W. (1983). Turnpike theory, discounted utility, and the von Neumann facet. *J. Econ. Th.* **30**, 330–352.

Mitra, T. & I. Zilcha (1981). On optimal economic growth with changing technology and tastes: Characterization and stability. *Intl. Econ. Rev.* **22**, 221–237.

Rath, K. (1986). On non-linear extensions of the Perron-Frobenius theorem. *J. Math. Econ.* **15**, 59–62.

Read, T.T. (1986). Balanced growth without constant returns to scale. *J. Math. Econ.* **15**, 171–178.

Turnpike Results for Dynamic Equilibrium Models

Recently, turnpike theory has begun to be extended to dynamic general equilibrium models—of exchange and with production and/or money. Closely related results for abstract and/or stochastic models will be cited later in these references.

Balasko, Y. & K. Shell (1980). The overlapping generations model. I: The case of pure exchange without money. *J. Econ. Th.* **23**, 281–306.

Becker, R.A. & C. Foias (1987). A characterization of Ramsey equilibrium. *J. Econ. Th.* **41**, 173–184.

Bewley, T. (1982). An integration of equilibrium theory and turnpike theory. *J. Math. Econ.* **10**, 233–267.

Coles, J.L. (1987). Equilibrium turnpike theory with time separable utility. *J. Econ. Dynamics Control* **10**, 367–394.

Duffie, D. & W. Shafer (1985). Equilibrium in incomplete markets: I: A basic model of generic existence. *J. Math. Econ.* **14**, 285–300.

Epstein, L.G. (1987). A simple dynamic general equilibrium model. *J. Econ. Th.* **41**, 68–95.

Gagey, F., G. Laroque & S. Lollivier (1986). Monetary and fiscal policies in a general equilibrium model. *J. Econ. Th.* **39**, 329–357.

Kehoe, T.J. & D.K. Levine (1984). Regularity in overlapping generations exchange economies. *J. Math. Econ.* **11**, 69–93.

Lucas, R. & N. Stokey (1984). Optimal growth with many consumers. *J. Econ. Th.* **32**, 139–171.

Polterovich, V.M. (1978). Equilibrium trajectories of economic growth. In: *Functional Analysis in Mathematical Economics*. B.A. Efimov, ed. Harke, Moscow. (In Russian.) *Econometrica* **51** (1983), 693–729.

Stacchetti, E. (1985). Analysis of a dynamic decentralized exchange economy. *J. Math. Econ.* **14**, 241–259.

Yano, M. (1983a). Competitive equilibria on turnpikes in a McKenzie economy: I. A neighbourhood turnpike theorem. II. An asymptotic turnpike theorem. Working Papers, Dept. of Economics, Cornell U.

Yano, M. (1983b). The turnpike of dynamic general equilibrium paths and its insensitivity to initial conditions. Working Paper, Dept. of Economics, Cornell U.

2. CHAPTER 2

Maximum Principles For Discrete Time Dynamic Stochastic Models

These papers concern appropriate versions of the maximum principle and related results for a variety of discrete time stochastic dynamic optimization models ranging from the Bolza problem of the calculus of variations, through optimal control—including the practically important class of models in which the data process is controlled—to the dynamic recourse problem of stochastic programming.

Arkin, V.I. (1984). The stochastic maximum principle. *Soviet Abstracts of the International Conference on Stochastic Optimization, Kiev, 1984*. V.I. Glushkov Institute, Ukranian Academy of Sciences, Kiev, 21–23.

Birge, J.R. & M.A.H. Dempster (1987). Optimality conditions for match-up strategies in stochastic scheduling and related dynamic stochastic optimization problems. Technical Report DAL TR-87-4, Dept. of Maths., Stats. & Comp. Sci., Dalhousie U.

Bordunov, N.N. (1983). Optimality conditions for multistage problems of control of random convex mappings. *Kibernetika* **1983.1**, 40–45. (In Russian.)

Dempster, M.A.H. (1981). The expected value of perfect information in the optimal evolution of stochastic systems. In: *Stochastic Differential Systems*. M. Arató, D. Vermes & A.V. Balikrishnan, eds. Lecture Notes in Control & Information Sciences **36**. Springer, Berlin, 25–40.

Dempster, M.A.H. (1986). On stochastic programming: II. Dynamic problems under risk. Technical Report DAL TR-86-5, Dept. of Maths., Stats. & Comp. Sci., Dalhousie U. *Stochastics*, to appear.

Flåm, S.D. (1985). Nonanticipativity in stochastic programming. *J. Opt. Th. Applns.* **46**, 23–30.

Flåm, S.D. (1986). Asymptotically stable solutions to stochastic optimization problems. In: *Stochastic Programming*. F. Archetti, G. Di Pillo & M. Lucertini, eds. Lecture Notes in Control & Information Sciences **76**. Springer, Berlin, 184–193.

Gihman, I.I. & A.V. Skorohod (1979). Discrete-parameter controlled stochastic processes. Chapter 1 in: *Controlled Stochastic Processes*. Springer-Berlin, 1–78.

Kushner, H.J. (1971). Necessary conditions for discrete parameter stochastic optimization problems. In: *Proceedings of the Sixth Berkeley Symposium on Mathematical Statistics and Probability. Vol. III: Probability Theory*. U. of California Press, Berkeley, 667–685.

Pavon, M. & R.J-B. Wets (1980). A stochastic variational approach to the duality between estimation and control: Discrete time. In: *Analysis and Optimisation of Stochastic Systems*. O.L.R. Jacobs, M.H.A. Davis, M.A.H. Dempster, C.J. Harris & P.C. Parks, eds. Academic, London, 347–360.

Pliska, S.R. (1982). Duality theory for some stochastic control problems. In: *Proceedings of the Second Bad Honef Conference on Stochastic Differential Systems*. M. Bohl & M. Kohlman, eds. Lecture Notes in Control & Information Sciences **41**. Springer, Berlin, 229–337.

Rockafellar, R.T. & R.J-B. Wets (1983). Deterministic and stochastic optimization problems of Bolza type in discrete time. *Stochastics* **10**, 273–312.

Wets, R.J-B. (1976). Duality for stochastic Bolza problems with applications to a model for economic growth and a liquidity preference model. Technical Report, Dept. of Mathematics. U. of Kentucky.

Discrete Time Stochastic Models of Economic Growth

The results reported in the following papers are related both to the references just given above and to stochastic generalizations of those given for Chapter 1. They concern existence, characterization and stability of optimal stochastic economic growth policies and related turnpike results. As such they are also related to the stationary stochastic turnpike theory of Chapters 4 and 5 of this book.

Brock, W.A. & M. Majumdar (1978). Global asymptotic stability results for multisector models of optimal growth under uncertainty when future utilities are discounted. *J. Econ. Th.* **18**, 225–243.

Epstein, L.G. (1983). Stationary cardinal utility and optimal growth under uncertainty. *J. Econ. Th.* **31**, 133–152.

Evstigneev, I.V. (1980). Homogeneous convex models in the theory of controlled random processes. *Soviet Math. Doklady* **22**, 108–111.

Evstigneev, I.V. (1982). Rapid turnpike theorems and the central limit theorem for stochastic models of economic dynamics. In: *Soviet-Japan Symposium on Probability: Abstracts*, 207–208.

Evstigneev, I.V. & Yu. M. Kabanov (1980). On the stochastic modification of the von Neumann-Gale model. *Uspekhi Matem. Nauk* **35.4**, 185–86. (In Russian.)

Evstigneev, I.V. & P.K. Katyshev (1982). Equilibrium paths in stochastic models of economic dynamics. *Prob. Th. Applns.* **27.1**, 120–128. (In Russian.)

Evstigneev, I.V. & S.E. Kuznetsov (1982). A nonstationary model of a developing economy. Technical Report 79 A-07835, Central Economic Mathematics Institute, USSR Academy of Sciences, Moscow. (In Russian.)

Evstigneev, I.V. & S.E. Kuznetsov (1983). The stochastic version of the turnpike theorem for homogeneous convex controlled models. *Mathem. Zametki* (*Math. Notes*), **33.1**, 147–156. (In Russian.)

Evstigneev, I.V. & S.E. Kuznetsov (1984). Recent progress in the mathematical theory of stochastic economic models. In: *Soviet Abstracts of the International Conference on Stochastic Optimization, Kiev, 1984*. V.I. Glushkov Institute, Ukranian Academy of Sciences, Kiev, 71–73.

MacLean, L.C., C.A. Field & W.R.S. Sutherland (1981). Optimal growth and uncertainty: The borrowing models. *J. Econ. Th.* **24**, 168–186.

Majumdar, M. & R. Radner (1983). Stationary optimal policies with discounting in a stochastic activity analysis model. *Econometrica* **51**, 1821–1837.

Pres'man, E.L. & A.D. Slastnikov (1980). Asymptotic behaviour of the utility functionals in stochastic models of economic growth. In: *Stochastic Models and Control.* Central Economic Mathematics Institute, USSR Academy of Sciences, Moscow, 83–103. (In Russian.)

Pres'man, E.L. & A.D. Slastnikov (1983). One approach to definition of the growth rate in stochastic von Neumann-Gale models. In: *Models and Methods of Stochastic Optimization.* Central Economic Mathematics Institute, USSR Academy of Sciences, Moscow, 123–152. (In Russian.)

Pres'man, E.L. & A.D. Slastnikov (1984). Growth rates and optimal paths in stochastic models of expanding economy. In: *Soviet Abstracts of the International Conference on Stochastic Optimization, Kiev, 1984*. V.I. Glushkov Institute, Ukranian Academy of Sciences, Kiev, 191–193.

Zaharevič, M.I. (1981). Ergodic properties of nonlinear mappings connected with models of economic dynamics. *Soviet Math. Doklady* **24**, 430–433.

Maximum Principles For Continuous Time Dynamic Stochastic Models

Although in general more difficult mathematically than in the discrete time case, considerable progress has recently been made in the provision of maximum principles for continuous time stochastic control models involving diffusion dynamics.

Arkin, V.I. & M.T. Saksonov (1979). Necessary optimality conditions in control problems for stochastic differential equations. *Soviet Math. Doklady* **20**, 1–5.

Arkin, V.I. & M.T. Saksonov (1980). On the maximum principle theory for problems of control of stochastic differential equations. In: *Stochastic Differential Systems, Filtering and Control.* Lecture Notes in Control & Information Sciences **27**. Springer, Berlin, 255–263.

Arkin, V.I. & M.T. Saksonov (1983). On the stochastic maximum principle in problems with continuous time. In: *Models and Methods of Stochastic Optimization.* Central Economic Mathematics Institute, USSR Academy of Sciences, Moscow, 3–26. (In Russian.)

Haussmann, U. (1983). On the approximation of optimal stochastic controls. *J. Opt. Th. Applns.* **40**, 433–450.

Haussmann, U. (1985). A stochastic maximum principle for optimal control of diffusions. Technical Report, Dept. of Mathematics, U. of British Columbia.

Haussman, U. (1986). Existence of optimal Markovian controls for degenerate diffusions. Technical Report, Dept. of Mathematics, U. of British Columbia.

Loewen, P.D. (1985). Proximal Normal Analysis in Dynamic Optimization. Ph.D. Dissertation, U. of British Columbia.

Saksonov, M.T. (1984). On the stochastic maximum principle for time optimal problems. In: *Soviet Abstracts of the International Conference on Stochastic Optimization, Kiev, 1984.* V.I. Glushkov Institute, Ukranian Academy of Sciences, Kiev, 207–209.

3. CHAPTER 3

The Bellman Equation for Discrete Time Stochastic Optimal Control

These works concern the fundamental dynamic programming approach to discrete time optimal stochastic control and its extensions.

Bertsekas, D.P. & S.E. Shreve (1978). *Stochastic Optimal Control: The Discrete Time Case.* Academic, New York.

Davis, M.H.A. (1986). Control of piecewise-deterministic processes via discrete time dynamic programming. In: *Proceedings Third Bad Honnef Symposium on Stochastic Differential Systems.* Lecture Notes in Control & Information Sciences. Springer, Berlin.

Dynkin, E.B. & A.A. Yushkevich (1980). *Controlled Markov Processes.* Springer, Berlin.

Futia, C.A. (1982). Invariant distributions and the limiting behavior of Markovian economic models. *Econometrica* **50**, 377–408.

Klein Haneveld, W.K. (1986). *Duality in Stochastic Linear Programming*. Lecture Notes in Economics & Mathematical Systems **274**. Springer, Berlin.

Pres'man, E.L. & A.D. Slastnikov (1983). On an approach to a growth rate notion in stochastic von Neumann-Gale models. In: *Models and Methods of Stochastic Optimization*. Central Economic Mathematics Institute, USSR Academy of Sciences, Moscow, 123–152. (In Russian.)

The Bellman-Hamilton-Jacobi Equation for Continuous Time Stochastic Control

The Bellman-Hamilton-Jacobi necessary and sufficient condition for optimal control of continuous time stochastic processes is treated in the following references. Although these are mostly for models involving diffusions, control theory for another very general class of controlled Markov processes—piecewise deterministic processes—is currently under active development.

Arkin, V.I. & M.T. Saksonov (1982). The role of second derivatives of the Bellman function in the stochastic maximum principle. In: *Studies in Mathematical Economics and Control Theory*. Central Economic Mathematics Institute, USSR Academy of Sciences, Moscow, 3–12. (In Russian.)

Davis, M.H.A., M.A.H. Dempster, S.P. Sethi & D.Vermes (1987). Optimal capacity expansion under uncertainty. *Adv. Appl. Prob.* **19**, 156–176.

Dempster, M.A.H. (1987). A computationally tractable necessary and sufficient condition for optimal control of piecewise deterministic processes. In preparation.

Dempster, M.A.H. & E. Solel (1987). Stochastic scheduling via stochastic control. Technical Report DAL TR-87-01, Dept. of Maths., Stats. & Comp. Sci., Dalhousie U. To appear in: *Proceedings of the First International Congress of the Bernoulli Society, Tashkent, 1986*. VNU Science Press, Utrecht.

Fleming, W.H. & R.W. Rishel (1975). *Deterministic and Stochastic Optimal Control*. Springer, Berlin.

Gihman, I.I. & A.V. Skorohod (1979). *Controlled Stochastic Processes*. Springer, Berlin.

Krylov, N.V. (1980). *Controlled Diffusion Processes*. Springer, Berlin.

Solel, E. (1986). A Dynamic Approach to Stochastic Scheduling via Stochastic Control. Ph.D. Dissertation, Dalhousie U.

Vermes, D. (1985). Optimal control of piecewise-deterministic processes. *Stochastics* **14**, 165–208.

4. STOCHASTIC ECONOMIC EQUILIBRIA

Perhaps the most important development since the Russian edition of this book appeared is the recent progress made in treating stochastic economic equilibrium models.

Abstract Equilibrium Models

Below are collected papers concerned with existence and characterization of solutions of abstract models of economic equilibrium and related matters which are useful for the dynamic, stochastic and spatial special cases.

Aliprantis, C. & D. Brown (1983). Equilibria in markets with a Riesz space of commodities. *J. Math. Econ.* **11**, 189–207.

Araujo, A. (1985). Regular economies and sets of measure zero in Banach spaces. *J. Math. Econ.* **14**, 61–66.

Cotter, K.D. (1986). Similarity of information and behavior with a pointwise convergence topology. *J. Math. Econ.* **15**, 25–38.

Duffie, D. (1986). Competitive equilibria in general choice spaces. *J. Math. Econ.* **15**, 1–24.

Florenzano, M. (1983). On the existence of equilibria in economies with an infinite dimensional commodity space. *J. Math. Econ.* **12**, 207–219.

Khilnani, A. & E. Tse (1985). A fixed point algorithm with economic applications. *J. Econ. Dynamics Control* **9**, 127–137.

Mehta, G. & E. Tarafdar (1987). Infinite-dimensional Gale-Nikaido-Debreu theorem and a fixed-point theorem of Tarafdar. *J. Econ. Th.* **41**, 333–339.

Rader, T. (1982). Utility over time: The homothetic case. *J. Econ. Th.* **25**, 219–236.

Richard, S.F. & W.R. Zame (1986). Proper preferences and quasiconcave utility functions. *J. Math. Econ.* **15**, 231–248.

Simons, S. (1984). Minimaximin results with applications to economic equilibrium. *J. Math. Econ.* **13**, 289–303.

Yannelis, N.C. & N.D. Prabhakar (1983). Existence of maximal elements and equilibria in linear topological spaces. *J. Math. Econ.* **12**, 233–245.

Yannelis, N.C. & W.R. Zame (1986). Equilibria in Banach lattices without ordered preferences. *J. Math. Econ.* **15**, 85–110.

Temporal Equilibrium Models

The following works concern themselves specifically with dynamic stochastic models of economic equilibrium—both constrained and unconstrained—including questions of existence, properties, information structure, expectation formation, finite-lived agents, stability, turnpikes, etc.

Allen, B. (1985). The existence of rational expectations equilibria in a large economy with noisy price observations. *J. Math. Econ.* **14**, 67–103.

Bewley, T.F. (1981). Stationary equilibrium. *J. Econ. Th.* **24**, 265–295.

Duffie, D. & C. Huang (1986). Multiperiod security markets with differential information: Martingales and resolution times. *J. Math. Econ.* **15**, 283–303.

Epstein, L.G. (1987). The global stability of efficient intertemporal equilibrium. *Econometrica* **55**, 329–356.

Grandmont, J-M., ed. (1986). Nonlinear Economic Dynamics. *J. Econ. Th.* **40.1**.

Hartman, R. (1987). Monetary uncertainty and investment in an optimizing, rational expectations model with income taxes and government debt. *Econometrica* **55**, 169–176.

Huang, C. (1985). Information structures and viable price systems. *J. Math. Econ.* **14**, 215–240.

Jordan, J.S. & R. Radner (1982). Rational expectations in microeconomic models: An overview. *J. Econ. Th.* **26**, 201–223.

Marimon, R. (1983). Stochastic equilibrium and the turnpike property: The discounted case. Discussion Paper No. 686, Cowles Foundation, Yale U.

McCall, J.J., ed. (1982). *The Economics of Information and Uncertainty.* U. of Chicago Press, Chicago.

Radner, R. (1982). Equilibrium under uncertainty. In: *Handbook of Mathematical Economics, Vol. II.* K.J. Arrow & M.J. Intriligator, eds. North Holland, New York.

Saari, D.G. (1985). The representation problem and the efficiency of the price mechanism. *J. Math. Econ.* **14**, 135–168.

Spear, S.E. & S. Srivastava (1986). Markov rational expectations equilibria in an overlapping generations model. *J. Econ. Th.* **38**, 35–62.

Wright, R.D. (1987). Market structure and competitive equilibrium in dynamic economic models. *Econometrica* **41**, 189–201.

Spatial Equilibrium Models

The final reference begins an interesting line of attack on spatial stochastic economic equilibria.

Evstigneev, I.V. (1984). An optimality principle and an equilibrium theorem for controlled random fields on a directed graph. *Soviet Math. Doklady* **29**, 89–93.

INDEX

(Bold numbers refer to pages on which topics are either introduced or formally defined.)

ECONOMIC THEORY, ECONOMETRICS AND MATHEMATICAL ECONOMICS

Edited by Karl Shell, Cornell University

Recent Titles

Haim Levy and Marshall Sarnat, editors, *Financial Decision Making under Uncertainty*

Yasuo Murata, *Mathematics for Stability and Optimization of Economic Systems*

Alan S. Blinder and Philip Friedman, editors, *Natural Resources, Uncertainty, and General Equilibrium Systems: Essays in Memory of Rafael Lusky*

Jerry S. Kelly, *Arrow Impossibility Theorems*

Peter Diamond and Michael Rothschild, editors, *Uncertainty in Economics: Readings and Exercises*

Fritz Machlup, *Methodology of Economics and Other Social Sciences*

Robert H. Frank and Richard T. Freeman, *Distributional Consequences of Direct Foreign Investment*

Elhanan Helpman and Assaf Razin, *A Theory of International Trade under Uncertainty*

Edmund S. Phelps, *Studies in Macroeconomic Theory. Volume 1: Employment and Inflation. Volume 2: Redistribution and Growth*

Marc Nerlove, David M. Grether, and José L. Carvalho, *Analysis of Economic Time Series: A Synthesis*

Jerry Green and José Alexander Scheinkman, editors, *General Equilibrium, Growth and Trade: Essays in Honor of Lionel McKenzie*

Michael J. Boskin, editor, *Economics and Human Welfare: Essays in Honor of Tibor Scitovsky*

Carlos Daganzo, *Multinomial Probit: The Theory and Its Application to Demand Forecasting*

L. R. Klein, M. Nerlove, and S. C. Tsiang, editors, *Quantitative Economics and Development: Essays in Memory of Ta-Chung Liu*

Giorgio P. Szegö, *Portfolio Theory: With Application to Bank Asset Management*

M. June Flanders and Assaf Razin, editors, *Development in an Inflationary World*

Thomas G. Cowing and Rodney E. Stevenson, editors, *Productivity Measurement in Regulated Industries*

Robert J. Barro, editor, *Money, Expectations, and Business Cycles: Essays in Macroeconomics*

Ryuzo Sato, *Theory of Technical Change and Economic Invariance: Application of Lie Groups*

Iosif A. Krass and Shawkat M. Hammoudeh, *The Theory of Positional Games: With Applications in Economics*

Giorgio Szegö, editor, *New Quantitative Techniques for Economic Analysis*

John M. Letiche, editor, *International Economic Policies and Their Theoretical Foundation: A Source Book*

Murray C. Kemp, editor, *Production Sets*

Andreu Mas-Colell, editor, *Noncooperative Approaches to the Theory of Perfect Competition*

Jean-Pascal Benassy, *The Economics of Market Disequilibrium*

Tatsuro Ichiishi, *Game Theory for Economic Analysis*

David P. Baron, *The Export-Import Bank: An Economic Analysis*

Real P. Lavergne, *The Political Economy of U.S. Tariffs: An Empirical Analysis*

Halbert White, *Asymptotic Theory for Econometricians*

Thomas G. Cowing and Daniel L. McFadden, *Macroeconomic Modeling and Policy Analysis: Studies in Residential Energy Demand*

Svend Hylleberg, *Seasonality in Regression*

Jean-Pascal Benassy, *Macroeconomics: An Introduction to the Non-Walrasian Approach*

C. W. J. Granger and Paul Newbold, *Forecasting Economic Time Series, Second Edition*

Marc Nerlove, Assaf Razin, and Efraim Sadka, *Household and Economy: Welfare Economics of Endogenous Fertility*

Jean-Michel Grandmont, editor, *Nonlinear Economic Dynamics*

Thomas Sargent, *Macroeconomic Theory, Second Edition*

V. I. Arkin and I. V. Evstigneev, *Stochastic Models of Control and Economic Dynamics*